# SECOND WARNING

**THE SMITH FAMILY**

*Left to Right: Barry, May, Andrew, Rachel and husband John holding their son Andrew James, Debbie, Becky and husband Dennie.*

# SECOND WARNING

BY

BARRY SMITH

Published by
SMITH FAMILY EVANGELISM

Reprinted 1985
Reprinted 1986
Reprinted 1987
Reprinted 1989
Reprinted 1990
Reprinted 1991
Reprinted 1992
Reprinted 1997

All Scripture references in this book are taken from the Authorised Version, unless otherwise stated.

Words in brackets are the Author's explanations, to enable a clear understanding.

ISBN No. 0-908961-01-4

TYPESET BY LINOTYPE SERVICE (P.N.) LTD,
PALMERSTON NORTH, NEW ZEALAND.
PRINTED AND BOUND BY WRIGHT AND CARMAN LTD,
UPPER HUTT, NEW ZEALAND

# CONTENTS

# PREFACE

This book I dedicate to the many thousands of once-born people who will become twice-born as a result of reading and thinking upon the things contained in these pages.

My wife May, children and I greet you and say, "We are your servants for Christ's sake".

Barry Smith,
Pelorus Bridge,
Rai Valley,
New Zealand

# SPECIAL TRIBUTES

Urs and Kathy Leimgruber and family, our Australian agents, for their continued love and help in setting up a base in that country.

Colleen Bolitho who gave herself unsparingly and typed this ever-increasing in size manuscript — very grateful thanks.

Mike and Anji Porter of Campbelltown, N.S.W. for the very clear artwork presented in this book. — The Lord's blessings be upon you all.

## ACKNOWLEDGEMENTS

Linotype Service (P.N.) Ltd: Managing Director, Mr George Young; General Manager, Mr Jeff Brown, and the staff of the above Company.

Thanks to Mr Barry Setterfield for permission granted to quote short extracts from his Manual, "The Velocity of Light and the Age of the Universe".

# RECOMMENDED READING

*Peace, Prosperity and the Coming Holocaust — The New Age Movement in Prophecy* by Dave Hunt. Harvest House Publishers — Eugene, Oregon, 97402.
*The Brotherhood — The Secret World of the Freemasons* by Stephen Knight. Granada Publishing Ltd., 8 Grafton Street, London W1X 3LA.
*In God's Name* by David Yallop. Publishers Jonathon Cape Ltd., 30 Bedford Square, London WC1B 3EL.
*The Cosmic Conspiracy* by Stan Deyo. W.A. Texas Trading, P.O. Box 70, Morley, W.A. 6062.
*Azaria — What the Jury Were Not Told* by Phil Ward. Published by Phil Ward, 41 Rawson Street, Epping, Sydney, Australia.
*Mystery 666* by Don Stanton.
*None Dare Call It Conspiracy* by Gary Allen.

Author's Note.—Because of reaction after publishing my first book "Warning" I state herewith that I am not a member of the League of Rights, the John Birch Society, nor any extreme right wing political or pressure group. I am simply a minister of our Lord Jesus Christ. I am also a friend of Israel and regularly speak of God's clear promises to them regarding their regathering and return to the Holy Land. The Arabs and Palestineans also have God's clear promises as to their position in the land.

This book is not a novel, but a collection of facts, many of which will probably astound you, but they remain facts nevertheless.

In order that you may further your understanding on these subjects, tapes may be obtained upon written application. For details see addresses on the last page of this book.

Jesus
is
born
Public
ministry
Apostle
Paul
is born
9
mysteries
revealed
Crucifixion
4 major signs
of the coming
of Jesus
10 nations
in Europe
Israel
a nation
World church
under W.C.C.
Spectacular Holy
spirit movement
Times of Gentiles
finished
in Jerusalem
Jerusalem
in Israeli hands
6 day June war
Fulness of the
Gentiles coming in
1 9 nations in E.E.C. – 1 to go.
2 Stage set for world leader
3 Israel more established
4 W.C.C. invites Eastern religions to observe meetings
5
Daniel 9: Prophetic clock ticks again. LAST 7 YEARS
Beginning of sorrows
PEACE TREATY IN
MIDDLE EAST
Christians – Start counting!
3½ yrs
42 months · 1260 days
Time, times and ½ a time
3½ yrs
The Great Tribulation
4bc 30ad
1948
1967
1977
19??

7 things happen
during great
tribulation
Christ on Mt Zion,
plus 144,000.
Archangel Michael
protects Israel.
Begins with Russian
invasion of Israel.
Closes with Chinese invasion of
Israel. This is Armageddon
Christ on Mount of Olives.
Divides mountain.
Builds the Temple.
Reigns with Saints.
1000 years
Reign of
CHRIST
ON EARTH
Peace generally
Satan cast
into
pit
1 Satan
released
2 Final
battle
3 Satan joins
E.E.C. leader
and world
church leader
in lake of fire
Great
white throne
of Judgement
Lamb's book of life
Heavens and Earth
burn
New Heavens
and new Earth
NEW
JERUSALEM
DESCENDS
LIKE
A
BRIDE
Whosoever
will
may come

# INTRODUCTION

The silence was so thick, you could cut it with a knife.

All who lived in that particular residential area had been summoned from their homes to witness the execution.

The portable guillotine, on a low slung trailer towed by a black police van was parked alongside the curb in the area's shopping centre.

All eyes suddenly focused on a middle-aged man who walked calmly between two tall policemen, towards the instrument of death — he was flung unceremoniously on to his knees, his neck resting on the lower semi-circular collar with his wrists strapped down to two arm-rests alongside.

As one lawman stood with his hand on the release trigger, another sharply addressed the unfortunate victim.

"You realise of course by now that you are a divisive force in society. This is your final opportunity to recant, receive your trading mark on your hand or forehead and publicly swear allegiance to our great world leader — you have 15 seconds to decide."

The crowd murmured encouragingly, "Go on, recant — give up — save your life".

The kneeling man spoke clearly and firmly. "You may take my life, but not my soul. A workmate and friend of mine who was for many years a Christian, warned me of this day. I laughed and would not listen. Now I am compelled to believe his words. To take this satanic mark now, would deprive me of receiving the name of my Lord Jesus Christ on my forehead later. Executioner, I am ready!"

"And they shall see His face and His name shall be in their foreheads."[1]

THIS BOOK IS FACT, NOT FICTION.

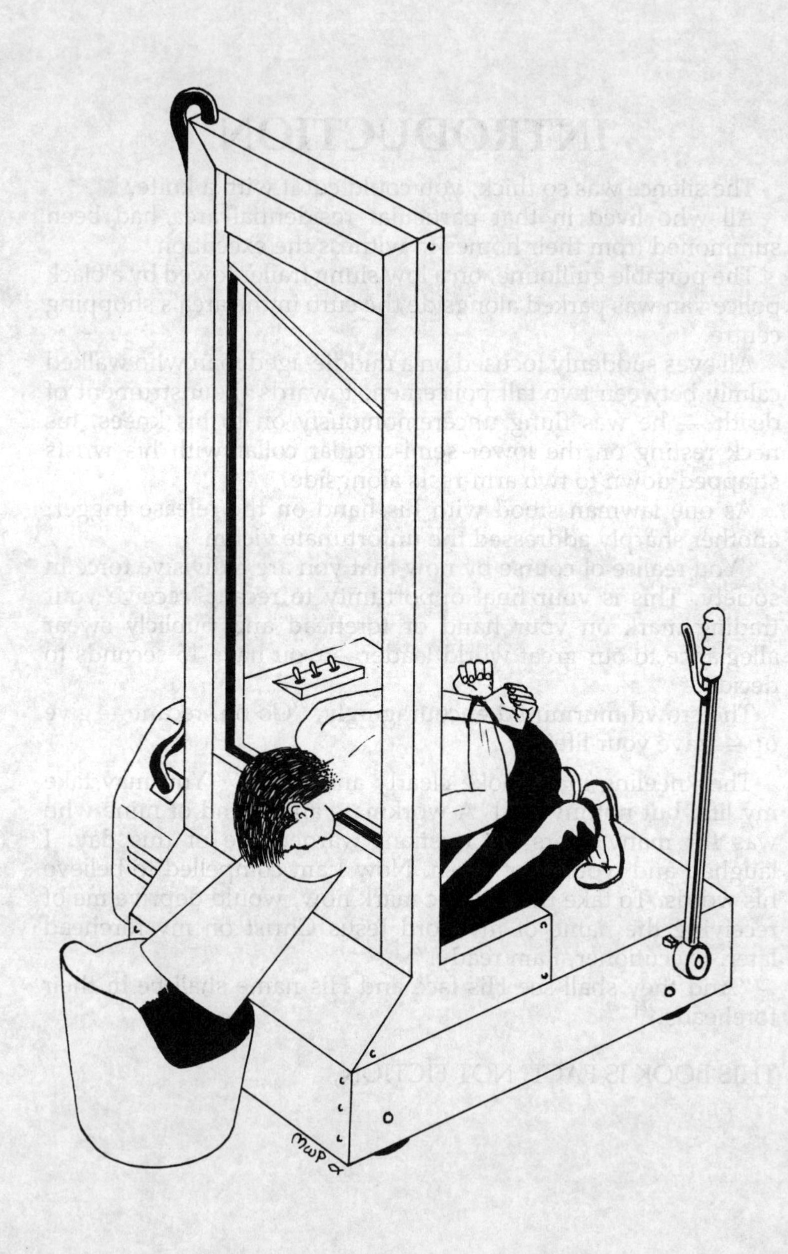

## CHAPTER ONE

# CASH WILL CRASH IN A FLASH

PREFACE: When I wrote the book "WARNING" I thought I had exhausted my sources of information. However, after reprinting that book a number of times, people from various parts of the world are now saying, "Please write an update".

Here then is that update in the form of a Second Warning.

In 1980 a Christian pastor boarded a plane in Miami Florida en route to Los Angeles, California.

He took his seat next to an elderly Jewish gentleman, and as the plane took off, he struck up a conversation with his fellow passenger.

I present here, part of that conversation that was spoken, the very next day in a public meeting and tape recorded.

After a short discussion centred around the elderly gentleman's solid gold watch with strange insignia on it, he was asked what his job was.

Answer: I am president of a group that is at present stabilizing the world currency system.

Question: What do you know about the Common Market?

Answer: I financed the Common Market.

Question: What are the aims of your Group?

Answer: We are working towards the formation of a one world government and a one world religious system.

Question: Do you know anything about a personalised numbering system?

Answer: Oh yes. This system has been prepared already. It is no longer a question of "IF" but "WHEN" we will allow the old monetary system to collapse and issue numbers to each individual to use for buying and selling.

Question: How do I know that you are indeed who you say you are?

By way of an answer, the elderly man opened his attache case and drew out numbers of photographs; each one showing him standing next to a prominent world leader.

Question: If you are who you say you are, why aren't you travelling first class?

Answer: Because I don't want certain people to know I'm on this plane.

Question: Do you know that all you are telling me, is right here in the Word of God?

Answer: You don't believe that book do you?

When shown the passage in the book of Revelation the elderly gentleman remarked . . . "Well, that's very interesting. I'll have to pay more attention to that book in the future."

This is what they read,

"And he causeth all, both small and great, rich and poor, free and bond, to receive a mark in their right hand, or in their foreheads, that no man might buy or sell save he had the mark, or the name of the beast or the number of his name.

Here is wisdom, let him that hath understanding, count the number of the beast, for it is the number of a man and his number is six hundred, three score and six."[1]

When the plane arrived at L.A. International Airport, the Christian pastor endeavoured to follow the elderly man to the baggage checkout but to his dismay noted that his fellow passenger's "friends" had whisked him away out a side door.

Let us put everything in order.

1. There will shortly be a world-wide money collapse. You may now ask, "Do the governments of the world know about this?"

   Answer — "YES".

   Why don't they warn us about it?

   Answer — Because banking is built upon one word — CONFIDENCE. If the powers that be said officially that the world monetary system was due to crash, this information would set off a bank scare and a run on the banks by clients wishing to withdraw their money. This in turn would bring about an impossible situation as the banks do not have enough ready cash to cover this.

   Therefore, in spite of the true facts, the public is barraged with a series of lies, designed to bolster up confidence, e.g. working on the basis that the average newspaper reader only takes notice of the larger headings, and ignores the smaller ones, we note the following examples, taken from Australian and New Zealand papers.

   Melbourne Age 1.12.82 (Large Heading) "AUSTRALIA'S FUTURE BRIGHT. U.S.

   The short-term economic outlook for Australia was for low growth and high inflation, but the country remained a land of great economic opportunity, the U.S. Department of Commerce said yesterday."

   New Zealand Herald 15.6.83 (Small Heading)

   "In the Red

CLOSED

Australia had a balance of payments deficit of $A106m last month, compared with a surplus of almost $A1billion in April."

Newswatchers will possibly remember watching Australian T.V. news during the second half of 1982 where there appeared a large map of America on the screen with stars dotted here and there. Each star represented a bank that had closed down that day.

As all in the room gathered together to watch the most graphic picture of all, we observed a man, leaning against a glass door of a bank. He had a very sad look in his eyes — Reason — above his head was written one word only — CLOSED".

I reminded all present that we were watching the beginnings of the crash we predicted years ago.

The next day we read in the paper that a giant U.S. Bank, Citibank, needed to borrow $US2 billion daily so that they could open their doors each morning.

Those who have made world finance their study will know that although most countries in the western world are borrowing continually to keep their economies afloat, many are now borrowing from the original money-lenders just to pay back the interest on the original loans.

The media then told us that if one country defaulted on repaying the interest on these loans, it would set off a domino style, worldwide, monetary collapse.

Readers, please note that many, many countries have defaulted on their loans, i.e. Poland, Denmark, Mexico and many South American countries, yet the crash that was forecast did not come.

WHY?

Because the International Bankers do not have things completely set up as yet, for the New World Monetary System.

This new system must be set up first, as a monetary crash could cause some folk to starve to death, not having any alternative means to buy and sell.

What have the International Bankers done then?

— They have rushed in with more money to bail out the defaulters and re-scheduled their loans.

Sydney Morning Herald 6.9.82: "Rich nations agree to pay more to bail out poor.

Ten leading western industrial democracies agreed yesterday to provide more funds to help financially ailing countries to pay their debts. The move represented a reversal in policy by the United States, one of the ten countries. The U.S. is working with other nations calling themselves the Group of Ten, i.e. Belgium, Canada, France, West Germany, Italy, Japan, the Netherlands, Sweden, Britain and the United States."

"Switzerland is an affiliated member."

Many ask, how do the money lenders expect the borrowers to pay their loans back?

Answer — they don't. Each time a country borrows, it yields up a measure of its sovereignty by way of collateral to the money lenders.

One such group of lenders is "The Federal Reserve", governed by a group of private individuals in the U.S. whose combined wealth is so massive it bails out the U.S. when they are in need, and wields massive control over the foreign policy of the United States.

Point to ponder — the Federal Reserve does not allow their books to be audited.

VERY IMPORTANT: In 1982, 19 words were quietly added to The Federal Reserve Act section 14(b) (i) "and obligations of, or fully guaranteed as to the principal and interest by a foreign government or agency thereof."

Big deal you say. What does that mean?

Well, this is a short term U.S. rescue operation. It is quite simple really — in the old days, the U.S. would simply print more U.S. dollars to cover the deficit. These days, the U.S. doesn't even do that.

All it does now is add a few zeros to the world's monetary reserves. Now the U.S. has agreed to take over the bad debts of other nations, and has become the central banker of the world. This means that third world countries no longer need to worry about their debts.

Quote from "Australian" newspaper 4th June 1984. "Federal Reserve chairman Mr Paul Volcker . . . has attempted to calm the markets by suggesting the world debt problem had been blown out of proportion. . . . the overall situation was 'intrinsically manageable'.

He would not elaborate on any particular schemes to resolve the debt crisis." — end quote. — Readers can now join the very few "ELECT" who have knowledge of this sneaky plan. — Mr Malcolm Fraser spoke of this cover up as being very unwise, in a recent interview.

This is important as many of the world government people work out of New York — Wall Street — Banking — Money Crash — New System.

Notice now, that all those nations in debt must now dance to

AUSTRALIA
100
100

the tune of the world government planners — alias, the international money lenders.

It was well written.

"The rich ruleth over the poor, and the borrower is servant to the lender."[2]

Question: When is the best time to crash the world monetary system?

Answer: Either, on a Sunday, when the banks are shut, or before banks open for trading during a week-day.

In 1948 in Germany the reichmark was heavily inflated and in Bonn, as they studied the economy, they decided a stroke of the pen and a cancellation of the old system was the best approach to starting all over again.

There was no warning to the populace.

The Sunday morning paper made the announcement "Reichmark cancelled".

Millions of folk lost their savings overnight.

N.B. The old system was not linked to the new system — Any money you had under the old system, was not credited to your account under the new system.

Rich and poor lost their money overnight. Each was given 40 deutschmarks to start again with.

The poor were delighted. They now possessed 40 D.M.

Some of the rich felt like buying a pistol with their 40 D.M. to use to attempt suicide.

"Suicide," I hear you cry. Was it that serious?

In 1948, the Stars and Stripes, the official organ of the U.S. Army published statistics of suicide, and showed pictures of the Rhine river filled with the bodies of the dead, many of them with their hair turned white overnight. — Their foundation for life, i.e. money, had collapsed like a pack of cards.

1929 was the year of the New York stock market crash. Many men jumped to their deaths from the skyscrapers.

Australia and New Zealand readers possibly will remember the following.

During the first part of 1983, Mr Bob Hawke was elected as Australia's new Prime Minister, replacing Mr Malcolm Fraser. Upon taking power he fooled would-be investors and financiers by suddenly devaluing the dollar.

A phone call to New Zealand aroused Prime Minister Muldoon after midnight. A hastily arranged cabinet meeting was convened in the early hours of the morning, resulting in the N.Z. dollar also being devalued. All overseas trading was suspended for the day until values were firmly established.

NEWS DAY
GIVE A TALK ABOUT THE OLD DAYS (MONEY, SHOPS ETC.)
MWPa

When the world currency goes, it will be just like that. Perfect timing is essential.

The notes you carry in your wallet will one day be useful only as a focal point for children to give morning talks about at school.

Picture a child in front of the class displaying a $1 note and saying, "My Mum and Dad used to use these to buy things with."

Class — "OO-OOOO!"

**BAD NEWS FOR ALL**

Readers who read my first book "Warning" will remember reading on pages 77-78 that unless you are amongst those organising this crash, you will lose all the money you possess as it will be cancelled and not credited to your new account.

I well recall speaking at a public meeting on the Gold Coast, Queensland, Australia in 1983, and once the meeting had concluded it was easy to identify the wealthy as they left the gathering with shattered expressions on their faces.

I'm truly sorry, but it will be exactly as I say. They tell us that to be forewarned is to be forearmed.

**S.D.R'S**

The International currency nicknamed 'invisible gold' or 'paper gold' is already destined to become the basis of the new world currency system.

Some years ago, my family and I were travelling in New Zealand pulling a large trailer caravan behind our car. Half way up a mountain, the engine began to overheat.

We pulled in to a rest area, where I observed another travel coach already parked.

I approached the driver, who very kindly offered me some water for my overheated radiator. Noticing his very clipped English army accent, I said, "You are from the old country I presume?"

"Yes indeed," he replied, and then volunteered further information as to his status.

"I am actually connected to the European Economic Community Finance Division."

Well, I was momentarily stunned and murmured, "Let's leave the water for a moment," and as we climbed into his vehicle, I suggested we discuss finance, and very quickly the conversation turned to:

**SPECIAL DRAWING RIGHTS**

Already destined to become the basis for the New World Monetary System, S.D.R's are simply bookkeeping entries used to credit or debit accounts. No cash is involved.

When will the new system commence?

It has started already with the introduction of the plastic credit card. The morning will come when you pick up your newspaper and read, "WORLD MONETARY SYSTEM COLLAPSES. Please go to the bank of your choice and pick up your plastic card."

I remember making that statement during a university meeting in north Queensland when a young man rose to his feet and asked for permission to speak. I gave him an opportunity to do so and he told the following story.

"Running short of money, I was anxious to procure an overdraft, and was therefore, at last willing to take out a plastic card and the overdraft facilities that were included.

I approached the bank teller with my request, and he asked me to wait just a moment.

Going to a drawer, he pulled out a plastic credit card with my name embossed on it. I said, 'Excuse me, I am only applying at this stage', to which he retorted,

'Oh, it's okay sir, we have them here already and just wait for our customers to come in and pick them up'."

It will be clear to you by now that it is not "IF" but "WHEN" all this commences.

**TERRIBLE CONFUSION**

During the changeover period, there will be a time of terrible confusion.

It is a bold venture, never undertaken before on a world-wide scale.

Telecommunications men will be seen everywhere, installing wires to the outback and obscure places, as all places of business must have computer link-ups.

Readers, please note that in early July 1983 the New Zealand newspapers announced that telecommunications were being installed and upgraded throughout the South Pacific region. This included small atolls, seemingly unimportant to the majority of people. Some suppose that this is being done to give better telephone links — WRONG — It is being done to computerise these islands, ready for the new world money system.

Countries such as Papua New Guinea will need a great deal of fast work to be done. During a lecture tour of Madang on the north coast during September 1983 I was asked a very relative question.

"When cash is cancelled, how will our local outdoor markets carry on, selling local produce, i.e. taros, bananas, yams?"

The answer I gave will apply to all markets worldwide in all countries, including those of third world classification.

(a) Barter will become popular for a time, i.e. I exchange my bananas for your taros.

(b) All sellers will finally be forced to receive a plastic credit card, and later a plastic debit card, or a combination of the two.

All markets, shops and businesses will require a computer link-up to operate.

Do bankers realise the cash system is about to collapse?

Yes, of course they do.

(a) Bank tellers everywhere are being instructed to sell the plastic card idea to customers.

(b) Personal overdrafts to non-card holders are becoming difficult to get. e.g. Arriving in Sydney, Australia, during the month of August 1983, I contacted the bank where I have an Australian cheque account, asking for an overdraft. I have had good credit ratings with this bank, but the manager refused to help me. He did say, however, that if I took out a credit card, a $2,000 overdraft could be arranged within a week. You may ask, "Did you accept the card?" to which I clearly reply, "No. I didn't at that stage."

(c) Note also that the banks have put a tax on cheques and I quote from a newspaper article in front of me, "it would appear at a glance, that we'll all be using our credit cards more, and our cheque books less."

**WHAT ABOUT CREDIT CARDS?**

These credit cards look good. Many times, when doing radio interviews, I am asked, "Why do you oppose this system? Surely it is much easier."

I reply like this, "Yes, there are many advantages:

(a) Burglaries for cash will be eliminated.

(b) Air hijackings for cash will be eliminated.

(c) Tax dodging will be almost eliminated.

(d) Groups involved in organised crime will suffer. Most of their deals are cash arrangements, e.g. drugs, prostitution, protection rackets. Mafia folk will go crazy.

There are many disadvantages

(a) Special concerts, dinners and evenings where cash is collected at the door will have to meet in special venues, where there is a computer link-up, which takes plastic debit cards.

(b) Churches and clubs, where offerings are made, will all need to be linked to computer outlets. Thus, all offerings will go through the computer. The government tax departments will favour those churches linked to the great world church which is forming under the auspices of the W.C.C. and drive evangelical, Bible-believing, Holy Spirit powered churches underground. It will be simple to tax them overmuch, and make life so difficult that they will not be officially recognised. — Please note, however, that those particular groups will thrive, as God's power is not limited to earthly systems.

"(c) Many bank workers and tax consultants will be out of a job. The computers will ultimately do the whole thing."

During the month of September 1983, whilst lecturing at Port Moresby, Papua New Guinea, I made this statement on the final night. "Papua New Guinea is running behind in the installation of computers plus computer link-ups at all places of business, including your outdoor markets where produce is sold. I predict that very soon, you will see masses of men rushing around with bundles of wires setting the place up ready for the plastic card system." (Date of lecture, Thursday 22nd September 1983.)

Travelling back to Australia on Friday, 23rd September I thought of the massive culture shock involved to many of the folk in obscure areas such as the Highlands.

Many of these, fresh to the idea of cash as opposed to centuries of bartering, suddenly find their cash is of no use, and they will move into the computer age along with the rest of us. This applies to all third world countries and even to jungle tribes, etc.

Remember the rule — no card, no number, no food can be bought or sold.

A friend connected with a leprosy mission in P.N.G. told me that it would not be that difficult to track individuals down through informants, head men, relatives, etc. This is being done already by the Health Department whilst looking for leper contacts.

It is obvious that a few folk will escape the net — e.g. nomads, some aboriginal tribes in Northern Territory, Australia, who have no need of shops or trade, but the vast majority of people will be caught in this worldwide net.

Imagine my surprise to pick up Brisbane's "Courier Mail" newspaper dated Saturday, 24th September 1983 and see my not yet two-day-old prophecy about to be fulfilled.

Under the heading, "Career and Professional Opportunities"

Telecommunications Opportunities
150 Positions
Papua New Guinea

During the month of April 1984 whilst speaking in Melbourne on these topics, a young man committed himself publicly to Jesus Christ in our meeting.

Afterwards he explained why. He said, "When you told that story, I was shocked, as the firm I work for in Melbourne supplies the computer hardware for P.N.G."

Make no mistake — it's all systems go for a cashless society.

**HOW DO WE PROTECT OURSELVES?**

Financiers around the world are all offering their "expert" advice.

1. Buy gold.
2. Buy silver.
3. Buy land and real estate.

Each of these solutions is wrong, wrong, wrong.

These would-be helpers each show a complete lack of understanding of what is ahead.

The new finance system is to be completely cashless. No negotiable commodities will be involved.

During the month of March 1981, whilst lecturing in Singapore, the Christian businessmen in that city arranged for me to speak on the "Wall Street" of that country, called Shenton Way. Lunchtime after lunchtime, these people gathered by the hundreds in large restaurants where luxurious 10 course meals were served.

Present were millionaires, stockbrokers, bank managers, sharebrokers and many others. I remember watching the sumptuous 10 course meals being wheeled out on trolleys, served, and much of it being returned to the kitchen, uneaten. Why was this, you ask?

To the Asian mind, gold is the all-important commodity. Imagine the consternation when these people heard a visitor to their country read this ancient prediction from the Word of God. Never before in history could these words have had any meaning. These financiers are very clear thinkers. This is what they heard read.

Quote — "Go to now ye rich men, weep and howl for your miseries that shall come upon you. Your riches are corrupted and your garments are moth-eaten. Your gold and silver is cankered, and the rust of them shall be a witness against you, and shall eat your flesh as it were fire. Ye have heaped treasure together for the last days."[3]

(Some might add) — In your numbered Swiss bank accounts.

No wonder appetites waned on this occasion.

Even as I write, I note an article from the Sydney Morning Herald.

"Hong Kong Dollar Near Collapse."

Quote — "As many people swarmed to buy gold, others desperately tried to withdraw their Hong Kong dollars and buy U.S. dollars. Most banks refused to sell greenback notes yesterday morning.

Many supermarkets were stormed by shoppers, stocking up on staples like oil and rice." — Signs of things ahead?

I'm sorry investors, but your buying of gold and silver bars is a complete waste of time. These bars will be used shortly for possibly two things only.

(i) Holding the door open on a hot day.
(ii) Holding down papers on your desk on a windy day.

**WHAT ABOUT LAND AND REAL ESTATE?**

Yes, it is good to have your own home, but even this is only temporary.

This new monetary system is also involved in plans for world government. Henry Kissinger stated that this system should be in place as a loosely-knit organisation by the end of 1982. The organisers are running slightly behind with their plans.

Their aims are:

1. Get rid of all democratic forms of government.
2. Get rid of all religion, as the final religion of the world will be pure satan worship.
3. Take over all ownership of private property.
4. Control each individual through a computerized numbering system.

**WHAT SECURITY IS THERE THEN?**

On this old world, absolutely none at all. I have examined this subject for 14 years from every possible angle and have come to the following conclusions:

Only a vital living relationship with God, through His Son, Jesus Christ, will act as a buffer against all.

Tempted to lay this book down?

Don't.

Just think carefully and try to offer an alternative place of refuge in these days.

Places of refuge:

1.
2.

3.
4.

## PLASTIC CARD PROBLEMS

These cards are being issued at a phenomenal rate and card holders should at this stage take them out and note the following.

Never mind the embossed name or number on the front.

Take a look at the piece of magnetic strip on the back. This little piece of tape has enough room on it to contain a computerised system about you as an individual, giving access to all other computer records or dossiers on you, through link numbers.

Ultimately, your history will be made accessible through that strip along with the linknumbers.

(a) Birth date (person number)
(b) Location (address)
(c) Medical file
(d) Banking history
(e) Marital status
(f) Passport details
(g) Car ownership
(h) Business details
(i) Social security
(j) Family statistics
(k) Tax details, etc.

A new card will be issued shortly. It will be an international one and will take the place of all existing cards.

There will be no apparent names or numbers on it but it will have all required information on the magnetic strip, or built into the card itself through a silicon chip or some other method. The computer will decipher and read it.

Warning: Be careful about this card. It is what you can't see that is dangerous.

Four problems with the card. These can be:

(a) Broken — I used to carry example cards in my back pocket for showing the audiences I spoke to. Each time I sat down, I would hear "crack" and pull out a stump by way of illustration.
(b) Lost — Imagine being on an overseas trip with the card as your only means of obtaining finance. If you lose it, you will agree with me that unless you meet a man called Mr Wong, you're sunk.

(c) When the Visa card first appeared in New Zealand, a boy reportedly stole his father's card and ran up $30,000 worth of sales before his father realised the card was missing.

When my son, Andrew, heard that, he asked "Hey Dad, do you have a Visa card?"

(d) Passing a magnet over the magnetic strip on the card can erase all the information recorded there.

**NEXT STAGE**

Newsweek, August 22nd, 1983 reports –

"A Vision of 1984 in Germany. A new identity card promises heightened security – and the shadow of Big Brother. The new law requires every West German citizen 16 and over to purchase the card ($3.75 and good for 10 years) and present it upon request to any authorised government office. Photos are embossed on each card." This card guarantees entry into a police surveillance state," warns a legal expert.

The government is churning out 30,000 cards per day.

No wonder folk are queuing up to leave Germany.

All this performance is very temporary. The old world government people are

CLEVERLY CONDITIONING PEOPLES' MINDS STAGE BY STAGE TO RECEIVE, WITHOUT PROTEST, THE FINAL MARK.

Do they know this final step you ask?

Oh yes — very well. If it was suddenly produced, the masses would resist it.

Like the story of the crayfish being boiled in the pot. If one starts with cold water and gradually heats it up, the creature doesn't notice until it is too late.

Don't be surprised Australia — you're next.

**WHAT ABOUT THE COMPUTER MARK ON FOOD?**

I'm glad you asked that.

Called UPC, developed in 1974, this universal product code is on most of the food you buy at your supermarket.

It looks like a lot of lines covering an area about the size of a large postage stamp.

Stage 1: Most of these have a five digit system with these numbers printed under the lines. As I write, I notice these digits have been increased to six in each of the two sections.

Stage 2: Smaller computer marks appear under the main computer mark. These help with further information as required.

Stage 3: There is another number on the left hand side of the two sections of the bar codes.

This is the number which signifies the country of origin. Five more digits will be added shortly, bringing the whole system to three lots of six digits, i.e. 666.

**SHOCKING NEWS**

Readers should now go to the shelf, take down a can bought at the supermarket and note that there are three sets of double lines, unidentified within the mark.

These lines are found at the beginning, the middle and the end of the mark and are slightly longer than the others. They are called guard bars.

Why do they not have an identifying number?

Because each of these marks is similar to the bars equalling 6 on the right hand side of the central guard bar.

Hence 666 would appear to be on all the food you buy at the supermarket, but it is cleverly hidden, as in actuality these guard bars have no numeric value.

Stage 3: UPC has now developed some more additions to the mark.

A laser tattoo machine has been developed by IBM and others. This mark will be printed invisibly on people's bodies and this new code now has the letters F and H at the beginning and the end of the smaller additional codes.

Remember what was written in 96AD. This was prophetic. It refers to the 1980's and it is here right now. Only an ostrich would bury his head in the sand.

"And he causeth all, both small and great, rich and poor, free and bond, to receive a mark in their right hand, or in their foreheads: and that no man might buy or sell, save he that had the mark, or the name of the beast, or the number of his name. Here is wisdom. Let him that hath understanding count the number of the beast: for it is the number of a man; and his number is six hundred three score and six."

Revelation 13:16-18

This F and H mark on the card will specify that the buyer has the required tattoo on either the forehead or the hand.

**WHO THOUGHT THESE MARKS UP?**

An American lawyer named Constance Cumbey sought out the answer to this question and this is what she came up with.

Quote — "When the product codes are set up, it is worked at different levels. Often the people who are doing the designing are the people who are deeply into the study of the occult. They are the ones who designed it (product codes) in the first place. . . . Some of those who set it up, did it in response to instructions they believed they were receiving from superior intelligences. — These were evidently demon instructions." — End quote.

**SUMMARY**

1. CASH WILL CRASH
2. CREDIT AND DEBIT CARDS ISSUED
3. TIME OF CONFUSION
4. COMPUTER LINKS EVERYWHERE
5. LEADS ON TO LASER MARK ON BODY TO AVOID THREE PROBLEMS
6. MARK WILL CORRESPOND WITH UPC NOW ON FOOD
7. F AND H ADDED TO CODE

SIMPLE CARD
JOHN CITIZEN
110177 971217 116904
SOC.
MED.
EMP.

## CHAPTER TWO

# A CLEVER CON TO CATCH CITIZENS

It is obvious that when the cash system does fold up criminals are going to get really angry about it all. However, lest we are tempted to feel sorry for these people, let us remember that they always have recourse to the Human Rights Commission.

Don't worry, it has been well written.

"The heart of man is deceitful above all things and desperately wicked."[1] They will think of something.

From the "Australian" newspaper, 16th November 1983 we read, "Credit Card Crooks go from Hot Dogs to Caviar in the Cashless Society.

He worked for a sophisticated criminal outfit. His job was to go on spending sprees, charging up to $5,000 a day on stolen credit cards."

Our computer society has spawned a whole range of new crimes. So has our cashless society.

It is estimated that the total loss in the United States from illegally used credit cards in 1982 topped $1,000 million — a threefold increase from 1979.

At a recent Congressional Hearing, representative Clay Shaw asked Detective Alex Ortega of the Economic Crime Unit of the Miami Police Department if there was any sure way people could prevent criminals from obtaining their credit card numbers.

"Unfortunately the answer is no," the detective said.

Obviously this detective is either ignorant of the next step, which makes him highly unsuitable for his present position, or has been told by his bosses to keep quiet.

Do you realise that what you are reading here, in very plain English, is information used in certain government departments. I come in contact continually with men and women who work on this information and they are amazed as to how we know all these things. Folk I have never met send me articles from all over the world.

The secret to our success is a book entitled the Word of God with the book of Revelation included. This latter book was written in 96AD and is being fulfilled in the 1980's.

I recently met a young man in inland Australia who listened intently to my lectures, then made known his desire to accept

God's offer of salvation through our Lord Jesus Christ. He told me that as I quoted the various Scriptures on this subject, he was able to repeat them with me as he had learnt them from a pop album of a group calling themselves 'Iron Maiden'. Their album's title is "The Number of the Beast".

Many readers will be familiar with the film "The Omen", both parts I and II, also its conclusion "The Final Conflict". Where do these stories come from? They are purely and simply the Hollywood version of these world-shaking events set out for us by God in His Word in 96AD.

"Proof — proof" I hear you cry. "I want proof." Keep reading because that is what you are going to get.

Leading on from the thought that F and H (Forehead and Hand) are on stage three of the UPC or Bar Coding, some Australian readers will have noticed this glaringly suggestive cartoon in the Sydney Morning Herald, Saturday, 1st October 1983.

A number of questions are in order here.

(a) Who inserted this series of four pictures?

(b) It is obviously not funny. Why insert it then?

(c) Why was there no accompanying article, by way of explanation?

A friend of mine in Sydney called the Editor of this newspaper for an explanation.

Editor: "No comment."

Assistant Editor: "No comment."

The artist was away on holiday so readers waited five months for the explanation; their minds — psychologically prepared.

Remember the crayfish?

Now, a further word about laser beam treatment.

In many countries around the world, women are submitting to a system called laser cosmetics. The laser beam apparently is used to smooth wrinkles from foreheads. However, in a letter to the newspaper, the Chairman of Dermatology, a Professor of Surgery and a Professor of Ophthalmology from Sydney Hospitals and the University of N.S.W. agree that, quote — "They (women) should not use the potentially dangerous therapy." — End quote. Dangers include skin cancer, tumours, etc.

With the mark indelibly etched in the skin invisible to the naked eye, it certainly is an EASY SYSTEM.

The banks will make a play on the word EASY or SIMPLE and no doubt we will be treated to some spectacular T.V. advertising, e.g. a man springs out of a bank doorway singing happily, "I've just taken the mark — it's easy."

Oh yes, it's easy all right but I regret to inform readers that the taking of this mark is the quick way to hell. Not only that, but before arriving there, you may get cancer of the skin as an added bonus. If receiving the mark is dangerous (it actually burns right through into the bone of the skull so that even a skin transplant cannot remove it) how about the continuous standing in front of ultra-violet lights at checkouts, etc., in the every-day business of buying, selling, travelling, making phone calls, buying petrol, etc.

Regarding the judgements of God on those who accept this mark on their bodies, a rather graphic picture is presented.

"And the first (angel) went and poured out his vial upon the earth, and there fell a noisome and grievous sore upon the men which had the mark of the beast, and upon them which worshipped his image."[2] (Word added for meaning.)

5
WE RES E THE RIGHT
TO CHECK
CUST MERS BAGS
THANK YOU
SPECIA
Billo
Soappo
ALCO
5

If you don't want cancer of the skin, nor to finish up in the lake of fire, my advice would be:

DON'T ACCEPT THE MARK

It now becomes apparent that there will be a choice given. This is sometimes called Hobson's Choice.

(a) Take the Mark — able to buy food — ultimately lose your soul.

(b) Refuse the Mark — unable to buy food — lose your head (execution).

I must confess at this stage that to those of us living in the comparative security of certain countries, enjoying a measure of freedom and prosperity, all this seems rather remote.

How do you explain this to a man who has just jumped up on the beach from his water skis, body tanned in the sun, white teeth flashing as he gives you a dazzling smile. Life is too good to think about such matters.

Talk to a man in prison in a communist state, and it will not surprise him at all.

You see, it all depends on where you live, yet within five years (by 1989) people will be fervently thanking God for this book and others like it.

NOTE: It would appear that when George Orwell wrote his book "1984" there was a power working in him, who even gave him a date which is exactly right. We see the beginnings of this world government system shaping up now. By the way, Orwell wrote his book in 1948 and simply interchanged the last two digits, making 1984.

HERE IT IS — an explanation for the cartoon.

The Sydney Morning Herald reported on 15th February 1984 on page 9 an article entitled,

"Cashless, paperless . . . defenceless."

I quote herewith some extracts. If your mind boggles, don't be surprised for so did mine.

Printed again at the top of the article is that picture of the man with the bar code on his head. Got it? First printed in October 1983, then after five months, thus allowing sub-conscious consideration by readers, it appears again, this time with an explanation.

Quote: "The cashless society is approaching, faster than most people realise. Financial institutions are spending an estimated $800 million on a grandiose scheme where cash and cheques will be replaced by electronic impulses. The government has given its silent nod of approval, as the elimination of cash is seen as the only way to combat tax fraud, the drug trade and all other cash-based crimes.

— In April Westpac will launch the world's first national retail electronic funds transfer (EFT) network in conjunction with Woolworths, Food Plus and B.P." — End quote.

Early in 1984, I received a telephone call from the Gold Coast, Queensland, Australia from a man who had attended our meetings held there in late 1983. — Here I was, at my home in New Zealand, listening to this man play a tape recording of that night's television news to me over the telephone. "In the month of April 1984, Queensland and Sydney will become the venues for the world's first EFT national system between Westpac, Woolworths, B.P. and Food Plus."

I trust that you, the reader, caught the significance of this initial quotation.

This is 'the world's first'. Apparently Australia is to be the test case.

**HELLO GUINEA PIGS**

Continue quote — "A customer will hand his card to the cashier who will feed the card into a terminal and enter the amount of the transaction. The customer will then authorise the transaction by entering a personal identification number (PIN) through a separate hand-held key pad. The funds will be then instantly transferred from the account of the customer to the account of the merchant."

This raises serious ethical questions.

— Through the scanners recording the Universal Product Code (UPC) on each item, the bank's computers will have the facility to store complete buying habits of each consumer. Thus, if the customer is given to buying articles of a doubtful or private nature, the computer would never forget and this information could be used against the individual at a later date.

— The use of EFT systems also facilitates the manipulation of computer related files to obtain information not only about the transactions, but also when and where they were conducted. In this way the computer can be used to survey the movements and activities of people, and actually locate them at the exact time and place of the transaction, i.e. if you were being sought by the police, the link numbers on your files would all be directed through their computers. Thus,even if you bought a packet of chewing gum you could be picked up at that very shop at the moment of buying the article.

For example, in Germany, while a customer uses his automated teller machine (ATM) his name flashes on a screen in the bank's consultancy area. A bank employee will then approach the customer with an offer to discuss other bank services.

Imagine standing on the street using your plastic card through an outside automatic teller and, suddenly, there is a man standing there who, not only knows your name, but hustles you into a discussion about banking — a quite unnerving experience.

Continue quote. — "Banks are devising ways to get customers to use automated facilities. Most prefer to use the example of Telecom, and the analogy of direct dial versus operator-assisted calls. Cheque charges have increased so much that many people prefer this direct system.

"All financial institutions advise their customers to memorise the PIN and then destroy any trace of the number, lest their spouse or best friend wipe out their savings. A lot of people will find it difficult to keep PIN a secret." — End quote.

By the way, the State Bank in Australia has devised a system for those who don't like to operate as a number.

A password containing SIX LETTERS is permissible, using their system. There is that No. 6 again.

**THE KEY THOUGHT**

Continue quote — "In the quest for the ultimate means of identification there is talk of BRANDING EVERYONE WITH A NUMBER. Any such action would surely cause an uproar, but as card fraud increases and customers get tired of paying for it in increased costs, IT IS SEEN AS THE ONLY POSSIBLE SOLUTION." (Emphasis added.)

Now on with more quotes from the same article. Please remember, this is from the Sydney Morning Herald, February 1984, and not the book of Revelation 96 AD. There is a striking similarity, however, you will agree.

Continue quote — "The Mastercard issued by Westpac will have the dual facility of credit and debit in the same card." — End quote.

As we travel the world lecturing on these subjects and others, we picked up this piece of information. Sydney Morning Herald 10th August 1982: "Banks will join SWIFTer Link."

"In November most of the major Australian banks are to become members of the SOCIETY FOR WORLDWIDE INTERBANK FINANCIAL COMMUNICATIONS (SWIFT), a system which links 1,000 banks in 46 countries through a highly sophisticated computer network" — end quote.

Readers of my first book "Warning" will recall reading of a giant computer in Brussels, nicknamed by an enterprising U.S. news reporter — "The Beast". Some wrote to me saying that there was no such machine. These dear folk must have got confused and written to the wrong sources for their information. Not only is it there, but it is collating masses of information on the billions of individual citizens in the industrialised world who have any connections or trade links with the E.E.C.

There is an even larger computer, almost completed, across the border in Luxembourg. These two machines will work in conjunction with each other.

Now back to our original quotes. Sydney Morning Herald 15th February 1984. This will help bring our thinking up to date.

"Since its foundation in 1973, SWIFT's membership has expanded rapidly. Today, it envelops 1,104 banks (which are also competitors) in 49 countries. According to the "Banker", SWIFT expects to have full worldwide membership within five years.

Australia joined the society in 1981 and today all banks depend on its service.

THERE HAS NEVER BEEN ANYTHING LIKE SWIFT IN THE HISTORY OF BANKING" (emphasis added)

With the world's banks depending on one monolithic organisation, for the trans-border flow of monetary information, THERE IS THE POSSIBILITY THAT AN OUTSIDE GROUP COULD TAKE CONTROL AND START PULLING STRINGS. (Emphasis added.) The average citizen in turn, would be connected to the system by way of the plastic card.

The vision of the future is the cashless, paperless society where money will move instantaneously and invisibly through a central joint operational centre, and consumers will possess one card that will access all financial services.

That vision is fast approaching reality." — End quote.

New Zealand readers should note that many of our banks joined SWIFT about December 1982, and many more have joined since. VERY IMPORTANT: At the end of the 1970's various members of the Club of Rome (a powerful world government body) had written books. One of their members in Australia pointed out that Australia would make a very suitable test case, as it had all necessary inherent characteristics. Their motto — "She'll be right mate" would be one of these characteristics.

This man, Professor Charles Birch in his book, "Confronting the Future" says, "Absolute freedom is not possible. There must be restraints on freedom. Not restraints to dissent, but restraints

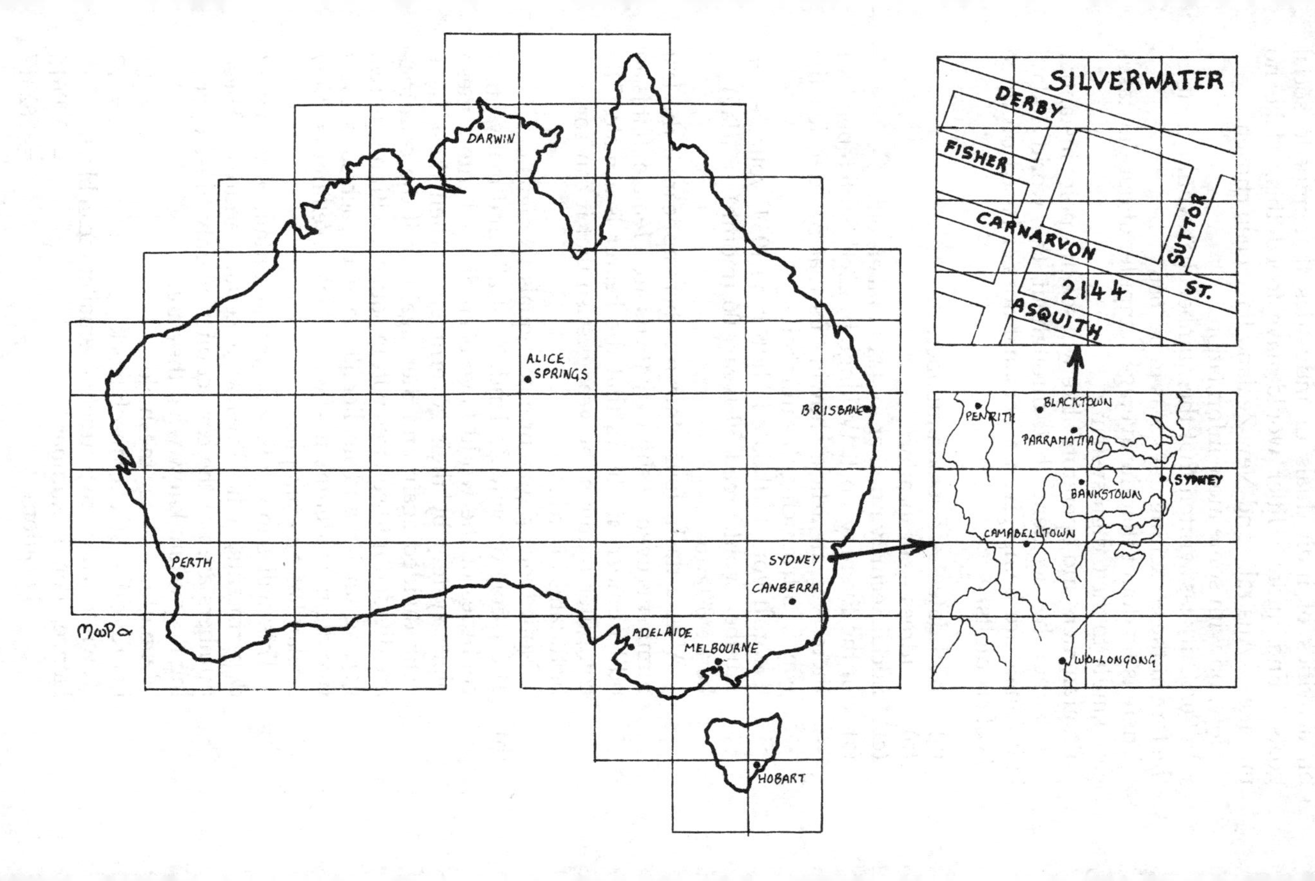
DARWIN
ALICE SPRINGS
BRISBANE
PERTH
SYDNEY
CANBERRA
ADELAIDE
MELBOURNE
HOBART
PENRITH
BLACKTOWN
PARRAMATTA
BANKSTOWN
SYDNEY
CAMPBELLTOWN
WOLLONGONG
SILVERWATER
DERBY
FISHER
CARNARVON
SUTTOR
ST.
2144
ASQUITH

on activities of individuals or industries that impede social goals." End quote. Hitler would have loved this. Make no mistake — Australia and New Zealand have been chosen.

Now, on with some more information.

In 96AD it was written that the number that would come to the fore in these exciting days was to be '666'.

There is no doubt that the average computer of our day takes very kindly to the 6 digit system.

Programmers and operators alike will see this point instantly.

It is not by accident that throughout the world today, individuals are being given a personal dossier based on three lots of six digits.

(a) Birthdate — or person number.
(b) Address — or location
(c) Social Security number, or tax number, etc.

(a) In the Evening Post, Wellington, 22nd September 1981 there was an article showing us that Sweden led the way in introducing this number.

e.g. If your birthdate is 16th June 1939, your person number would read 39 (year) 06 (month) 16 (day) — hence 390616.

After a dash, four other numbers appear. If the last number is even, it shows that you are a female. If it is an odd number, it shows that the bearer is a male. The computer requires the year first so that it can sort out birthdates in order.

Notice the original number equals six digits.

(b) The whole of New Zealand, Australia and many other countries of the world have been divided into a mesh block system by their governments. Then these have been divided again and then again until the countries are divided into squares within squares within squares, getting smaller and smaller all the time. Each square has two digits to identify it — we will take Wellington, New Zealand as an example.

This will show folk working at certain government departments, who lives at a certain address. These numbers are not the correct ones as only those operating the system know what they are.

Wellington — large mesh block = 06
i.e. Karori — smaller mesh block = 23
Down to within two streets — smaller mesh block = 17
Hence, Person number = 390616
Location = 062317

(c) Add to these first two lots of six digits a tax number, or social security number and there you have it: 666.

| | | |
|---|---|---|
| i.e. | Person Number | = 390616 |
| | Location | = 062317 |
| | Soc. Sec. or Tax | = 413824 |

When an individual moves and hands in a change of address form to the Post Office, these changes are noted and fed into the computer.

When World Government comes in, people will not travel freely outside their areas without a permit as is the case in Communist countries now.

VERY IMPORTANT:

The whole point of this becomes obvious when you see that it would be a very rare occasion for two persons with the same birthday to be living in the same mesh block. Thus, you become an individual person.

A rather amusing anecdote may assist here. One of my relatives from Australia came to stay with us in New Zealand.

He applied for a taxation number to enable him to go to work in our area. There was great consternation at the Tax Department when it was discovered that there was another young man of the same name living not too far from us. Obviously in the same mesh block.

This exercise may now be entitled: How to confuse a computer without really trying.

I can almost see people's minds opening up as they read.

Now it becomes clear to New Zealand readers as to why the New Zealand Government suddenly introduced a space for your birthdate on your Electoral Roll Voters form. Also the Tax Department now requires your birthdate on your annual tax form.

Australian readers will recall that when the last census forms were distributed, there was a space for your birthdate to be inserted for the first time in history.

I was speaking in Queensland on this subject when a professional man came up to me at the conclusion of my address. He told me that when the lady brought his census form around, he had deliberately omitted to fill in his birthdate. The lady returned later with a new form and demanded that this space be filled in also. — "Invasion of privacy," I hear you cry. That's correct, and that is exactly what this man was getting at; as he explained this to me.

This World Government's plan is very "sneaky" and how

angry people are going to be when they find out what has happened to them.

The New Zealand Police have just sent out a computer form to all gun owners. This form has a birthdate space prominently displayed.

Shortly, there will be a tremendous disturbance in the Middle East. With the Iranians threatening to close the Gulf of Hormuz, which is the main oil route, and the U.S. Government saying that they won't let that happen, and with Russia watching from the north, things are looking quite shaky.

Those who have read "Warning" will recall that we are now watching for a Jewish leader to confirm a SEVEN YEAR PEACE TREATY.

The first period of 3½ years will be called prophetically "Beginning of Sorrows".

Already, the average man in the street knows intuitively that something is amiss, but he doesn't know what. We must be careful not to blame bankers and their employees for all this, recognising that many of them are mystified and apprehensive as to the future. Some of these will be losing their jobs, along with tax consultants, etc. Slip them a copy of this book and ease their frustration into understanding. Do not assume your bank manager knows all this. He probably doesn't — as he has approached banking with different concepts in mind.

ONCE THIS SEVEN YEAR TREATY HAS BEEN SIGNED AND CONFIRMED IN THE MIDDLE EAST a number of things will take place during this first period.

1. A tremendous increase in false Christs and religions, all claiming to be the way to God.
2. An increase in wars.
3. Famines.
4. Pestilence.
5. Earthquakes in unusual places. (There will be a strange lack of atheists at this stage.)
6. A world-wide monetary crash involving three major currencies — U.S. Dollar, West German Deutchmark, Japanese Yen.
7. Weather going crazy.
8. Children hating their parents, for their not providing necessary discipline and security.
9. A flood of filth in book stores, theatres, T.V. and video tapes.
10. A worldwide hatred and persecution of Christians.
11. A massive REVIVAL will burst out with many super-

SHOPPING CE

natural signs including dreams, visions and prophecies. Tens of thousands will turn to the Lord Jesus Christ for His salvation. The spiritual hunger will be initiated by the apparent collapse of all seemingly secure foundations.

12. Churches who believe the Word of God will be inundated with anxious enquiries.

IT IS WRITTEN

"And it shall come to pass afterward, that I will pour out my Spirit upon all flesh, and your sons and your daughters shall prophesy, your old men shall dream dreams, your young men shall see visions and also upon the servants and upon the handmaids in those days will I pour out my Spirit."[3]

13. As cash will now be cancelled, plastic credit cards and debit cards will be the short term medium of exchange, and the mark on the hand or forehead will be voluntary at this stage.
14. Christians will be very excited, coping with the massive increase in converts to Christ. Church buildings will be too small to cope with the masses of new folk and meetings will be held everywhere. It will be the day of Pentecost, multiplied over and over again.

Imagine this scene, amplified in our day.

"Be glad then ye children of Zion and rejoice in the Lord your God, for He hath given you the former rain — moderately" (3,000 souls).

"And He will cause to come down for you the rain. The former rain (Pentecost) and the latter rain (a final spiritual revival) in the first month".[4] (Words in brackets added to assist meaning.)

Get excited, you Christians, all is not doom and gloom.

Just as the early Christians thrived under pressure, so will we. Even now, I chuckle from time to time at the power of God, and the way He gives the enemy a little rope to hang himself with.

I also get a personal kick out of watching people trying to escape from the only one who can save them. If it wasn't so serious, it could sometimes seem to be amusing.

God has any amount of time on His side.

We either bow now or burn later.

To those who try to dodge or ignore God during this life, I seem to hear a voice from heaven saying, "I'll catch you later".

Some time ago I was travelling through the area of Parramatta, Sydney, in our pick-up truck.

I record herewith a C.B. conversion I held with an Aussie truckie. Time — about midnight.

Self: "Hello. Anyone got their ears on?"

Truckie: "Yeah mate."

Self: "We're looking for some L.P. gas for our truck. Do you know where there is a station open?"

Truckie: "Jesus Christ mate, I dunno."

Self: "I was interested to hear you mention that name. I am a preacher myself, at present travelling around your country. You will possibly notice us sometime in a blue G.M.C. twin cab pick-up. We travel continually, inviting people to come to know the Lord."

Truckie: "He hasn't done much for me mate. I've worked my . . . off but He hasn't given me a break."

Self: "I'm not surprised. He works for His own people. You'll need to get born again into His family first, then you'll notice the difference."

Truckie: "Aw, rubbish. When you die, that's all there is."

Self: "You mean you die like a dog."

Truckie: "Yeah, that's right."

Self: "I believe you only want to die like a dog so you can live like one."

— PAUSE —

Truckie (Amidst laughter from many other truckies who were also tuned in): "You might be right there mate."

Others then made some stupid comments.

"Enough", I said, switching off my C.B.

I really believe it is time some folk switched their brains on.

We all know inside that this life is not the end, no matter how vocal we become in our protests.

Death-bed scenes all around the world bring us face to face with the moment of truth. These folk suddenly have it revealed to them that they are going somewhere, and will remain conscious throughout all eternity.

Even Chairman Mao of China, when dying said, "I am going to meet God".

Better to meet Him as a Saviour — now, than as a judge — later.

You say, "I need God — can you help me?"

Yes, at the end of this book, I will set out clearly the way to receive God's way of salvation through our Lord Jesus Christ.

Now this pressure will drive Christians together — but some will give up and finish in hell.

This born again Christianity is the life. No substitutes. Only the real thing will satisfy. In the words of St. Augustine, a man saved from a life of depravity, "Oh God. Man was made for thee, and man will never find rest until his soul finds rest in thee." Not in parties, money and pleasure. But in the Lord.

"But if that servant say in his heart, my Lord delayeth His coming, and shall begin to beat the men servants and maid servants, and to eat and drink and to be drunken,

The Lord of that servant will come in a day, when he looketh not for him, and at an hour when he is not aware, and will cut him in sunder, and will appoint him his portion WITH THE UNBELIEVERS."[5] (Emphasis added for meaning.)

Looks like hell, doesn't it?

However, the Christians who mean business, will be having a great time. — The key word here is "Fellowship".

Birds of a feather still tend to flock together.

IT IS WRITTEN —

"Not forsaking the assembling of ourselves together as the manner of some is (who stay home watching T.V.) but exhorting one another, and so much the more, as ye see the day (coming of Christ) approaching."[6] (Words in brackets added to assist meaning.)

NOW

A major event then takes place. Just prior to the second lot of 3½ years.

(a) Christ lifts His people off this earth, and meets them in the clouds.

(b) The world leader places an image in a large place of worship in Jerusalem (probably the Great Synagogue) and the second lot of 3½ years commences.

This image will demand the worship of men. Satan, who stands behind it, then receives the allegiance of all who succumb to this pressure through the new world monetary system.

First then — the catching away of the Christians.

It is written —

(a) For the Lord Himself shall descend from heaven with a shout.

(b) With the voice of the Archangel

(c) And the trumpet of God

(d) And the dead in Christ shall rise first

(e) Then we which are alive and remain

(f) Shall be CAUGHT UP (not down or out, but up) together with them, in the clouds

(g) To meet the Lord in the air

(h) And so shall we ever be with the Lord. (Emphasis added for meaning.)[7]

MEANWHILE back on earth, the second lot of 3½ years commences. This is

**GREAT TRIBULATION**

"And there shall be a time of trouble such as never was, since there was a nation even to that same time.

It will be so bad, listen to Jesus' words:

"And except those days should be shortened, there should no flesh be saved."

You ask, how will folks know when this period starts?

(a) A great mass of people will go missing, all over the world. The police stations of each country will not have room on their missing persons boards for all the names of those who have gone.

(b) Not only that, this Jewish world leader will then, without warning, stop all the Jewish sacrificial systems in Jerusalem, and horror of all horrors, put up an image to be worshipped by all, and also force everyone ultimately to go along with the New World Money System, involving a mark on the hand or forehead (printed with a laser beam). This image is called "the abomination that maketh desolate".

IT IS WRITTEN

"And from the time that the daily sacrifice be taken away (Jewish Sacrificial System) and the abomination that maketh desolate set up (image standing to be worshipped) there shall be 1,290 days.[8] (Words in brackets added for meaning.)

Now, note that the full length of the second lot of 3½ years is 1,260 days, therefore there is 30 days (or a Jewish month) extra.

TIME BREAKDOWN

| | |
|---|---|
| 30 | days warning for Jews to run from trouble centre |
| 1,260 | days of tribulation with folk worshipping satan through this image, with his mark tattooed on their bodies. (New World Monetary System) |

TOTAL 1,290 days

The Great Tribulation will now commence, but in the midst of the bad news, many people can still be saved by the grace of God — that is good news.

Now for more bad news. In order to be saved at this time, one will need to refuse the worship of satan through the image, and also refuse the mark on the hand or head.

You see, at this point, whoever accepts this mark becomes the currency of the day. A walking piece of money. Whoever controls these individuals controls the money system of the day.

Satan will control it all, through his front man, 'the Beast'. This is why it is called, "The Mark of the Beast".

"Why should we refuse this mark?" I hear you ask.

Because each human head is reserved for the name of his or her creator, our Lord Jesus Christ.

"And they shall see His face (Jesus) and His name shall be in their foreheads."[9] (Word in brackets added for meaning.)

NEVER FORGET. With all your reading and listening;

"If any man worship the beast and his image, and receive his mark in his forehead, or in his hand, the same shall drink of the wine of the wrath of God."

AGAIN

"And the smoke of their torment ascendeth up for ever and ever, and they have no rest day nor night, who worship the Beast and his image, and whosoever receiveth the mark of his name."[10]

Heavy words, you will agree. God must really hate this system. I'm getting to hate it the same way because it is SATAN'S MASTER STROKE for taking people to hell.

Reason — Hell wasn't created for you and me.

Obviously, the Lord's people are pictured as sheep, and the others as goats. The end of the goats is very clear.

"Depart from me ye cursed, into everlasting fire prepared for the devil and his angels."[11]

Billy Sunday, a great evangelist of the early 1900's era was speaking on the platform of an American University.

B.S. "If you students by-pass the Cross of Christ, you'll end up in hell, for the wages of sin is death."[12]

A professor also on the platform stepped forward, removed the microphone from Billy's hand and said, "Excuse me, Mr Sunday, you are entitled to your opinion, but we are intellectuals here, and do not generally believe in the concept of hell."

Retrieving the microphone, Billy pointed to the professor and said,

"That man will not be in hell three seconds before he changes his mind. Jesus said there is a hell, you say there isn't. Who knows more, you or Jesus? If there is no hell, why on earth did Christ suffer such a terrible death on the cross if there is nothing to save us from?"

Did you know that Christ spoke more about hell than about heaven?

During the early 1980's, we were on a lecture tour of North Queensland. Arriving at Innisfail, we stayed with a lovely family who were not only Christians but had access to the local sugar mill.

On a tour of inspection one day, we gazed into the giant furnace, situated on one of the upper floors. One word could describe what we saw — terrifying. The cane stubble was fed in the top, and was burnt before it hit the floor. A mass of white hot flame surged and billowed. Each member of my party who viewed all this, passed exactly the same comment — "it looks like hell".

Leave the 'mark' alone.

## CHAPTER THREE

# THE NET CLOSES

Writing a book like this is quite a venture. People seem to love misquoting others, so I require that each public lecture is tape recorded also.

In one place, I was accused of saying that Christ would return again on 1st January 1973, when what I actually did say was, "Three more nations will join the E.E.C. on that date."

A sign on the wall of a truckstop in Australia seems to sum it up.

CONFUCIUS SAY
WHO SAY I SAY
ALL THEY SAY I SAY

Up until this point, you will agree most of what I have written is fairly clear to the average speaker of the English language.

Readers may have noticed the absence of such words as might, could be, hope, presume, etc.

The book that I use as my source is very definite. As my daughter Becky said to me one day, "God is very precise, isn't he Dad?" To which I replied, "He sure is!"

**HOTELS**

The computer is obviously here to stay. I see that the Japanese now have a hotel where guests can check in and out without any human contact. Only a membership card is used.

A paper key card then opens the door to the room, turns on the electricity and operates most of the other equipment in the room.

**LAW**

In Victoria at the end of 1983, the Victorian Council for Civil Liberties criticised the gigantic computer link up for law enforcement in that State. Operation Noah is a phone-in campaign using 200 computer terminals around the State to feed the gathered information into a police communications centre in Melbourne. Its critics said that it had the makings of an Orwellian Big Brother.

**N.S.W. LAND TITLES**

This is a multi-million dollar plan to record the State of N.S.W. land titles on computer — this will aid in their general

MwPa

"location" scheme and assist in setting up a dossier on people's movements.

## N.Z. TAX DEPARTMENT BIRTHDATES

An Auckland accountant has queried the addition to the information the Inland Revenue Department already collects in its computers. . . .

"What is the reason?" he asked. "If you are a taxpayer, you are a taxpayer. I do not see what your age has to do with it. It is another example of creeping bureaucracy."

The Assistant District Commissioner of Inland Revenue in Auckland, Mr B. A. Swift, said the Department had decided to ask for taxpayers' birth dates to make it easier to identify people.

"There is nothing sinister about it," said Mr Swift.

"Oh yes there is," says Barry Smith.

Continue quote — "Some people refused to give their birthday, but now we insist on it," said Mr Swift — Christchurch Press 16th March 1983.

The reader now understands why this is. The birth date or person number is the first piece of information to go on your own personal dossier, ready for the control of your life once World Government takes over.

## THIRD WORLD ON PHONE

Today, my writing schedule was interrupted whilst I took part in a radio interview at the Taupo radio station.

The interviewer asked me, amongst a lot of other questions, how the third world countries would fit into all this computerisation.

I returned home, opened my files, and now have the answer in front of me.

Taken from "The Australian" 22nd November 1983, "$1200m Plan to Put the Third World on the Phone."

"Plans for putting a telephone within reasonable reach — not more than an hour's walk of the many millions in rural or isolated Third World areas, are being put forward by the International Telecommunication Union of the 24 nation OECD Organisation for Economic Co-operation and Development" — End quote.

Most discerning readers will instantly see that these people, live in their own little worlds, and that this scheme is nothing more than a false front, pretending to give them a telephone, yet we know now that it is really to link up computers to capture these folk along with the rest of the world. Some of these, clad only in a loin cloth, will soon require a pocket sewn on to it, in which to carry their plastic card.

By now, some will be asking a valid question.

## WHO OR WHAT IS ORGANISING ALL THIS?

Although there are literally thousands of groups involved, each little group or large power sector cannot see beyond their own back door, yet there is a master POWER in the background. It is too clever to be human.

"His name?" I hear you cry.

LUCIFER — The bright and shining one (alias Satan).

In my book "Warning" I referred to a power group, entitled "The Club of Rome". In a report to this group, a book entitled "Reshaping the International Order", reads like this.

Quote (P185) "The achievement of this global planning and management system calls for a **"conscious transfer of power"**. A gradual transfer to be sure from the national state to the World Organisation.

Only when this transfer takes place can the organisation become effective and purposeful.

Whether this historical challenge will be adequately met by nations is one of the key questions of the New International Order" — end quote. This N.I.O. is simply code for

WORLD GOVERNMENT

It is quite clear already that this "historical challenge" is being met by the governments of the two GUINEA PIG NATIONS of Australia and New Zealand.

Certain individuals, who either do not understand the New Monetary System or are genuinely sincere in their efforts are making speeches on world monetary reform. What a waste of time.

In New Zealand we have a number of Parliamentarians (including Mr Richard Prebble) who belong to a group called "Parliamentarians for World Order". There's nothing sinister in this they say. Mr Prebble speaking in Parliament on June 16th 1981 confirmed that P.W.O. would challenge N.Z's independence. — Quote "We will not be able to tackle those problems unless we are prepared to co-operate and give up some of our national sovereignty . . ." End quote. I personally feel that New Zealand is not his to give away.

## MONETARY REFORM 50 YEAR CYCLE

The system promoted by God for the Hebrew race was obviously a good one and finance experts would do well to (figuratively) take a leaf out of the Word of God.

Four thousand years ago, God gave Moses laws for his people.

He created a cycle of seven years. Every seventh year the land was to lie fallow.

Then after seven lots of these seven years (i.e. 49 years) the land was to lie fallow, two years in a row.

In this 50th year, which was called "The Year of Jubilee",

(a) Not only was the land to lie fallow
(b) All debts were to be cancelled
(c) All indentured servants were set free
(d) All land reverted back to the original owners.

There was a natural flushing out of the economy.

As the cycle began to draw to a close, money would only be available for a few years, and in the 49th year people would only loan money for one year, because on the 50th year those debts would be cancelled.

**REAL ESTATE CYCLE**

If you bought land at the beginning of the cycle, it was expensive. If you bought it 40 years into the cycle, it was cheaper, because in 10 years, the title reverted to the original owner.

All this kept the Hebrew race going for over 2,000 years. Men have tried to improve upon it, but failed.

In God's way using this 50 year cycle, the economy was flushed out and purified. People could count on it, and it worked.

**THE FRANKLIN DAM — TASMANIA**

The Tasmanian State Government intended to dam the Franklin River to provide another power source.

The environmentalists (Greenies) from different parts of the world began to exercise their muscle.

Finally, the Federal Government of Prime Minister Bob Hawke stepped in, and, because of international pressure, interfered with and finally cancelled out a State Government decision.

Thus, for the first time in the history of Australia, we see the beginnings of "a conscious transfer of power".

The Federal Labour Government in Australia has a number of Fabian Socialists in power (i.e. those who take over for socialism by stealth.)

The following examples are points to note.

Bills foisted upon this country by international power groups, many of them avowedly communistic, are being debated and passed by parliamentarians who have "not a clue in the wide world" that their country is being subtly taken over. The same obviously applies in New Zealand with the new Government elected in 1984. For example, the Anti-discrimination Bill — which looks good, but gives people of unusual lifestyles a measure of respectability and even power to teach the children of honourable people.

In New Zealand most of us laughed when we heard that when advertising for an employee, we could no longer write "Man" or "Woman". We were sure our friends were joking — they weren't. We now use the word "Person" which I beg to add, finishes with the suffix "son" and the word woman finishes with the suffix "man". It's indeed a strange old world. There are a few anomalies to be ironed out yet. For example:

— pictures of persons and persons on toilet doors at public places — discrimination I cry.

— Women's Charter, again from overseas. Endorsed by a number of Communist States.

Someone says, "Aha, he sees a red under every bed," to which I reply, "We don't mind them under the bed, it's the ones in the bed that worry us." Many concerned folk see the end result of this bill as a further aid to the distintegration of the family and home unit, e.g. there is now a move afoot to abolish corporal punishment from schools. This is so in some Scandinavian countries where a father recently went to prison for punishing his son. The boy was heartbroken and said, "I didn't mean this to happen".

Of course, these do-gooders never bother to read the textbook on life. Their intellects apparently are far superior to that of He who created them. Someone replies, "You brute. You mark the children's bodies with your rod of correction!"

Hark, I seem to hear a booming voice from heaven,

"The blueness of a wound cleanseth away evil, so do stripes, the inward parts of the belly." Proverbs 20:30.

By the way, did I hear correctly that the British monarchy is being eased off the Australian scene. Oh well, we must make way for progress, mustn't we.

Readers from other countries must not be too smug. For example, the Club of Rome has plans for the whole world.

Having read their writings, I was able to give a definition, by way of explanation of their aims, to my family.

Smith definition — The Club of Rome is a group of very sincere, but sadly misguided persons, who, having left God and His Word out of their lives and thoughts, are terribly concerned as to how this old world can continue on very much longer.

They have fed masses of information into computers covering the following subjects:

1. Population
2. Environment — air pollution, etc.
3. Land
4. Minerals
5. Resources
6. Farming, crops, etc.
7. Politics
8. Economy

and to their alarm, the machines have naturally churned out answers that give these dear folk very sleepless nights.

The world cannot continue on very much longer, at its present rate.

It's very strange you know, but we Christians already knew that without the aid of a computer.

A friend of mine at a mining conference heard the 'experts' bewailing the fact that we appear to be running out of certain minerals. He chuckled quietly to himself, knowing that God had put just enough into the earth to get us through until the return of His Son, our Lord Jesus Christ.

I feel genuinely sorry for folk without the Lord in their lives.

THIS IS THE MOMENT OF TRUTH.

I can clearly see that it all comes back to one foundation question — WHERE DID WE COME FROM?

**CHOICE OF ANSWERS:**

**1. GOD** **or** **2. NOTHING**

Believing No. 1 is the obvious answer. I must say here to you, the reader, surely you are too intelligent to believe No. 2. Is life an accident? Even Charles Darwin who died a Christian, a firm believer in Christ, said that people should never take him seriously. "I was only thinking aloud," he said. To him, the intricacies of the human eyeball were a tremendous stumbling block to his theories which he later discarded.

An article in the N.Z. Herald dated 3rd March 1984 tells of the adventures of an anthropologist, Richard Leakey, who is all excited because he found some fossilised fragments of an ape jaw. The unbelievers love it. "Amazing," they will say as he builds what he wants to around these things, in the form of an ape-man.

Listen to his arrogance. "So many years after Darwin and with the improvement of education, there are still well educated people who don't believe in evolution" — end quote. If that amazes him, my amazement must supersede his as to how learned people with a brain in their heads don't even betray a hint of a smile around their lips as they proceed to solemnly inform us, that this world of design came from nothing, no architect, no designer.

Mr Leakey and his family obviously are not very deep thinkers.

I think I remember reading somewhere "The fool hath said in his heart, there is no God".[1] An amplification of this passage reads like this, "The empty headed fool hath said in his heart, there is no God".

Someone retorts, "Aha, but scientists say . . ."

Wait a moment. I have also given my family a definition of a scientist. "A scientist is a person who is gradually and little by little discovering some of the things which God has created."

No wonder many of these are now becoming committed Christians.

"For the invisible things of Him from the creation of the world are clearly seen, being understood by the things that are made, even His eternal power and Godhead, so that they are WITHOUT EXCUSE."[2] (Emphasis added for meaning.)

The world is now hastening on towards a final show-down. There is no neutral ground. We all belong to one side or the other:

GOD'S or SATAN'S

**BACK TO THE CLUB OF ROME**

These folk have plans to arrest this coming cataclysm as they see it.

They have taken a number of very positive steps. One such step has been to divide the world into "10 Regions".

As we are working in the main in Australasia, and as these two countries of Australia and New Zealand are the test patterns for the whole world I will list here Region No. 4 on the Club of Rome's list:

New Zealand
Australia
South Africa
Israel
Oceania — the Pacific Islands

It is interesting to note that C.E.R. has been introduced between New Zealand and Australia. This stands for 'Closer Economic Relations'. The Australians for many years have allowed travellers to bring in $200 of duty free goods while the New Zealand Government generously allowed us $50 worth. Since this treaty was signed, New Zealand has fallen into line with Australia and now allows $200 worth New Zealand duty free goods. This of course is not exactly the same as there is a currency value difference at this time of writing. We have been told that this trade difference should all but disappear within five years.

"Why five years?" I hear you ask. Because World Government should be in by then.

Whilst lecturing in Canberra recently, a friend took me up the hill to show me the new Federal Parliament buildings. I was told that in the building there will be a chair provided for our New Zealand Prime Minister so that he can attend the Australian State Premier's Conferences. Mr Doug Anthony, Leader of the Australian National Party, alluded to this in his recent retirement speech where he suggested an extension of C.E.R. could be C.P.R., i.e. Closer Political Relations, possibly making us virtually one country.

Speaking at a public lecture recently, I wrote the list for No. 4 group on the blackboard and made the statement that as we were all in the same list, very soon sporting and other contacts with South Africa will, of necessity, need to be re-established. Picking up the newspaper, the very next day, I read where a well-known sportsman said that all this anti-South African feeling should be discontinued and normal sporting contacts resumed. Mark my words, it must come to this.

Bankcard holders in Australia will notice No. 4 as the initial digit on their card. Note the new Government in New Zealand has expelled the South African Consul. They will look extremely foolish when they invite him back as we are in the same region, i.e. No. 4.

Other Regions of the Club of Rome:

1. North America
2. Western Europe
3. Japan
4. (Mentioned above)
5. Eastern Europe
6. Latin America
7. North Africa and Middle East
8. Main Africa
9. South and South East Asia
10. Centrally planned Asia.

## A FRIGHTENING FACT — SEEDS UNDER ATTACK — PVR

I am writing herewith something which very few people know about.

In almost every country of the western world, a bill has been passed, making it legal for plant breeders to emasculate the seeds and make them into hybrids, with only one good season of growth, thus requiring the grower to return annually to the plant breeder for more seeds.

Ultimately the World Government group will handle all seed distribution. In New Zealand the two main groups were Yates and Coopers, but now a large group has taken over seed distribution.

Some years ago I learnt that giant food companies were merging with energy (oil) companies, as has happened so much in Australia. Now, take notice. These hybrid seeds will only grow when planted with an oil derived fertilizer produced by the same firms that distribute the seeds.

The name of the Bill is P.V.R., i.e. Plant Variety Rights or P.B.R. i.e. Plant Breeders Rights. New Zealand passed this diabolical legislation in the early 1970's with very few Kiwis realising what was going on.

The excuse of the Plant Breeders is that they want to protect their new hybrid breeds and take out a patent on new strains, forbidding others to copy.

A definition of P.V.R. — taking a natural resource — fiddling with it — selling it for a profit.

The only country which seems to have struck some opposition with this bill is Australia. It has been before Parliament many times, but there is so much opposition it will finally have to be pushed through somehow as this is essential for World Government.

By the way, this seed bill will ultimately bring all the alternative lifestyle people out of the bush for new seed supplies and bring them also under the benevolent umbrella of Big Brother.

Whilst lecturing in Queensland, I had opportunity to visit and hold a discussion with Senator Flo Bjelke-Peterson. She is a very gracious born again Christian woman. I gave her a copy of my book "Warning", read her some scriptures and asked her to fight this bill in Canberra. All that can be done really is to delay it, and by the time this book goes to press, the bill will probably be well and truly passed.

Here are the Scriptures I read that day.

"And God said, let the earth bring forth grass, the herb yielding seed, and the fruit tree, yielding fruit after his kind, WHOSE SEED IS IN ITSELF, upon the earth and it was so."[3]

"And God said, Behold I have given you every herb bearing seed, which is upon the face of all the earth, and every tree, IN THE WHICH IS THE FRUIT OF A TREE YIELDING SEED, to you it shall be for meat."[4] (Emphasis added for meaning.)

"While the earth remaineth, seedtime and harvest, and cold and heat, and summer and winter, and day and night shall not cease."[5]

It is quite clear that anyone who is involved in this PVR is in direct confrontation with the will of almighty God.

"Oh come now," I hear you answer, "It has been proven that these hybrid strains, now being patented bring forth greater and better quality yields." That is what we are told by the greedy lads whose eyes sparkle as they examine their current bank statement.

Let us now read excerpts from an article entitled
SEEDS OF DISASTER — Taken from the Soil Association's Quarterly Review

"Multinationals are patenting plant life, and weeding out variety. They may be sowing seeds of disaster."

**IRISH POTATO FAMINE**

When Sir Walter Raleigh returned from the new world in 1588, with a mysterious new plant called the potato, no one could have foreseen that he was carrying the seed for the greatest natural disaster since the Black Plague. The potato took well to the fog-soaked soil of Ireland. Within 50 years, it was the universal staple of the Irish diet.

Then came the blight. The first signs appear in the summer of 1845, when the tops of the unripe potato plants turned an ugly black. A stench hung over the fields. Underground the potatoes shrivelled and began to rot.

That year, half the Irish crop was ruined by the same fungus; the next year almost the entire crop was devastated. The primary potato strain, known as the "Lumper" had no resistance to the new disease. Over the next three years, one million Irish people (most of them peasants), nearly one in every eight, died from starvation or disease. One and a half million more emigrated.

**IOWA CORN BLIGHT**

The year is 1970. It is hot but rainy in Iowa, unusual weather for August. Row upon row of green corn stalks vibrate in the still air. In a couple of months, the corn, one of the two largest food crops in North America, will be ready for harvest. But in Story County, Iowa, farmers are uneasy. From the early spring reports in Florida, at the southern edge of the corn belt, plant pathologists learned that a fungus was causing trouble. It was a new strain of an old fungus, and it was spreading with a virulence never seen before. The blight destroyed up to half the crop in parts of the south and scientists feared the infestation would spread north. By summer, it did, and it spread quickly.

By August, farmers all over Iowa were helpless, their crop scarred with small ink-like spots. In October, when the infested fields were harvested, black spores sailed over nearby towns like locusts.

Millions of plants — 15 per cent of the nation's total corn crop, more than 50 per cent of the yield in some regions of the country — were killed by the leaf blight.

. . . The corn seeds planted in tens of millions of acres across the U.S. contained "Texas Male Cytoplasm". This ingredient made the male plants genetically sterile, eliminating the need for expensive hand de-tasselling to prevent cross pollination. But breeding a new strain to solve that problem, caused a larger one."

**WHAT MISTAKES WERE MADE?**

"What the Irish Potato crop of 1845 and the American corn crop of 1970 had in common, was an OVER-RIDING UNIFORMITY. The seeds for both crops were from a single genetic strain, and were sown over very large areas.

In both cases, the seed strains had some real agricultural advantages. But also, in both cases, the crops were vulnerable to diseases, that might not have struck other strains. Had Sir Walter brought home three or four varieties of potatoes, and had corn farmers from Florida and Iowa planted different strains of corn, alternating them from field to field, neither blight would have caused as much damage as it did, and both would today be only minor footnotes in agricultural history.

**DANGER FAMINE AHEAD**

. . . Royalties have contributed to making seeds, next to fuel, the most inflationary agricultural production factor, with prices rising more than 150% over the past 10 years.

. . . The European Economic Community (EEC) governs the seed trade with its common catalogue, which lists only the varieties that are legal to sell through the continent. In 1980, a revised catalogue was issued that made more than 2,000 vegetable varieties illegal to sell in Europe. To sell them would be violating a patent owned by one of the new corporate seed merchants.

. . . It has been estimated that 75 per cent of the vegetable varieties, currently planted in Europe will be "extinct" by 1991 if current policies continue.

. . . Just 100 years ago the world's farmers grew literally thousands of different grain and produce items. Today 30 crops provide 90 per cent of the world's calories. Four of these — corn, wheat, rice and sorghum — supply more than half of those calories. There's more food, to be sure, but fewer varieties. . . . End quote.

Where did I read this, I wonder?

"For they have sown the wind, and they shall reap the whirlwind, it hath no stalk, the bud shall yield no meal, if so be it yield, the strangers shall swallow it up."[6]

I reckon these strangers sound a little bit like the Plant Breeders.

**FISHERIES**

It is also worthy of note that World Government sources are also tying up the fisheries. Laws are being passed to limit who may fish, where he may fish, width of mesh, a special radio band, the numbers of certain species allowed to be caught.

Can you see now how food supplies are, along with the New World Money system, also being cleverly tied up, to exclude any who wish to live outside the system.

Please keep watching for more restrictive laws being passed.

I recall an event which took place some years ago when I was a teacher at Seddon High School in Auckland, New Zealand.

The Auckland Mayor at the time, Sir Dove Meyer Robinson, speaking at a morning school assembly, gave us all a very worthy piece of advice.

Quote: "Young people, be very slow to elect a new committee, because each new committee feels obliged to pass new laws to justify their existence." End quote.

As a Christian, I can state with conviction, that true born again folk have "now" a freedom second to none.

"If the Son therefore shall make you free, ye shall be free indeed."[7]

**ON TO ENERGY**

In my first book "Warning", I mentioned on p. 92 three major problems, each of them false, which are being continually presented to us by the media.

1. Money
2. Food
3. Energy

Whenever I see the words "Go easy on Energy" presented, I ask "Why".

There obviously is plenty of oil round. Why are these people telling us lies? By now, you can answer that question yourself.

By presenting three major problems, the citizens of this world are being continually bombarded until they submit through downright fear. When these world leaders say, "give us World Government, there is no other way," folk will be so weary of it all, they will like a regiment of robots say, "Yes, we must have World Government".

A couple of examples will assist in our understanding of this false energy crisis.

From the Sydney Morning Herald, 12th February 1980 we read:

"Enough Oil for 120 Centuries."

"Canberra — The Acting Prime Minister, Mr Anthony, claimed yesterday that Australia had enough reserves of shale oil to last 12,000 years at the present rate of consumption."

NOT ONLY AUSTRALIA — U.S.A. IS ALSO OVERSTOCKED WITH OIL.

In March 1980, Hugh M. Chance, Former Senator of the State of Colorado endorsed the findings of the Chaplain in charge of work camps on the trans-Alaska oil pipeline.

An official on this job was questioned by the Senator. We will call this official Mr X to protect his identity.

Senator: "Mr X, how much crude oil is there under the north slope of Alaska?"

Mr X: "In my estimation, from the seismographic work, and the drilling we have already done, I am convinced that there is as much oil under the north slope of Alaska as there is in all Saudi Arabia.

Senator, there is no energy crisis. There is an artificially produced energy crisis and it is for the purpose of controlling the American people. You see, if the government can control energy, they can control industry, they can control the individual, and they can control business. It is well known that everything relates back to crude oil.

. . . And there is enough natural gas here to supply the entire United States of America for over 200 years. The gas comes out when the oil does, but they won't let us pipe it to the lower 48, and they won't let us burn it. At a cost of millions and millions of dollars we are being forced to pump that natural gas back into the ground — thus adding to the cost of the oil."

Just off the coast, there was great excitement as oil was discovered on Gull Island. The official in charge, said, "Chaplain, within one year, we can build a pipeline and flood America with oil, Alaskan oil, and we won't have to worry about the Arabs. This ought to hit the front page in every paper in America."

The next day, the official was very quiet and subdued.

Chaplain: "I listened as that official said to me that the government had ordered the oil company to seal the documents, withdraw the rig, cap the well, and not release the information about the Gull Island find. — The truth about it has never been told until NOW." End quote.

Now my wife and I verify that, whilst we were visiting the West Cost of America in 1979, we read that the headlines in the Alaskan newspapers were asking the obvious question, "Why Don't You Want Our Oil?"

I remember an old quote attributed to Dr Henry Kissinger who once said,

"By controlling energy, you can control nations; By controlling food, you can control individuals."

**RECAP**

1. Computer files being extended.
2. 3 lots of 6 digits.
2. Traitors in Parliament.
4. Club of Rome — Gradual Transfer of Power.
5. 10 Regions.
6. Seeds, Fisheries, Energy being manipulated.

# CHAPTER FOUR

# KISSINGER KAPERS

In our last chapter, we referred briefly again to

**HENRY A. KISSINGER**

In my first book I had quite a bit to say about this man and his activities.

I pointed out that a world leader had been predicted first in 586 B.C. and then again in 96 A.D.

Here again I list the qualifications for this man, whoever he may be.

From "Warning" p. 29-33.

1. Jewish, and possibly German.
2. A man of boasting arrogance.
3. Something special about his eyes (the eyes being the windows of the soul).
4. Outstanding in the field of diplomacy.
5. Not to be trusted.
6. Good people rely on him.
7. Party type man (swinger and jetsetter).
8. Travels a great deal.
9. His aim is World dominion.

I should add here also that his name will add up to 666, as the name Kissinger does.

I am more than aware of an over-eagerness in the human spirit to be the one to be the first to discover the identity of the elusive One World Government Leader.

Countless books have been written exposing the ultimate antichrist person or group, as the case may be. By this phrase, any person or group who denies the authority of the Word of God, and the method of salvation set out for us by God, through our Lord Jesus Christ alone, through his substitutionary sacrifice on the cross, once and for all, is clearly ANTICHRIST or against Christ, and all He stands for.

You reply, "That form of thinking is a little naive isn't it?" To which I reply, "Please show me one book other than the Bible which has the same success rate in changing lives, and also one that speaks with authority on WHERE WE CAME FROM — WHAT WE ARE DOING HERE — WHERE WE ARE GOING TO?

I challenge you. It is not me, it's you who are naive and plain careless regarding your own future unless you come up with such a book of authority.

I call the Bible, the manufacturer's handbook. During the early 1900's, there was a man named Ivan Panin; a Russian mathematician who was also an avowed atheist who set out to prove the Word of God incorrect.

For the following 50 years, he wrote on his findings. The irony of the whole exercise was that he finally proved that no person, other than God himself, could possibly be the author of this wonderful Book, and Panin committed himself wholly to God, and to His son the Lord Jesus Christ.

"How can this be?" you ask. "I thought such a thing was impossible to prove."

Actually, most unbelief stems from lack of knowledge. It was well written, "My people are destroyed for lack of knowledge."[1]

I was in the school teaching profession for 15 years and regularly came up against poor boys, girls and even staff members, who when they tried to discuss things with me about spiritual matters, simply parroted off what their fathers or mothers had taught them, from their own ignorance.

It is a tremendous responsibility to teach others, because if you are wrong, you are also responsible at the judgement for all those you have put wrong.

"My brethren, be not many masters knowing that we shall receive the greater condemnation."[2]

**IVAN PANIN**

Panin discovered early in his investigations into the Old Testament (written in Hebrew) and the New Testament (in Greek) that both of these languages have a numeric system built into their alphabets.

During his many years of research, he found an incredible pattern emerge in these original languages. Patterns of numerics quickly took shape, criss-crossing right through the word of God. Students have for many years accepted No. 7 as God's number of perfection. It was notable, therefore, that there was this number, over and over again with its multiples — 7, 14, 21, 28, etc. These numbers are so incredible that only a mastermind could have designed them.

1. These numerics only apply to the inspired books, i.e. Genesis-Malachi and from Matthew-Revelation. N.B. The Apocrypha is not included.
2. These numerics do not apply to any other book, e.g. Koran, Book of Mormon — thus proving them to be uninspired by God.
3. So overwhelming was his evidence that he put an open challenge in the "New York Sun" newspaper inviting

the intellectuals of his day to go with him to the highest court in the land, together with a dozen mathematicians of the highest calibre they could muster and he would establish that the Bible was indeed the Word of God.

He also named the Principals of Harvard, Yale and Cornell Universities along with the Editor of the Encyclopaedia Britannica as possibly wishing to debate with him. This challenge was put in the form of an open letter to the "New York Sun" newspaper, but remained unanswered as he was dealing with "Facts" which tend to be stubborn things.

The Nobel Foundation examined his works and said, "We cannot fault the findings of Ivan Panin".

Young people and old everywhere are looking for an authoritative voice.

It was interesting recently to read again of another event in the life of Malcolm Muggeridge. — Converted to Christ in later life, he became a voice to be listened to, with his years of experience and nimble mind, together with a brilliant vocabulary, spoke on many issues.

Born again Christians all around the world were recently shocked to read that he had joined the Roman Catholic Church. — A friend of mine eased my surprise with the following explanation: Malcolm, in his declining years began searching for an authority which he felt he needed. Not having had years of exposure to the Word of God and its truths, he looked to the wrong source for his authority, i.e. The Roman Catholic Church, instead of the Word of God. Many others have in their ignorance done the wrong thing, yet the Lord's love and mercy is still operating in many of their lives.

By way of illustration let me tell of an actual happening in my own experience.

In the year 1978, together with a team of Christian Cook Islanders, we were on a lecture preaching tour of the island of Rarotonga. This was my fourth trip to this island and I had made many friends there. One such, a non-Christian man, because of his interest in the gospel, loaned us his picture theatres, free of charge in most cases, in which to hold our meetings.

One night, right in the town of Avarua, I made the following statement — "God will not judge you at the judgement."

"For the Father judgeth no man, but hath committed all judgement unto the Son."[3]

I then went on to say, "Neither will you be judged by Jesus the Son, but by the Word of God."

Leaving the building that night, after the meeting, we were met at the door of the theatre by one angry man.

"How dare you teach such false information," he said. I replied, "What do you mean?"

"Teaching that Jesus himself will not do the judging," was his answer.

Picking up my Bible, I turned to the following passage which clarified the whole matter not only to this man, but to all the others who had gathered around to see the fun.

"And if any man hear my words, and believe not, I judge him not, for I came not to judge the world but to save the world.

"He that rejecteth me, and receiveth not my words, hath one that judgeth him.

The word that I have spoken the same shall judge him in the last day."[4]

Having read this, we are now responsible to declare, wherein the source of our authority lies.

(a) A Protestant Church? — No! The Word of God.
(b) The Roman Catholic Church? No! The Word of God.
(c) Eastern Religion?— No! The Word of God.
(d) Humanistic Thought? — No! The Word of God.

**MEANWHILE, BACK TO KISSINGER**

As we travel, I am constantly asked, "Do you still have your eyes on Kissinger?"

Answer — "Yes, more so than ever."

Kissinger is a German Jew by nationality, which fits the prophecies perfectly, however, someone else may arise who will

(a) Settle the Mid-East conflict, by giving his seal of approval to a Seven year Peace Treaty.
(b) Be appointed a loosely knit leader of the European Economic Community (EEC).

These two details added together with other qualifications equal Antichrist.

**WHAT IS HENRY UP TO NOW?**

1. He is one of the executives of Kissinger Associates, a powerful group who in an advisory capacity give advice on strategic planning. Lord Carrington from Great Britain who resigned over the Falkland Islands war, also works for this firm.

   A retainer of $250,000 is requested initially to get Kissinger started in any business assistance required. It is interesting and important to note that both these men have had interests in Middle East Peace negotiations.

2. He worked for the NBC in America for five years, vetting the news and letting out to the media, that which he felt was suitable for the masses to see and hear. This was a $1.5m contract.

3. He has been called the public relations man for the One World Government people, and works in close conjunction with David Rockefeller, formerly of the Chase-Manhattan Bank, on preparing the world for a takeover. When he gives a breakfast speech, he may earn up to $12,500 and $20,000 for a dinner address.

4. He has been described as an egomaniac. This behaviour can stem from a number of factors. His background in Nazi Germany where he was continually pushed around by arrogant Nazis, before his emigration to the U.S. with his parents. Here he was, a German Jewish boy, very average at school, yet upon his arrival in America, suddenly began to collect 'A' passes. "Brilliant" his Professors called him.

   Have you ever met an egomaniac? You have; then you will be familiar with their aggressive arrogant behaviour. When you speak to them, they don't wish to listen. Your ideas are of no value to them and are dismissed with a flick of the hand. Nothing interests them like the sound of their own voice.

   From a news article. Quote — "Dr Kissinger has invited a reporter to attend the party on the condition that his apartment would not be described in print ('Nancy would go into orbit' — he says of his wife) and that none of his guests be quoted," but he added, "if you want to quote me that's okay." — End quote.

   Here is another quote. "The longer I am out of power, the more infallible I appear to be to myself." — End quote.

5. In a book entitled "The Price of Power", by Seymour Hersh, Kissinger is shown up in a very poor light. Hersh was offered $200,000 to write the book and does not feel antagonistic towards Kissinger. To make sure none of the money went out in libel payments, Hersh employed three lawyers to check his manuscripts.

   Hersh claims Kissinger was involved in

   (a) Lies
   (b) Watergate
   (c) Phone tapping (friends included)
   (d) False peace in Vietnam

(e) Secret bombing of Cambodia (Kampuchea — 1967-70)

(f) Misuse of power — quote from another source in a news article 21st June 1983: "So consistently did he circumvent the limitations placed on his use of power by the constitution and by Congress, that subversions became the norm, not the exception . . . Dr Kissinger, the record shows, presided over the secret bombing of Kampuchea in 1967-70 without the advice and consent of Congress. . . . But this discussion is not about personalities. It is about the laws and constitutional rules that are fundamental to our Government (i.e. U.S.A.). The alternative is an authoritarian form of Government". — End quote.

6. On 6th March 1984 we read,"President Reagan has named the former Secretary of State, Dr Henry Kissinger, as a member of his Foreign Intelligence Advisory Board."

7. He has recently given a speech, recorded in the Time magazine, to N.A.T.O. (North Atlantic Treaty Organisation).

8. He recently brought about a temporary truce in Central America. It took him one week, whilst critics said it should have taken at least three months observation and negotiating.

"How did he do it so quickly?" I hear you ask.

Answer: "Money — he used the American tax payers money and spread a little love around."

9. It is quite possible that he will be used in the Middle East area to confirm the future Seven Year Treaty. — Let's watch and see.

10. During his visit to Australia in 1983, he gave the odd speech, looked into minerals, natural resources and banking.

Interested persons will note that it was just after he left that the Cashless Society took off. "Coincidence" you cry. Maybe so, maybe not. During this visit he addressed the heads of the banking system.

Cloak and dagger type characters shepherded him around during his visit — shades of James Bond.

11. On his own admission, whilst negotiating for peace, etc., Kissinger uses the following ploys:

(a) Threats of force

(b) Innuendo

(c) Downright lies are permissible on occasions.
(d) The use of monetary gifts works wonders.

Many of his skills were learnt from his studies of the lives of three great personalities in history:

(a) Bismarck — a man of war and force.
(b) Metternich — a man of lies and deceit.
(c) Castlereagh — a man of peace settlements.

"But in his estate he shall honour the god of forces, and a god whom his fathers knew not . . ."[5]

Please do not forget that the ancient prophecies make it very clear that this new world leader, whoever he turns out to be will be a non-religious Jew.

AGAIN

"Neither shall he regard the God of his fathers (Jehovah) nor him to whom women desire to give birth (Jesus Christ the Messiah) nor regard any god, for he shall magnify himself above all."[6] (Words in brackets added to assist meaning.)

Henry Kissinger is a non-religious Jew. In 1973, he deliberately took over the job of Secretary of State on the Sabbath Day, to show the distance between him and the religion in which he was raised.

When asked by a reporter if he ever prays, H.K. replied, "Oh yes. Each night I ask God if there is anything I can do for him."

12. We realise of course that all these activities are being undertaken under a supposed cloak of secrecy, yet, in spite of all the nefarious scheming, spies, false media reports, unreported visits to various places, envelopes marked 'Secret' — 'Personal' — 'Burn Before Reading', etc., all is known by the author of the world's best seller.

"He disappointeth the devices of the crafty, so that their hands cannot perform their enterprise. He taketh the wise in their own craftiness. . . . They meet with darkness in the daytime, and grope in the noon-day as in the night."[7]

**STATEMENT**

If I did not have a very personal knowledge of the Lord and His Son Jesus Christ, and have a copy of His book in my possession, at this stage, all this information would shatter and terrify me, as we all appear to be so vulnerable.

However, I hasten to add, all is not doom and gloom. God is not particularly impressed with all this, and neither are His people — just mildly interested.

"There shall no evil befall thee, neither shall any plague come nigh thy dwelling . . . because thou has made the Lord . . . thy habitation."[8]

## LAWLESSNESS

I well remember an incident from my school teaching days. The school bus was leaving to take the high school students home. A girl aged about 15 years of age sat in one of those departing buses, smiling and waving cheerfully to a poor woman teacher who was almost frantic, calling out, "Get off the bus and come to the detention room." I later helped escort this teacher into the staff room. Weeping and shaking she drank the cup of tea offered to her.

Weakened discipline, children's rights, etc., have weakened the fabric of our society.

This must needs be the state of society when this new World Leader arises — a slack law system.

"Therefore the law is slacked, and judgement doth never go forth for the wicked doth compass about the righteous, therefore wrong judgement proceedeth."[9]

EXAMPLE No. 1

An excellent example of a case of wrong judgement is the famous dingo/baby case in Australia. A Christian woman goes to prison for the presumed murder of her baby, who in fact was taken from its bassinet by a wild dingo, which is not a dog, but a wolf. The dingo's name was Ding, and was shot by a local policeman soon after the baby was taken, although it was supposed to have been shot by a ranger before this baby was taken.

The witnesses who were on the spot are disbelieved to a man — cleverly worded loaded questions are used in the court case — the facts are ignored — result — woman goes to jail on a hypothetical case built up by forensic science on a false premise, i.e. that blood found in the parent's car was foetal haemoglobin, when in fact it was the blood of an adult accident victim, picked up and helped by the parents some time before. The spray pattern under the dashboard of the car was a preservative paint — not blood at all.

Therefore upon further investigation the original forensic science report has been shown to be faulty, and by the time this book goes to press the woman involved should have been released from prison, scarred for life — put away by false circumstantial evidence. Eleven persons who were involved at

Ayers rock know the truth and I, along with many others, know their names. — The media in Australia told so many lies that they are too embarrassed to print the truth, even though it is clearly set out in a book entitled "AZARIA — WHAT THE JURY WERE NOT TOLD" by Phil Ward. Avalable from 305 Pitt Street, Sydney, N.S.W., Australia.

EXAMPLE No. 2

A similar thing happened in New Zealand to a man called Arthur Alan Thomas. Ten years in prison for a murder he did not commit, whilst the real murderer and cohorts remained free to travel around at will, spend money and enjoy life generally. Why? Police corruption — planted evidence — scapegoat needed.

EXAMPLE No. 3

A well-known scientist in Tasmania, Australia, cuts up his wife and feeds her into the sewer system, having first of all practised on a sheep's carcase.

The newspaper reports. Quote — "He was found not guilty by reason of insanity of murdering his wife and declared a mentally disordered person. This means that he cannot be sent to prison because he was not convicted or sentenced to jail." — The article goes on to say, "the scientist would be more easily supervised in the prison hospital, where facilities could be made available for him to continue his highly valued research work." — End quote. Who is really insane here?

**RECAP**

1. Kissinger's latest movements.
2. Ivan Panin proves authority of Bible.
3. Law systems becoming corrupt, thus making way for world government.

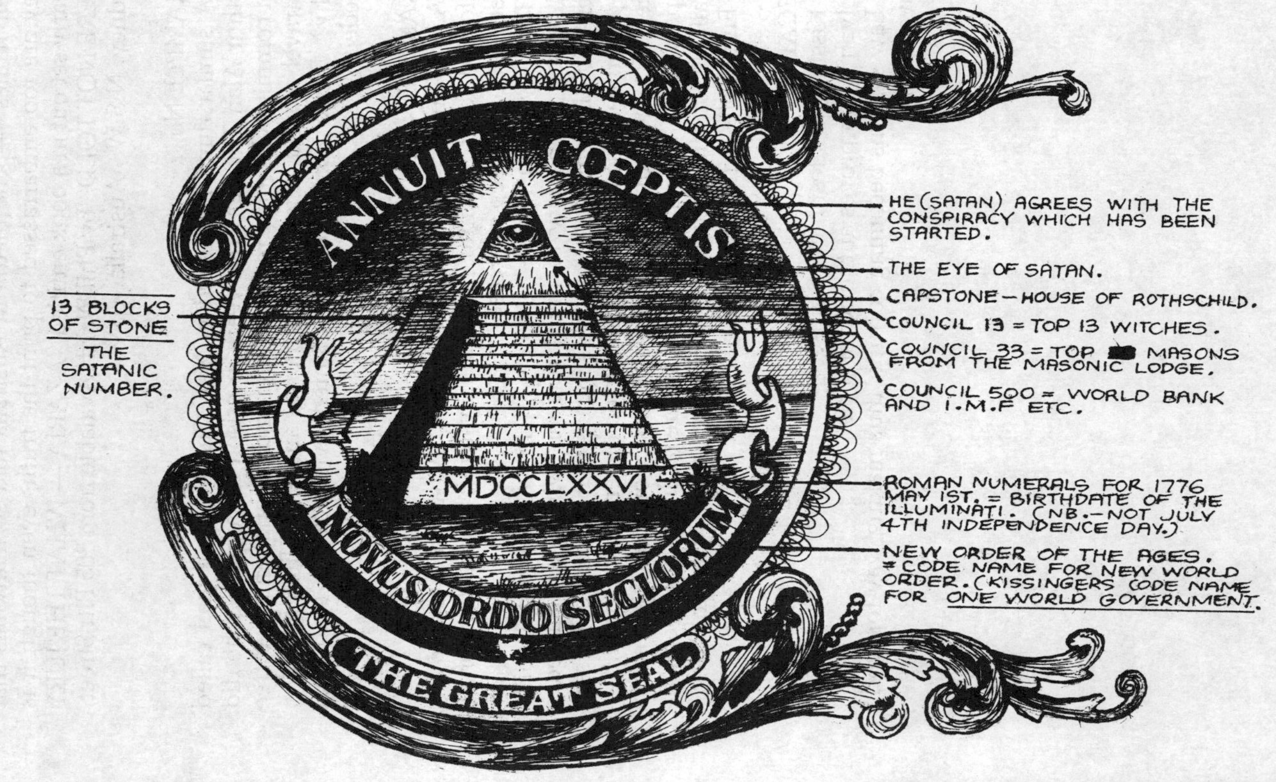

(ONE WORLD GOV'T ADVOCATES.)
ANNUIT COEPTIS
MDCCLXXVI
NOVUS ORDO SECLORUM
THE GREAT SEAL
13 BLOCKS OF STONE
THE SATANIC NUMBER.
HE (SATAN) AGREES WITH THE CONSPIRACY WHICH HAS BEEN STARTED.
THE EYE OF SATAN.
CAPSTONE — HOUSE OF ROTHSCHILD.
COUNCIL 13 = TOP 13 WITCHES.
COUNCIL 33 = TOP MASONS FROM THE MASONIC LODGE.
COUNCIL 500 = WORLD BANK AND I.M.F ETC.
ROMAN NUMERALS FOR 1776 MAY 1ST. = BIRTHDATE OF THE ILLUMINATI. (NB.—NOT JULY 4TH INDEPENDENCE DAY.)
NEW ORDER OF THE AGES. = CODE NAME FOR NEW WORLD ORDER. (KISSINGERS CODE NAME FOR ONE WORLD GOVERNMENT.

## CHAPTER FIVE

# WORLD GOVERNMENT

This strange seal found on the reverse side of the American $1 bill is the seal of the One World Government advocates.

We will attempt herewith to present a logical explanation. Anything the reader finds unpalatable, please bear with me and continue reading as the matter will be fully documented in this chapter and the next.

The Arch-enemy of the true and living God is named satan or Lucifer (bright and shining one):

(a) He originally lived in God's heaven.
(b) Was involved in music.
(c) Was very beautiful.
(d) Was full of wisdom.
(e) Mis-directed praise due to God to himself.
(f) Was thrown out of heaven to the earth.
(g) His titles — Prince of the power of the air — Prince of this world — God of this world.

His aims are recorded for us clearly:

"I will ascend into heaven." i.e. Paradise, clouds, place of natural beauty. This is entitled the "third heaven" where Christians go at death.

"I will exalt my throne above the stars of God" i.e. the starry heavens, showing a portion of God's skill and variety in creation. This is the "second heaven."

"I will sit also upon the mount of the congregation in the sides of the north"[1] i.e. this is the "first heaven" — the throne room of God.

The prophets make it quite clear that Lucifer will, in a day to come, have this dream fulfilled, for the short duration of 3½ years only (i.e. 42 months, or 1,260 days, or time (1 year), times (2 years) and a half (6 months) ). These calculations are correct when one uses the time scale used by the Jews for centuries, i.e. a 360 day lunar year or a series of 12 x 30 day months.

At the end of this 3½ year period, Lucifer, plus his political front man (i.e. Antichrist) running the EEC through the New World Money System and also his religious front man (i.e. false prophet) running the One World Church System, linking with eastern religion and the occult will come to their end, in hell (i.e.the lake of fire).

1. Lucifer — Boss Man

2. Beast — Politics
3. False Prophet — Religion

Some years ago in San Francisco at the Berkeley University the following took place.

A young Christian man, nicknamed the footpath preacher ran services in a large building. During his preaching he observed a group of satan worshippers taking their places in the balcony, zapping him as they moved, by the pointing of the fingers and diabolical mutterings.

Noticing these attempts to hex him he said, "I notice you satanists up there trying to put your curses on me. Firstly, I wish to remind you that your curses do not work on me, because of the power of the Lord Jesus Christ who lives in me. Secondly, I hear that you, in your satanic church read the Bible backwards.

I intend to now read it to you forwards, and this will show you the end of your master, plus the judgement of his helpers.

"And the beast was taken, and with him, the false prophet that wrought miracles before him, with which he deceived them that had received the mark of the beast, and them that worshipped his image. These both were cast alive into a lake of fire burning with brimstone."[2]

And then, 1,000 years later, after being released from falling in the bottomless pit . . . Here goes No. 1 to join No's 2 and 3 forever.

"And the devil (No. 1) that deceived them was cast into the lake of fire and brimstone, where the beast and the false prophet are (Nos 2 and 3) and they shall be tormented day and night forever and ever."[3] (words in brackets added for clarity.)

The preacher pointed up to the white faced, tense little bunch in the balcony and said, "And you will join them unless you turn to God in repentance from sin and have faith in our Lord Jesus Christ."

Immediately, they rose as one man and walked down to the front of the building, where they individually committed their lives to Christ.

**EXPLANATION OF SYMBOL**

This eye inside the triangle is taken from Egyptian mythology and is called "The Eye of Horus" and is actually the eye of Lucifer.

As explained in my first book "Warning" in the year 1776 a group called the Illuminati was formed in Bavaria by one Adam Weishaupt, a former Jesuit who defected and became a Satanist or a Luciferian. Date again, 1st May 1776.

Their aim was to replace Christianity with a system of reason.

To destroy democracy, create a world government, along with a world church based on the adoration of Lucifer.

This seal you see drawn here in this book is the seal of the Illuminati (i.e. bearers of the light).

The eye in the triangle was called by Weishaupt, the "Insinuating Brethren" or a satanic eye previously known as Horus, that looks down on and controls society.

Doubters are invited to read an account in the Encyclopaedia Britannica where we are told that the Illuminati became so powerful that is was ultimately banned by the Bavarian Government in 1785.

However, three years later, they began to make contact with various Masonic Lodges and often managed to gain a commanding position in the upper degrees. So it is today that on many Lodge walls, worn also as jewellery by the Grand Master, we find this same eye in the triangle. This will be fully explained in the chapter entitled "Freemasonry".

Away back in 1776, Weishaupt's aim was to promote Lucifer to the throne room, governing world affairs.

Society was likened to the 13 layers of stone in the form of a pyramid. Witches and satanists who have been converted to Jesus Christ tell us the meaning of the symbolism.

**PLAN**

(a) Satan's eye in the triangle.
(b) Top block of stone — Council 13 of witchcraft on the east coast of America — controlling Wall Street, N.Y. — Finance.
(c) Next block down — Council 33 of Freemasonry. An honorary degree which issues statements and directives to those below, from those above.
(d) Next block down — Council 500 — The 500 richest banking families in the world who are in the know.
(e) The two Latin words at the top "Annuit Coeptis — Agreement with that which has been started", i.e. Lucifer in the triangle is in full agreement with this plan.
(f) The three Latin words at the bottom "Novus Ordo Seclorum" mean "New World Order of the Ages".

NOW CAN YOU SEE IT?

**EXPLANATION**

Lucifer agrees with this plan for One World Government which has been started because, ultimately he will be in charge (for a season only, i.e. 3½ years).

Now then: how did it get on to the back of the U.S. $1 bill?

Answer: By order of President Franklin D. Roosevelt in the year 1933, just as America was climbing out of the Stock Market crash of '29 — Roosevelt was a 32° Mason.

Why the American $1 bill? Because for many years this was the world's leading currency. Travellers always yearned for U.S. dollars to take on their trips.

Remember the surreptitious whispering, "Got any Yankee dollars?" Why was this you ask?

It was powerful, stable, and highly acceptable in most countries.

**A MONEY DEVIL**

Thus the spirit of this One World Luciferian system has already infiltrated the world systems in the form of finance.

The date 1776 on the base of the Pyramid stands for 1st May (the date the Illuminati was inaugurated) not 4th July (i.e. Declaration of Independence). In this same year of 1776, however, just two months after the inauguration of the Illuminati in Bavaria permission was given to a small group of illumined Masons to design a seal for the new Republic, i.e. 13 States of America.

This great seal of America was cast in two plates, and carried to Thomas Jefferson by a hooded figure on 17th June, 1782.

Jefferson, a Freemason, received the red velvet bag containing the plates, in his drawing room in Virginia. Later, he was appointed American Ambassador to France in 1784, thus giving him opportunity to examine the European Illuminati in detail.

Many world famous men have favoured the concept of World Government, but only Christians with their Bibles open know the end result of this thing.

"The fear of the Lord is the beginning of wisdom."[4]

Names like F. D. Roosevelt, John Adams, Benjamin Franklin, Cecil Rhodes, come readily to mind.

Regarding this latter name, it is important to realise that anyone trained under a Rhodes Scholarship is also subtly trained in the art of INTERNATIONALISM.

Even in our school Social Studies classes, the concept of INDEPENDENCE is giving way to the concept of INTER-DEPENDENCE.

Here is a riddle for Australian readers — Which man high in the field of politics in Australia was a Rhodes Scholar? Bob Hawke, your Prime Minister, of course!

In my last book "Warning", I outlined the four Power

FIBRE
OPTIC
COMPUTER
VIEWER
NEWS
CABLE
T.V.

Groups, significantly right in the front row of World Government plans.

(a) C.F.R. Council on Foreign Relations
Advise U.S. Presidents on Foreign Policy — Leader: D. Rockefeller.

(b) Bilderbergers in Europe.
Counterpart of C.F.R. in U.S.A. Annual Meetings held secretly. Discussion on Finance and World Government.

(c) Tri-Lateral Commission. Leader: D. Rockefeller
Meetings held between leaders of U.S., W.Germany and Japan on World Government matters.

(d) Club of Rome
You will remember reading something about this Group in Chapter 3, where we discussed the ten world regions, and Australasians belonging to Group 4.

By the way, Prime Minister Hawke of Australia is passing U.N.-sponsored World Government bills as quickly as possible whilst he still retains power.

## BACK TO THE EYE IN THE TRIANGLE

Hitler used a similar concept in his day to subdue the masses — particularly six million Jews. He called his eye — "The Blackshirts" or the S.S. Each of these men were irrevocably dedicated to Lucifer. Because they believed in reincarnation the six million victims became a sacrifice to satan himself.

Mussolini called his eye — "The Blackshirts", a small group of thugs that terrorised the masses.

The Russian communists of today call their eye — "The K.G.B.". By the way, Russian communism was paid for by World Government people in the U.S.A. in 1917.

It was to be a test case to see whether a large nation like Russia could be controlled by the eye principle — spying, lies and misery are the result.

It is not by accident, therefore, that communists, socialists and others like them march on 1st May.

— Remember 1776 — now communism is almost finished and will be swallowed up in World Government through the new economic system.

## BIG BROTHER

This is satan's final eye. By using fibre optics, which are a series of minute fish-eye cameras being built into cable T.V. sets, one person sitting in front of a computer console can monitor

10,000 homes. Even if your T.V. is switched off, the system still operates.

This system is being installed already in certain New Zealand and Australian cities and is being used widely in the United States and some other countries. Australia, for example, estimated 250,000 subscribers were ready back in 1982. This system has advantages — i.e. 50 or more additional channels.

It also has very distinct disadvantages.

According to the Deputy Federal Director of Australian Radio Broadcasters in a letter to the Editor,

Quote: "It represents a danger to the privacy of the cable subscriber. Tests based on subscriber responses has already been conducted in the United States involving a range of product preferences, including the "political" product. Just before the last Presidential election, at least one interactive cable television was used as an instrument to predict the poll and extraordinarily accurate last minute figures were achieved." End quote.

**RECAP ON THE EYE**

STAGE 1
Satan's Plan — Eye of Lucifer
STAGE 2
Egyptian Concept — Eye of Horus
STAGE 3
Weishaupt's Plan — Insinuating Brethren
STAGE 4
Freemasonry's Plan — Great Architect of the Universe
STAGE 5
Hitler's Eye — Black Shirts Gestapo S.S.
STAGE 6
Mussolini's Eye — Black Shirts
STAGE 7
Russian Communists' Eye — K.G.B.
STAGE 8
Satan's World Govt. Eye — Big Brother

N.B. All of these eyes represent Lucifer himself; and not the Christian God. Some church people from the Roman Catholic Church, the Greek Orthodox and others, will recall seeing this eye on their buildings.

**RELIGIOUS ASPECTS**

During the course of my lectures, I find the most difficult concept to get across to the listeners, is this fact.

ECONOMY AND RELIGION WILL LINK TOGETHER.

Rule No. 1: The word religion must be cloaked and veiled until it is unrecognisable by the masses.

**STATEMENT**

The New Age Movement is very rapidly moving in our societies and is infiltrating

(a) Religion
(b) Politics
(c) Health
(d) Agriculture
(e) The Arts
(f) Philosophical thought
(g) Education

Catch phrase — "Powers of the Mind" are subjects of discussion world wide, i.e. ESP Telepathy, Clairvoyance are now being accepted as scientific facts and are demonstrated to be so.

**NEW AGE CONCEPTS**

The Universe is a great mind. Our minds can tap into it. We must learn to alter our states of consciousness.
Witchcraft and demonism merge into a ONENESS with good.
Eastern religion is based on this concept of oneness, e.g. Chinese Yin = Feminine whilst the Yang = Masculine.
Get in touch with "yourself" is the catch cry.
The Feminist Movement believes that it is a political crusade to gain equality with men.
It is also a spiritual movement — reawakening goddess consciousness.
Goal = matriarchy — not equality = women ruling men.
The spiritual force behind it is a mystical relationship with MOTHER NATURE and MOTHER EARTH.
Any witch will tell you that this nature religion is witchcraft. This is the oldest spirituality on earth they say — i.e. Wicca (Witchcraft).

Therefore, the new Psychic Powers being investigated are in reality — Old occult powers dressed up and made semi respectable.

For example: During the month of October 1982 at a "Women's Spirituality and Healing Conference" held in Los Angeles, California, one seminar was entitled, "Introduction to Goddess Consciousness and the Craft."

The "craft" mentioned here is the same craft the Masons refer to, i.e. Witchcraft.

The Founder of the Universal Goddess Centre in Malibu, California, says very clearly: Quote — "The Healing of the planet depends upon women." End quote.

Wicca (witchcraft) is a so-called natural religion centred around

(a) The Mystery
(b) Sexuality
(c) Psychic abilities of the female
(d) Overthrow the global rule of men.

Out of all this, what have we learnt so far?

Playing with words is a clever way to deceive people.

**ILLUSTRATION**

I well remember an incident that occurred in Samoa whilst I was teaching there.

At a school called Palauli, a senior staff member made up some bush beer and distributed it to the school's older pupils. These boys, in turn got drunk, then violent and attacked various members of the staff including the principal who had been seconded from New Zealand. The lads actually had him up against a wall as they brandished bush knives in his face. — This principal wisely beat a hasty retreat home to New Zealand, accompanied by his family.

The Education Department from then on found it very difficult to recruit staff, so they were forced to do the only thing possible.

Change the name of the school. It is now Salafai High School.

Some years ago, a man from India entered the U.S.A. to try and introduce Hinduism. He failed. God's Spirit was there like a wall around the land. "In God We Trust" was on their coins. Prayer was conducted in schools and in government.

A woman called Madeleine O'Hair had prayer banned from the schools, eastern religion came in surreptitiously at first and then, one day, the same Hindu man reappeared onto American soil with a "new" philosophy. It took on immediately. What was it called?

Trascendental Meditation (T.M.) which is Hinduism with a new name.

Now, to link this with Antichrist's reign.

(a) The undermining of Judaeo-Christian beliefs (being widely assisted by U.N. Charters to Australia).
(b) "The Plan" for World Government based on economy (coming in through the plastic card).
(c) The declaration — Self is God (coming in from the East, i.e. Gurus, mantras, New Age Movement).

The main power therefore behind the New Age Movement worldwide is to use deceptive code words to veil what they are up to.

| OUT | IN |
| --- | --- |
| Witchcraft, Spiritism, Voodoo | Traditional Healers |
| Spirits | Mind Powers (which we all possess) |
| Demonic | Psychic |
| Pagan Occultism | Alternative Medicine |

KEY THOUGHT:

"ALL IS ONE"

Therefore,

Evil is good
God and satan are one
Everything there is can be found with the self.
Alternate lifestyles, e.g. homosexuality, lesbianism, free sex — frees one from moral restraints, they suppose.

"There is a way which seemeth right unto a man, but the end thereof are the ways of death."[5] — Sad isn't it.

**EDUCATION AND NEW AGE**

Educators in many places now use the term "Values clarification".

(a) This does away with Biblical morality.
(b) Student looks inside for inner guidance.
(c) How does the student "feel" about a situation.
(d) Student must be "true to himself (herself)"
(e) Forget the taboos of society.

Our kids in many cases are being trained like this in many of our public schools, and need to be decontaminated at home each evening with a good old dose of the Word of God.

In many public schools, the very young are being subtly trained in this manner.

Teacher — "Close your eyes and rest. Imagine you are going up a mountain. Through the mist you meet a very 'wise person' (this later will become a 'spirit guide'). This wise person is now speaking to you. What do you hear, etc., etc?"

This all sounds quite harmless, but that teacher has now opened the door to a demon spirit who seemed good, yet later on shows its real self and becomes evil, abusive and violent.

Many psychologists reject this explanation yet when confronted with a problem case in this realm, are powerless to deal

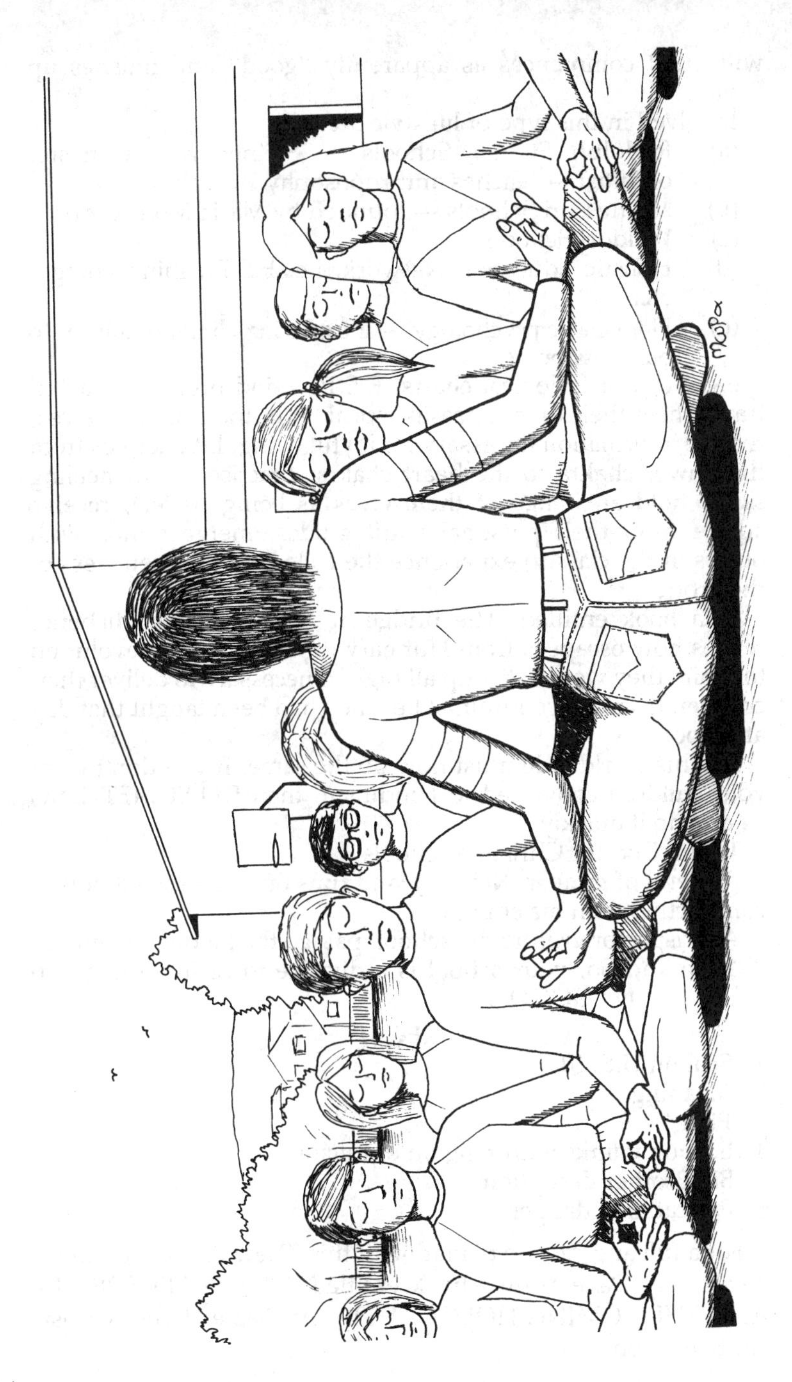

with it. It commences as apparently "good" and finishes up "evil".

Involved in this type of lifestyle are:

(a) Rudolph Steiner Schools — Steiner was a master occultist — teaches anthroposophy.
(b) Montessori Schools — founded by Maria Montessori.
(c) Waldorf Schools
(d) Holistic Education Network, i.e. E.S.P., mind energy, etc.
(e) Humanistic psychology – introducing Hindu occultism to our classrooms.

e.g. yoga, astrological charts, E.S.P., mind projection, astral travel, heal their own illnesses, speak with their higher selves, receive information necessary for joyful living, lift energies from the power chakra to the heart chakra, practise colour healing skills, hold an image of themselves as being perfect, receive advice from their personal spirit guides, merge minds with others in the class to experience the collective consciousness of the group.

In a book entitled 'The Bridge at Andau' James Michener relates how escapees from Hungary during the 1956 revolution told him they would stay up all night if necessary to deliver their children from the communist lies they had been taught that day at school.

Parents worldwide must now do the same. If you don't want your children converted to Hinduism, then DO SOMETHING — and do it quickly.

Thank God for Christian schools.

A friend of mine in New Zealand runs one of these schools in conjunction with his church.

An Inspector visiting the school, passed the following remark, "Mr So and So, your school is a divisive force in society", to which I reply "GOOD".

**RECAP**

1. Seal on U.S. $1.
2. Meaning.
3. Plan.
4. Economy links with religion of Lucifer.
5. Big Brother deception.
6. Educational dangers.

For a full and clear explanation of this "New Age Deception", please buy Dave Hunt's book entitled "PEACE PROSPERITY AND THE COMING HOLOCAUST". Available at your Christian Bookshop.

## CHAPTER SIX

# ANY LIGHT IN THIS DARK TUNNEL

"Jesus is Coming" was the proclamation on the Christian T-shirts during the Jesus Revolution in America.

Under a newspaper article heading entitled "Quit Worrying, It's The Second Coming," we read . . .

Quote "One of the most curious aspects of President Reagan's America is the number of people who believe a long trail of disasters, presages the imminent return to earth of Jesus Christ.

. . . Since President Reagan assumed power, with the massive assistance of the religious right, millenialists are to be found in every level of government, bureaucracy and legislature. . . .

Effect on Policy: Liberals fear, indeed that millenial thought may be having a discernable effect on United States policy-making.

. . . James Watt, Secretary of the Interior, recently told the House Interior Committee that 'I do not know how many future generations we can count on before the Lord returns,' prompting his critics to assume that his apparent lack of interest in conserving the wilderness lands of America springs from his belief that Christ is coming soon, so why bother. . . . A senior aide to one New York senator speaks of dozens of young men and women on Capitol Hill, in the Pentagon, in the various Departments of Government, insisting that we are the generation who will be lucky enough to see Christ return.

A few years ago, we would have thought of these people as just a bunch of wackos. Now they are in important positions in Government, we have to take them seriously. . . ." End quote.

Even away down south in little old New Zealand, this subject is with us in our newspapers.

Wellington's "Dominion" newspaper, 29th October 1983 reads,

Quote — "Shearer Ponders Second Coming".

"The Minister of Science, Dr Shearer, has asked the three government departments he controls for reports on the likely impact of the second coming of Christ. . . .

Dr Shearer asked for reports from the Department of Scientific and Industrial Research, the Broadcasting Corporation and the Commission for the Environment. . . ." End quote.

Dr Shearer would be one of the more thoughtful members of Parliament.

Many people assume, wrongly, that when one is elected to a high government appointment these individuals suddenly undergo a remarkable metamorphosis and know everything. This is simply not true.

I remember a parliamentarian saying to me once, over a meal eaten whilst surrounded by politicians from both sides of the house:

"The ignorance in here is appalling" — it is for this reason that these men and women need:

(a) To be prayed for — God allowed them the privilege of this office temporarily. "But God is the judge. He putteth down one and setteth up another."[1]

(b) To be spoken to by Mr and Mrs Average Citizen, recognising all the while, that these people are also flesh, blood and spirit.

(c) To be sent good reading material for information (such as this book and others like it). We must get them asking questions.

The story is told of an old Texas farmer and his son travelling into town in a cart pulled by a horse. The conversation went like this:

A motorcycle passed them.

Boy: "Say Dad, what's that?"

Old man: "I don't rightly know son!"

They pass a fire-engine.

Boy: "Say Dad, what's that?"

Old man: "I don't rightly know son!"

A jet swishes by in the sky.

Boy: "Say Dad, what's that?"

Old man: "I don't rightly know son!"

Later in the day, their business in town all completed, whilst on their way home the boy turns to the old man.

Boy: "Say Dad."

Old man: "Yes son."

Boy: "I hope you don't mind me asking so many questions."

Old man: "That's O.K. son. How do you expect to learn if you don't ask questions."

Imagine being a parliamentarian. Consider the hours and hours of wasted time spent at council meetings, clubs, societies, cocktail parties, listening much of the time to inane speeches with very little substance in them.

Then, upon ascending the ladder of success, daily in their offices, they are deluged with yards and yards of irrelevant information from all the different committees. Remember each new committee must continue to pass laws and make new policies to justify their existence.

Not only that, they attend endless conferences and seminars where nothing of importance happens, yet no doubt, a good time is had by all.

It is a strange old world that's for sure.

Consider the following news item, taken from the Mercury Newspaper, Hobart, Tasmania, 19th March 1984.

Quote . . . "Tidal Wave Overdue say Experts." . . . "A big Pacific-wide tsunami or tidal wave is long overdue, according to the scientists meeting in Honolulu.

. . . Experts from the United States, Canada, Chile, China, Japan, New Zealand, the Soviet Union and Hong Kong were among the scientists attending the meeting in the East-West Centre.

. . . The most recent major tsunami in Hawaii occurred in 1975 and killed two people.

. . . The conference ended today with a resolution calling for countries in the area to provide more funds to support an extended tsunami warning and information system." End quote.

Result:

(a) These scientists no doubt have had a great time in Honolulu and I am truly glad for them.

(b) However, what concerns me is what they have done, for example, in Hawaii since 1975.

(c) Tidal waves, in my opinion, come when they are ready, destroy and pass on.

(d) Men do not really know anything about them, apart from reading their instruments which tell of their coming and reporting to the newspapers after their passing.

(e) In the light of the following, Bill Brown who runs the corner store could have made the same prediction without the added expense of a trip to Honolulu.

My country, New Zealand, is volcanic in some areas. Occasionally a volcano will erupt, sending clouds of ash and smoke far and wide, polluting rivers, filling gutters and roofs with debris and fouling the surrounding air.

It is a standing joke in our family that the following little saga will then take place.

In spite of the fact that the local inhabitants have been almost driven out of town by the falling clouds of ash, a solemn voice announcing the national news one or two days later informs us:

(a) Mount Ngaruahoe has erupted.

(b) The chief government volcanologist has confirmed this by flying over the crater lake in a helicopter.

My family by now, well prepared, roar with laughter as we hear:

(c) The chief government volcanologist warns that further eruptions could take place.

Life can be amusing, can't it.

**ILLUSTRATION**

A man goes to the doctor down the road, to obtain help for an upset stomach.

Newly accredited doctor: "Hmmm, have you had this pain before sir?"

Patient: "As a matter of fact, yes, I have Doctor."

Newly accredited Doctor: "Hmm, er yes. It is my considered professional opinion that you've got it again."

Enough of this nonsense. Back to the subject. We must try to get copies of books like this one to our Parliamentarians. They need our help.

Signs of World Government are certainly here, as you can now clearly see.

When the communist Russians took over Poland through their puppet allies, I took careful note of all the details.

The two most outstanding aspects of this operation were:

**CONFISCATIONS OF ALL WEAPONS AND COMMUNICATIONS**

It is of note that in the vast majority of countries in the western world, all guns or owners thereof are licenced or registered. New Zealand readers will note that in 1984 all firearms owners were required to be registered on the computer. "Aha", I said.

In the U.S.A., however, in many of the States, a different situation exists.

People involved in World Government are pressing strongly for gun laws and take every opportunity to press their case, e.g. the attempted assassination of President Reagan by John Hinkley.

Do you realise the ownership of an unregistered weapon, plus ammunition give you a degree of independence. This independent spirit for many years has been the hallmark of Americanism.

These gun owners can

(a) Kill their own food.

(b) Protect themselves and families from zealous big brother informants.

(c) Have a measure of self-sufficiency and security.

I predict gun laws must be passed soon in America, because World Government is upon us.

Secondly, if you can cut off people's ability to communicate and thus organise against the system, you leave them as weak, helpless individuals, apparently unable to do anything against the repressive laws of the new regime.

**THE ANSWER**

At this point, I respectfully suggest that there is still a firm foundation in life amidst all these shifting sands of mans' confusion and nebulous schemes, i.e. The Living God and His Son — The Lord Jesus Christ.

Will the true God please stand up.

When you have finished reading the chapter entitled Freemasonry, the above catch phrase should become a sincere cry from your heart.

I remember, one morning in 1982 watching a telecast of a well-known American preacher. One of his statements stuck to me.

**STATEMENT**

Every person in their own way is looking for God, but God has ordained that there is only one way that mankind can ever find Him: That one way is a person, and his name is the LORD JESUS CHRIST.

"By the name of Jesus Christ of Nazareth . . . Neither is there salvation in any other, for there is NONE OTHER NAME under heaven, given among men, whereby we must be saved."[2]

Salvation of your soul is not in:

1. Any Protestant church denomination.
2. The Roman Catholic church.
3. The Greek Orthodox church.
4. The Mormon church.
5. The Seventh Day Adventist church.
6. The Jehovah's Witness group.
7. The World Wide Church of God (Armstrongs).
8. The Hare Krishnas.
9. The Divine Light Mission (Maharajah Ji)
10. Revival Centres (speaking in tongues for salvation).
11. Buddhism.
12. Hinduism.
13. Taoism.

14. Confucianism.
15. Moslem religion.
16. Anthroposophy OR ANY OTHER — ONLY IN JESUS CHRIST.

During the course of my travels I meet a number who tell me, "I believe in God but not in Jesus".

I have news for those people and it is all bad.

"For the Father judgeth no man, but hath committed all judgement unto the Son that all men should honour the Son, even as they honour the Father. HE THAT HONOURETH NOT THE SON HONOURETH NOT THE FATHER that sent him."[3] (Emphasis added.)

Obviously you can't have one without the other.

There is a real spiritual hunger in the world today. I receive letters and telephone calls continually from folk who are seeking out God's salvation, and thousands and thousands are accepting it.

If you are one of these seekers, please turn to the back of this book right now and pray the SINNERS PRAYER.

"The gift of God is eternal life through Jesus Christ our Lord."[4]

**NO MAN'S AN ISLAND** is the title of a film. It is true, we all affect other people for good or bad.

Back in the early 1900's, an ex-baseball star turned preacher named Billy Sunday was holding meetings throughout America.

Arriving in a certain town, his "Tabernacle" was erected on a vacant lot. The boards were all held on with one nail only, so that in case of fire, people could escape easily.

The aisles were liberally sprinkled with sawdust for people to walk down and receive Christ when the invitation was given.

Billy Sunday attended the local ministers fraternal meeting, where he was asked to go and invite the local "mill manager" to the meetings.

"Have any of you ministers been?" he asked. None had and so he set out on his errand. Down at the mill he saw the sign marked "Manager" on the door and knocked.

"Come in," said a voice.

Once inside, Billy observed the mill manager over at a cocktail cabinet pouring himself a whisky.

"I've come to ask you to give your life to God! My name is Billy Sunday, the visiting evangelist in town."

There was a pause, the manager strode to the door, opened it, flung his glass, whiskey and bottle into the bushes outside, and when he turned around, Billy saw tears glistening in his eyes.

Manager: "You are the first man in 20 years who has ever talked to me about my soul."

B.S. "Good. Then I take it, you will heed my invitation and come along to my meeting tonight."

Manager: "No I won't, because the church is full of hypocrites."

B.S. "So's hell, so if you don't want to live with them forever, why not come to church where you will be with them for a short time."

Manager: "No, I won't".

B.S. "Listen. If your dog bit you, would you kick your wife?"

Manager: "No, I would kick the dog."

B.S. "Therefore would you please stop blaming God for the hypocrites. Will you come?"

Manager: "Yes I will".

That night the building was jammed with listeners. Billy observed the manager standing away at the back listening to his message. When he gave the invitation for folk to walk forward and commit their lives publicly to Jesus Christ, he saw the manager was so keen he just couldn't wait for all the other people to move. He literally ran across the backs of the seats where he took Billy Sunday by the hand.

"Do you commit your life publicly to Jesus Christ tonight?"

The answer rang out loud and clear. "I do" and the grip as he shook Billy's hand removed any further doubt.

The manager returned to work, BORN AGAIN and before one week had passed, 60 members on his staff had also committed their lives to our Lord Jesus Christ.

The message is clear. We take people with us, to heaven or hell.

Please turn to the back of the book immediately and pray your prayer of commitment to Christ.

**RECAP**

1. Parliamentarians need sensible help.
2. World Government will confiscate guns, ammunition and communications equipment.
3. The only light in this tunnel.

# CHAPTER SEVEN

# FREEMASONRY

At the beginning of Chapter 5, we have a drawing of the Illuminati One World Government seal found on the reverse of the American $1 bill.

We noted that the eye in the triangle is none other than Lucifer, the bright and shining one. We also noted that the Grand Master wears this eye as part of his jewellery in the Masonic Lodge meetings, having been told that it is the eye of the Great Architect of the Universe whom we will later identify.

## REASONS FOR JOINING THE LODGE

Only men may join and there are a variation of reasons for them doing so.

(a) Upon invitation from another Lodge Member. This was not previously allowed, but owing to a decline in membership, this new dispensation has come in.

Recruits may be taken from any sphere, but such men's groups as Lions, Rotary, J.C's, etc., are of course fertile recruiting grounds, although none of these three aforementioned has anything sinister about them.

(b) Prospects of business assistance by other brothers.

(c) A good fraternal fellowship is promised. Men become very attached to one another when in continual close proximity, e.g. soldiers during the war continue this feeling of comradeship in R.S.A. or R.S.L. clubs, recounting the old days over a jug of ale.

(d) The opportunity to do good to others, in the form of retirement villages, hospitals, hostels, loans and advice to widows and others. — Morality is much spoken of.

(e) The secret knowledge learnt in Lodge rituals brings feelings of satisfaction.

If this was all there was to the Masonic Lodge there would not be a chapter on it, included in this book.

## BRITISH ROYAL FAMILY INVOLVEMENT

Most male members of the British Royal family have been members over the years, including Prince Philip (Lord Mountbatten), who admits that he does not now attend but is nevertheless linked.

The Queen Mother, a committed Christian, is right against it.

**CHURCH LEADERS AND MEMBERS INVOLVED** (INCLUDING OTHER FAITHS)

Anglican priests, Presbyterian elders, Methodist ministers, Salvation Army officers, some Baptist elders and members of many so-called Christian denominations are involved. The latest Roman Catholic Pope has spoken out strongly against it, yet many Catholics belong to the "craft". This is a word we will use to describe this movement from time to time.

David Yallop who wrote "in God's Name" has proof that well over 100 Vatican Priests belong to the Masons. Also, it is known that the Jesuits' Black Pope has the Masonic symbols on his signet ring.

Men from any other religion may also join provided they believe in a supreme being (who remains unidentified until the top degrees). Catholics, Protestants, Jews, Brahmins, Buddhists, Mohammedans, Hindus, Sikhs, etc., are all welcome. Atheists are excluded.

**DEGREES**

There are 33 degrees, although the 33° is an honorary degree. Very few go beyond the 32°.

**HOLY BOOKS USED**

The Craft calls them V.S.L. or Volumes of the Sacred Law which include all books which are considered to be the major Holy book of each major religion: i.e. The Grand Lodge of India keeps all the five V.S.L's — 1. Bible, 2. Gita, 3. Koran, 4. Granth, 5. Zenda Avesta — placed separately. In some Indian Lodges, there could be as many as 16 V.S.L. When the Master Elect takes his obligation, the square and compass are placed in position on the appropriate book, depending on the man's faith. — A sacred volume is always open whilst the lodge is in session.

**THE FIRST NIGHT**

When a man becomes involved with the craft, unless he has read a book like this, he will not know what is going to happen to him. It is quite shattering, therefore, to hear for the first time what he is obliged to say.

In my opinion, it is simply unethical to have the candidate for each degree, repeat line by line, his oath not knowing how it will end. In contrast, in my public meetings, I write on a board what is going to be said by those wishing to commit their lives to Jesus Christ.

"For by thy words thou shalt be justified and by thy words, thou shalt be condemned."[1]

## PROGRESSIVELY BINDING

Note again please that Weishaupt, when closed down by the Bavarian government, had others infiltrate many lodges in the upper degrees. In particular a man called Baron von Knigge (see Encyclopaedia Britannica).

**STATEMENT** — Sad to relate, hour upon hour has been wasted by tens of thousands of men, repeating their vows, secrets and oaths, depriving their wives and themselves of valuable sleep, not knowing that the secrets are of no value — just deception upon deception which fact Masonry freely admits.

"Masonry . . . conceals its secrets from all except

(a) Adepts
(b) Sages — or the
(c) Elect, and uses false explanations and interpretations of its symbols to mislead those who deserve only to be misled. To conceal the truth which it calls light from them, and to draw them away from it."

Who are these Adepts, Sages and Elect? you may ask.

Those who practice the occult, and many who are in the top degrees of Freemasonry have learnt through the years

(a) Astrological symbolism
(b) Kabalistic doctrine
(c) Ancient mysteries
(d) Occult symbols
(e) Many of these embroidered with Bible names and phrases to make it sound Christian to the so-called Christian's ear — clever, isn't it.

For example, when a man reaches the 28° "Knight of the sun" or "Prince Adept" his jewel is the occult pentagram which is used in witchcraft.

## APPRENTICE DEGREE (1st°)

(a) The candidate is blindfolded (hoodwinked).
(b) His trouser leg is rolled up.
(c) A noose is placed around his neck.
(d) His left breast is bared over the heart.

It is made clear that if he tries to run forwards he will be stabbed because at this stage he is being pricked over the heart with the point of a compass. If he runs backwards, he will be hung by the running noose.

At this stage he takes this fearful oath:

"Binding myself under no less a penalty, than that of having my throat cut across (he draws his right thumb across his throat like a knife), my tongue torn out by its roots and buried in the rough sands of the sea at low water mark when the tide ebbs and flows twice in twenty-four hours, should I ever willingly or knowingly violate this my solemn obligation as an Entered Apprentice Mason. So help me God and keep me steadfast in the due performance of the same."

Candidate seals his oath by kissing the V.S.L. once.

**FELLOW CRAFT (2nd°) OATH**

"Binding myself under no less a penalty than that of having my left breast torn open, my heart plucked out, and given as a prey to the wild beasts of the field and the fowls of the air. . . ." (Claw-like hand draws across chest.)

Candidate seals his oath by kissing the V.S.L. twice.

**MASTER MASON (3rd°) OATH AND PRACTICE**

"Binding myself under no less a penalty than having my body severed in twain (thumb of right hand is drawn across stomach), my bowels taken from thence and burned to ashes, the ashes scattered to the four winds of heaven, so that no more trace of remembrance may be had of so vile and perjured wretch as I should ever knowingly or willingly violate this my solemn obligation as a Master Mason. So help me God."

Candidate seals his oath by kissing the V.S.L. three times.

In a darkened room, the candidate is dealt three symbolic death blows to the head, after being placed on a stretcher and carried around the room to view a coffin, including skull and crossbones (a real coffin, black cloth or hole in the floor may be used). This is the symbolism of death. Is it any wonder that the wives stare with a sick feeling in the pits of their stomachs when they learn this for the first time.

I saw one dear lady cry, "No, no" upon hearing it. The poor husband confessed, "Yes dear, it is true." Thank God he renounced it all and got delivered that very hour in Jesus' Name.

By the way, the Name of our Lord Jesus Christ may not be spoken in the precincts of the lodge whilst the men are in full regalia. This applies to the first three degrees in particular.

No wonder. This could bring offence to a Jewish "brother" also present.

**RE-CAP**

The candidate starts off believing that he is joining a Christian-based society, but now finds himself taking witchcraft oaths which he swears over an open Bible. This is only of course where the candidate nominates the Bible as his V.S.L.

Is that clear? It is to me. This goes from stage to stage.

1. Apparently a good, moral, Christian-based society.

2. Witchcraft oaths. All prayers finish in the Lodge with that which witches also say, "So mote it be".

3. Blasphemy is now added.

By the way, didn't Christ say, "Swear not at all".

These curses, say the Freemasons do not really mean anything. They are only words tied up with some ancient rites. How sad. I actually see some men nervously chuckling when I reveal this in my meetings.

Man, you have just put a curse from hell on

(a) Yourself.

(b) Your wife.

(c) Your children.

(d) Your ancestors up to the third and fourth generation.

". . . visiting the iniquity of the fathers upon the children unto the third and fourth generation of them that hate me."[2]

How often have we seen homes wrecked by the witchcraft spirit behind this thing.

I remember seeing an advertisement on T.V. for wood products.

"How can you be sure of growing healthy trees?"

"Choose your ancestors."

Many of us cannot choose our ancestors but we can still choose Christ.

The homes of witchcraft in the western world are the gaelic speaking countries. Scotland, Ireland and Wales. England had and has a great deal to do with it also, e.g. Stonehenge.

If a man wishes to continue on, he moves out of the Blue Lodge into the Royal Arch Degree.

Here he moves on to learn the highly secret and sacred name of God. JAH-BUL-ON (J.B.O.)

This equals

1. Jahweh of the Hebrews

2. Bul or Baal of the Assyrians

3. On or Osiris an Egyptian god.

We have now reached a stage called "Syncretism", which is the joining together of many religions.

"I the Lord your God am a jealous God."[3] . . . "I will not give my glory unto another."[4]

This Jah Bul On creature certainly has nothing to do with the Christian religion.

"Aha" triumphantly laughs the Mason. "Freemasonry is not a religion, or so I've been told."

That's correct, you have been lied to. Even your Universal Pontiff said it was, many years ago.

If I see a four footed animal that moos, eats grass, has horns on its head, swats flies with its tail and gives milk through four spigots attached to a bag underneath, please excuse me if I presume I am looking at a cow.

If I meet a man who attends a temple, which has altars, sings hymns, says prayers, speaks of a Worshipful Master and using a number of religious books, hopes one day to make the grand lodge above by means of climbing Jacob's ladder, will you excuse me please for saying — Freemasonry is a religion.

Don't be so silly, stop playing with words.

Whilst on a lecture tour of Malaysia in the early 80's, I addressed a group of businessmen on the subjects contained in this book.

Seated in the audience was a brilliant professional man who trained the Master Masons.

Having heard what I had to say, he waited until afterwards to talk to me. "Mr Smith", he said, "You were wrong when you referred to Freemasonry as a religion".

"How is it then," I replied, "that it is written in your own writings — 'A man is never closer to God than when he kneels at the sacred altar of Freemasonry'."

There was a stunned silence as this man murmured that as the hour was late, it was time for him to go home.

Whilst in Malaysia and Singapore I learnt a lot of interesting things that I will outline here.

Many of my informants were ex 32° men who had come to our Lord Jesus Christ and had become committed Christians.

(a) In the Chinese dialects, taxi drivers call the Masonic Lodge — the house of devils. They should know — many of these folk are right into ancestor and spirit worship.

(b) In that area, only the so-called Christian Mason is allowed to progress beyond the third degree.

When my Chinese informant told me this, he asked, "Do you know why?" to which I replied,

"Yes, it is quite easy to understand. Satan (Lucifer) has all other eastern religions and others in his hands already. Three degrees is enough to bind them up with the witchcraft oaths."

**MERGING**

Most Eastern religions believe in the merging or mingling of opposites.

Darkness and light
Male and female
Night and day
Good and evil makes up perfect religion

The Chinese yin and the yang (good luck sign).

The hexagram is an eastern symbol, picked up by King Solomon from one of his 1,000 women, many of them heathen.

This is one of the most powerful signs in witchcraft today. The merging of one triangle for good and the other for evil. When a witch puts a "hex" on a person this is what it refers to.

I state in my public lectures that once Israel receives the Lord Jesus Christ as their Messiah, they will need to change the symbol on their flag, sometimes known as the Star of David.

## THE KEY TO DESTROYING FREEMASONS' FALLACY

Unfortunately for the Freemasons this merging concept does not apply in the case of Christianity.

Our God is good — full stop.

"God is light and in Him is no darkness at all."[5]

This is why Freemasonry takes the unsuspecting so-called Christian only, on this devious path which leads to the final secret.

## MOVING ON

Up through the degrees he goes as an ox to the slaughter. Each degree has another spirit behind it.

He reaches the 18° and to his delight, he begins to feel secure as suddenly out of the gloom he sees.

(a) An incense censer.
(b) A processional cross and a scroll, etc.
(c) An altar.
(d) A blasphemous communion in witchcraft surroundings. A broken biscuit with salt added — bread is forbidden. (Jesus is the bread of life, you see.)
(e) Two loving cups — drinking of wine.
(f) Reference to the veil of the temple being rent in twain.
(g) Mention of the Chief Corner Stone.
(h) The Rose of Sharon nailed to a cross.

"So far so good", the candidate mutters. "I'm on the right track now."

Satan is a cunning specimen. He bottles up all his lies in strawberry icing of truth. If he gave the Masons straight lies, very few would receive it.

Now, notice.

(i) "The pelican has shed its blood for its young." (Notes

from general directions 18° and the Chapter of the Princess Rose Croix.)

This is not a reference to the Lord Jesus Christ obviously. He is not a pelican. (They say it is a symbol of Christ.) The rose, they say is an emblem of secrecy and silence. Who wants to be silent about Jesus?

(j) Later comes a mention of the blessed Jesus.
(k) Later comes a mention of Christ.
(l) And then, the Calvary Room, also the Lamb and the Word. Isaiah 53 is read.

"Hooray" shouts the religious Mason.

However, Jesus Christ has another Name, and the three are clearly never put together in the Lodge.

LORD — JESUS — CHRIST

(a) There are many called Jesus in South America.
(b) Others call themselves the Christ, e.g. Maitreya.
(c) There is only one Lord (Master) — Jesus (Saviour) Christ (Anointed One).

"That at the Name of Jesus, every knee should bow of things in heaven, and things in earth, and things under the earth, And that every tongue should confess that JESUS CHRIST is LORD to the glory of God the Father."[6]

A preacher of the Gospel recently had this experience. Upon his quoting the above verse a young man looked at him with an arrogant gaze and said, "Never will that happen to me. God would need to break my back before I ever did that."

The preacher replied, "That shouldn't be too difficult," and continued on with his message.

If you, a Mason, are reading this chapter and feel very angry inside, do not be surprised. This book, in very simple English, under the power of the Spirit of the Living God is stripping away, layer by layer, all that you believed and held dear.

You cannot lay it down because I haven't finished yet.

I was in a town lecturing a little while ago when, (as is quite common in my meetings) a man stood up and began to yell at me. He felt that I had no right to say what I was saying about the craft.

I was quick to ask him, "Which degree are you in?"

"18th degree" was his reply.

"Thank you," I said, "You do not know enough yet. Would you please be seated."

Remember that there are secrets from those about to join the Lodge, and secrets also from those in it who are still climbing.

This particular man, I heard later, worked in a professional capacity in town and showed some interest in removing some teeth from my mouth with his fist. My suggestion was this, that unless he was connected with the dental profession, he would do well to read again the Eighteenth Degree Constitution on p.36-37 the three virtue steps,

Faith — Hope — Charity (love) — The latest news I hear is that he died a mysterious death part way through 1984. He now knows better, I am sad to relate, as I tried to warn him.

I also learned from my South East Asian informants that many men are deceived owing to the fact that many of the passwords are taken from the Bible.

**RECAP**

1. Candidate thinks it is a good Christian (or godly) system.
2. Takes witchcraft oaths. Immediately under a curse.
3. Blasphemes by kissing the Word of God, linking this sacred book with witchcraft. (We are discussing the so-called Christian Mason here.)
4. Moves on to discover that the Freemason's god is a triple headed monster — Hebrew — Assyrian — Egyptian. This links him now with eastern religion and mysticism.

This is certainly not the God of the Bible.

5. Stage by stage until the 18th degree he is further bound and enmeshed by the forces of witchcraft (that is why it is called "the craft") and eastern mysticism sprinkled with a few Bible words and phrases to make it palatable.
6. In the 18th degee a great relief comes over him. Any doubts he held to that point are instantly dispelled as the scriptures are read, and a communion feast is held, usually in the presence of non-born again men.

Satan loves this. It has been his strategy throughout the ages to entrap men and women with his cunning use of scripture.

Remember when he tempted Jesus? He said, "IT IS WRITTEN"[7] but Jesus knew the scriptures himself. Why? He wrote them.

**UPWARDS AND ONWARDS**

I had known for some time that the Adepts, the Sages and the Elect belonged to the 30th-33rd°. All I did know was learnt from my ex-32nd° informants who told me the details.

(a) In the 32nd° a man partakes of a communion feast, drinking wine out of a human skull.

(b) When these men die their screams and their panic is horrific.

I personally prayed for a 32nd° man one night in front of a gathering of over 1,000 people. As he renounced Freemasonry and was set free through the power of the Lord Jesus Christ, the spirit of Freemasonry which was in him jumped on to his teenage daughter who stood alongside. Her mouth twisted up, also her hands went into grotesque shapes. They cried out, "This is horrible," to which I replied, "Yes and if your father had known all this, he would never have joined the wretched thing."

I have witnesses galore to prove all this.

The reader may feel that I am coming on a little bit strong. This is true, and you will discover why, when you read on.

**WHO IS THE GOD OF FREEMASONRY?**

During a meeting one night, another man complained about my revelations and so I invited him up to prove I was wrong. I let him speak for 10 minutes. The audience probably thought I had gone mad. Actually, what can you lose by being fair.

The next night this Mason returned and before the meeting we had a discussion.

Here is an account of that discussion:

Self: "Are you a Christian?"

Mason: "Yes, I am also a lay preacher in the Methodist Church."

Self: "Are you a Mason?"

Mason: "Yes."

Self: "Which degree are you up to?"

Mason: "32nd°."

Self: "Excellent. As you are in that degree you are in a position to answer some of my questions.

"As a 32nd° Mason, and also a preacher in a so-called Christian church, can you tell me, are you familiar with the statement of Albert Pike, as written here in my book 'Warning'."

He agreed that he was familiar with it.

I quote herewith the statement. A copy of instructions issued by a 33rd° Mason and Grand Pontiff of Universal Freemasonry, on 14th July 1889 to the 23 Supreme Councils of the World. This will show you who the God of Freemasonry is —

Albert Pike, Sovereign Pontiff of Universal Freemasonry said: Quote — "That which we must say to the crowd is, we worship a God, but it is the God which one adores without superstition. To you Sovereign Grand Inspectors General, we say this, and you may repeat it to the brethren of the 32nd, 31st and 30th degrees; the Masonic religion should be by all of us initiates maintained in the purity of the Luciferian doctrine. If Lucifer were not God, would Adonay (God of the Christians) bother to spread false and harmful statements about him. YES, LUCIFER IS GOD. Unfortunately Adonay is also God. For the eternal law is that there is no light without shade, no beauty without ugliness, no white without black, for the absolute can only exist as two Gods; darkness becoming necessary to light to serve as its foil, and as the pedestal is necessary to the statue and the brake to the locomotive. . . . The doctrine of satanism is a heresy and the true and pure philosophic religion is the belief in Lucifer, the equal of Adonay, but Lucifer, God of Light and God of Good, is strugging for humanity against Adonay, the God of Darkness and Evil." END QUOTE. (In A. C. De La Rive *La Femme et l'enfant dans la Franc — Maconnerie Universelle* p.588 and Queenborough *Occult Theocracy* pp. 220, 221.)

Mason: "Yes, I will explain it to you. Have you not read Isaiah 14 where Lucifer is named 'Son of the Morning'or 'Oh Day Star' ".

"Quote — 'How art thou fallen from Heaven, O Lucifer, son of the morning. . . . End quote"[8]

Self: "Yes," I replied. "I read that regularly in my public meetings."

Mason: "Haven't you read in the book of Revelation, Chapter 22:16 where Jesus is called the Bright and Morning Star?

"Quote — 'I Jesus . . . am . . . the Bright and Morning Star.'[9] End quote"

Self: "Yes, I've read that."

Mason: "Can't you see it then?"

Self: "See what?"

Mason: "They are one and the same person. Lucifer and Jesus."

Self: "How dare you. I don't want to hear any more of this."

End of conversation.

**RECAP AGAIN**

1. Candidate thinks it is a good Christian (or godly) system.
2. Takes witchcraft oaths. Immediately under a curse.
3. Blasphemes by kissing the Word of God, linking this sacred book with witchcraft. (We are discussing the so-called Christian Mason here.)
4. Moves on to discover that the Freemason's god is a triple-headed monster — Hebrew — Assyrian — Egyptian. This links him now with eastern religion and mysticism. This is certainly not the God of the Bible.
5. Stage by stage until the 18th°, he is further bound and enmeshed by the forces of witchcraft (that is why it is called "the

MwPa

craft") and eastern mysticism, sprinkled with a few Bible words and phrases to make it palatable.

6. In the 18th° he feels safe in so-called Christian surroundings with familiar ritual, words and Bible readings, but never hears that JESUS CHRIST IS LORD — WHY? Because he will possibly go on in his deception to the top degrees.

7. He now learns the secret that eastern religion devotees learnt years ago, thus it was not necessary for them to go beyond the 3rd degree.

Remember: Merge — Mingle — Merge.

Good and evil

Light and darkness, and finally

Jesus and Lucifer

One further step. Lucifer is God. Jesus becomes the negative, evil force. Here Jesus is identified with Adonay, God's Name in the Old Testament.

This is the ultimate blasphemous lie.

No wonder they scream and thrash about on their death beds. These poor deluded souls.

Lucifer says his five 'I wills' in Isaiah 14, but listen,

"And the devil that deceived them was cast into the lake of fire and brimstone, where the Beast and the False Prophet are, and shall be tormented day and night for ever and ever."[10]

As for the Lord Jesus Christ —

"Wherefore, God also hath highly exalted Him, and given Him a name which is above every name. That at the name of Jesus, every knee should bow, and every tongue confess that JESUS CHRIST IS LORD to the glory of God the Father."[11]

Even Lucifer will bow and confess in a day to come, along with all those he deceived in Freemasonry.

No wonder that man knew the Albert Pike statement. It matters not which country you live in, Pike spoke on behalf of worldwide Freemasonry.

Even the lodge floor is chequered. Black, white, black, white, like a chess board: Evil — merge — Good — Evil — merge — Good.

Over the years, a number of evil things have been associated with Freemasonry.

(a) The murder of a man called Captain William Morgan in the U.S.A. for divulging the Lodge secrets. Date: September 19th 1826 — out of about 50,000 Masons, about 45,000 quit the Lodge as a result of this uproar.

(b) Its suspected involvement in Jack the Ripper murders where the prostitutes were killed by means of Masonic ritual to hush up a scandal in the British monarchy. See videotape "Murder by Decree".)

(c) The death of "God's Banker" — Signor Roberto Calvi, found hanging from a bridge over the Thames with the ritual stone (brick in this case) being placed over his testicles to symbolise castration.

Remember these words, "Where the tide washes over his body twice daily" — this happened to Calvi who was a member of the P2 Lodge, the ultra-secret group which was a hotbed of corruption and its exposure led to the Follani Government, and the resignation of the heads of Italy's two secret services, both Lodge members. Readers may have heard of David Yallop's book linking all this with the murder of Pope John Paul 1st. See p.70 of my first book 'Warning' — first printed 1980. Many Vatican priests are also Lodge members.

Note at time of writing Sindona has been extradited to Italy for trial and Yallop's book is being vindicated as the truth (see also the chapter on the World Church). Also, Pope John Paul II continues to shield some crooked priests within the Vatican walls. This point Yallop establishes.

(d) The K.G.B. has used Freemasonry to penetrate the most sensitive areas of authority in Britain according to a study of the 750,000 strong secret movement.

Our newspapers in 1984 continue to print articles revealing the unethical nature of Freemasonry. In quotes from "The Brotherhood" — the secret world of the Freemasons, the author, Stephen Knight says, "The K.G.B. has instructed recruits to become Freemasons, then exploited the 'jobs for the brethren' network to place spies at the highest levels of both MI5 and MI6.

A British diplomat who worked with MI6 for nearly 20 years, urged a ban on Masons holding top security jobs and personnel jobs, and he also says that security officers who are Masons should be forced to declare their membership."

I personally believe this rule should apply to all police, judges and magistrates also, to safeguard our democratic law systems, not only in Great Britain but also N.Z. and Australia and around the world.

For example, in the New Scotland Yard, headquarters of the metropolitan police, there is a private Lodge room for their rituals and functions. This is of interest in the Jack the Ripper case where it is alleged that senior

Freemasons were involved in a Royal scandal, and carried out ritual murders on prostitutes in the know.

Mr Knight also speaks of allegations of Masonic corruption in the police, including unfair promotion, charges being dropped against fellow Masons by police Masons, etc.

New Zealand readers should look up the Nelson Evening Mail, 26th January 1984 or the Christchurch Press, 28th January 1984 for further information. Australian readers could look up the Townsville Daily paper dated 28th January 1984.

Readers, in the light of all the foregoing, can now see the link-up between the Illuminati symbol on the U.S. dollar — Lucifer — and the Masonic lodge.

It is not by accident that the rite of the 33rd° was established on 1st May.

As a result, many will wish to get out immediately and my next chapter is written to Christian leaders, born again Christian pastors and to all those who wish to set these men, their families and their ancestors free in the Name that is above every name.

The LORD JESUS CHRIST.

P.S. By the way, some Masons upon reaching the top degree, go on into further acts of stupidity by joining the "Shriners".

Grown men,

(a) Walk blindfolded along a board emitting electric shocks through the candidate's feet. He is told this represents hot sands of the desert. They are about to be auctioned off.

(b) Wives are invited with purses loaded with money to buy back their husbands or some other man (dressed in women's clothing) from an auction block.

**DANGERS TO THE LAW SYSTEM**

The Royal Arch Mason's oath says,

"I will aid and assist a companion Royal Arch Mason, when engaged in any difficulty, and espouse his cause so far as to extricate him from the same, if in my power, whether he be right or wrong (note the last six words).

He also swears, "A companion Royal Arch Mason's secrets, given me in charge as such, and I knowing them to be such, shall remain as secure and inviolable in my breast as in his own, without exception."

Readers please notice that there are NO EXCEPTIONS, such

as murder or treason and it doesn't matter whether the brother is RIGHT or WRONG.

No wonder, strange decisions are recorded in the courts from time to time in various countries around the world.

A Mason on trial in court will, from time to time, pass his right thumb across his forehead, from right to left, as if removing sweat from his brow. (The phrase well known to Masons is "Is there no help for the widow's son?")

The judge if a Mason himself, and has reached the Royal Arch degree — this also applies to the prisoner, he is bound by Masonic oath to get the prisoner off, if at all possible. This becomes a perversion of justice.

We Christians trust that this will be stopped by a complete cleansing of the system, very shortly. As a result of Mr Knight's book, an investigation is already underway in Great Britain to stop these abuses.

"There is nothing covered that shall not be revealed . . ."[12]

Readers observing any strange decisions being handed down from now on should investigate and find out if the (a) accused, (b) the policeman involved or (c) the judge, is a Freemason.

It will then all add up.

**RECAP**

This chapter is of vital importance in understanding the top degree Masons' link-up with the One World Government and One World Religion.

The only real threat to this concept are the born again believers in Christ and their belief in the authority of Scripture.

Jesus said in John chapter 14, I am THE WAY, I am THE TRUTH, I am THE LIFE. Please notice, the definite article THE is used, and not the indefinite article A.

In order to counteract all this, modern theologians teach the lies —

(a) The Fatherhood of God over all mankind.
(b) The Brotherhood of all men.

In actual fact there are two Kingdoms in opposition to one another. God — and the twice born believers in Christ; Satan — and the once born submissive flock. Link God and satan and the damage is done. Therefore, this final secret of Freemasonry is of vital importance.

If other degrees are involved use the following formula and renounce them also.

# CHAPTER EIGHT

# HOW TO SET A FREEMASON FREE

First of all, any person who belongs to any society using that Luciferian eye will need a good clean up.

i.e. Masonic lodge — and Order of the Eastern Star; Oddfellows; Buffaloes, etc.

Check your membership card and look for that eye. Check all documents, walls of lodges, etc.

Any born again Christian who attends a church where any of the leadership is involved in these lodges should ask them to read the preceding chapter, and leave the lodge. This applies to:

Bishops
Ministers
Pastors
Elders
Deacons

If they refuse, you must leave that church, for it is under the sway of witchcraft and finally the dominion of Lucifer.

Picture in your mind, this church leader drawing his right thumb across his throat, with a black hood over his head and ask — "Do I really need spiritual assistance from this person?"

## FOUR WEAPONS — NO! FIVE

(a) The Name of our Lord Jesus Christ
(b) The Blood of our Lord Jesus Christ
(c) The anointed praise of God's people
(d) The Word of God read by a Spirit-filled believing Christian
(e) The Baptism in the Holy Spirit is essential

## THINGS TO LEAVE AT HOME

(a) Prayerbook
(b) Holy Water
(c) Crucifix

The enemy is not impressed with any who are not truly born again. Religious robes are meaningless in this situation. Take warning and read the story of the seven sons of Sceva in Acts 19:14-16.

I was holding a meeting one night when, at the conclusion of the message, I commenced delivering Masons and families from these spirits in Jesus' name.

A pastor who was visiting that evening sidled up to me and said, "Can you teach me how to do this please?"

I agreed, and later on in the evening commenced to write it down for him on a piece of paper. A few minutes went by and when I looked up, there was a young man about 20 years of age swaying on his feet, standing just a few yards away.

I said to the pastor. "There is no need to write any more. Watch this. His father will be a lodge member."

Sure enough — I was right. The discernment of spirits gift found in 1 Cor. 12:10 never fails.

Others from overseas have also written for help.

**REMEMBER THIS . . .**

We are not there to spook people. Be very natural. Nothing must sound weird.

**Rule:** Light will always destroy darkness, e.g. walk into a dark room — with the sweep of the hand proclaim 'Darkness depart!!!" Results: nil.

Go into a dark room, switch on the light switch. Result: light.

Jesus said, "I am the light of the world. He that followeth me shall not walk in darkness, but shall have the light of life."[1]

**A FORMULA TO FOLLOW**

1. Have the candidate stand next to you.
2. Get him/her to say, "I renounce the spirit of Freemasonry with all its oaths, secrets and curses." (repeat after Christian worker.)
3. I renounce every ancestral spirit of Freemasonry in my family line.
4. "I confess Jesus Christ is my Lord and Saviour."
   At this point, stop and ask candidate if they are truly born again. If not, lead them in the sinner's prayer found at the back of this book, or one of your own involving:
   (a) Repentance from sin.
   (b) Believing that the Lord Jesus Christ died for me.
   (c) I receive Him into my life now and CONFESS this with my lips. Rom. 10:9-10
5. Leader speaks — candidate follows.
   1st°
   "I renounce my spirit of the Entered Apprentice Degree as taken by me (my father, my grandfather, etc.). I renounce all these curses with the oaths in the name of the Lord Jesus

Christ. I reject the cutting of the throat, and the tearing out of the tongue. This no longer belongs to me."

2nd°

"In the name of the Lord Jesus Christ, I renounce the oath and the curses of the 2nd° as taken by . . . I reject the tearing open of the chest, and the ripping out of the heart. This curse no longer belongs to me."

3rd°

"In the name of the Lord Jesus Christ, I renounce all the curses connected with the oath of the 3rd degree. I reject the slitting open of the stomach, the tearing out of the bowels and the burning of them to ashes.

I reject the demonic name Ma Ha Bone.

I reject the spirit of death from the death blows to the head.

I reject falling into the stretcher and observing the death symbols.

I reject the blasphemous kissing of the Bible, on a witchcraft oath.

I reject the spirit behind a false resurrection. Only Christ rose from the dead of His own free will."

Royal Arch°

"In the name of the Lord Jesus Christ I renounce the false secret name of God.

I reject Jah Bul On as the demonic monster that he is.

He is not the living and true God.

The God that I worship is the Lord.

The God of Abraham, Isaac and Jacob.

The Father of our Lord Jesus Christ.

He is my God and my Father through the new birth.

I renounce with my lips, any other subsequent oath or curse taken by . . . and I confess that Lucifer will go to the lake of fire where he will burn forever.

My Lord Jesus Christ is in heaven from whence He will reign forever over all. King of Kings and Lord of Lords."

Leader then invite candidate to breathe out gently, long breaths. As he continues like this,

Leader speaks to spirits.

(a) "In the Name of the Lord Jesus Christ whom I serve, I speak to the spirit of the Entered Apprentice Degree. Come out on the breath and set him free. — In the Name of Jesus I break this oath and this curse over . . . life and pronounce him free."

(b) "I come against the Spirit of the 2nd° in the Name of the Lord Jesus Christ. I break the oath and the curses of the

2nd° in Jesus' name. — You are no longer welcome here. Come out on the breath."

(c) I speak to the demonic spirit of the 3rd° with the oath and the curses. I release . . . from these cursed things, in the Name of our Lord Jesus Christ. Set him free now. His body is the temple of the Holy Ghost. You have no right to be in him. Leave on the breath, now in Jesus' Name, Spirit of Death — leave him."

(d) "In the Name of the Lord Jesus Christ, I come against the false name of God. Jah Bul On is false. You devil, come out in Jesus' Name. I SET THIS MAN FREE IN THE NAME OF THE LORD JESUS CHRIST."

(You may also pray over his family.)

"WHAT GOD HATH CLEANSED, LET NO MAN CALL UNCLEAN."[2] Praise the Lord.

Whisper in candidate's ear, "You are now free in Jesus' Name.

1. Go home and read thoroughly II Cor. 6:14-18 — now.
2. Now that you are born again, get baptized by immersion, receive the baptism in the Holy Spirit.
3. Hand in your resignation to the registrar of your lodge. Say, 'As I am now a born again believer in Christ alone, please strike my name from the register. I no longer require a Freemason's funeral.'
4. Burn your gear — all of it. Apron, scrolls, belt buckles, should be disfigured with a hammer. Rip Masonic symbols off Bible. The book itself is good – minus Masonry symbols. Get it re-covered. Deut. 7:25-26.
5. Join up with a live, born again, spirit filled men's group, e.g. a live church group, or Full Gospel Businessmen's Fellowship International — or both. Read Heb. 10:25."

**RECAP**

Those involved in Freemasonry up until this point will find that if they mean business with the Lord their spiritual life will suddenly take off like a rocket.

Freedom comes from knowing the truth.

# CHAPTER NINE

# THE WORLD CHURCH

We have dealt with the World Government plans. Remember the words of the gentleman on the plane in our initial story.

"We are working towards the formation of a One World Government and a One World Religious System."

Any newspaper reader in the 1980's can sit back, Bible in one hand, a paper in the other, and watch the following take place.

Dr Runcie, the Archbishop of Canterbury on a tour of New Zealand was asked by a radio interviewer if it was true that the Anglican Church was going to link with the Roman Catholic Church.

Runcie said, "Oh yes, It is not a question of 'if' but 'when'."

Interviewer: "When this union takes place, will you be the leader of this new church?"

Runcie: "Oh no, I have no interest in that."

Now from that statement it is very clear that Dr Runcie is implying that Rome will be in charge.

"And I beheld another beast coming up out of the earth and he had two horns like a lamb and he spake as a dragon."[1]

This is the world religious leader. He looks good on the outside — a lamb, but inside he is full of the power of Lucifer.

The word 'religion' comes from a basic word 'religare' — 'to bind'. Notice, it was Christ himself who said,

"If the Son therefore shall make you free, ye shall be free indeed."[2]

What a tremendous thrill comes to the human soul when one finds out —

That religion "binds" and Jesus sets "free".

The predictions therefore tell us that this World Church will be based on seven mountains. This World Church system is likened to a woman described by the prophets in capital letters, "MYSTERY BABYLON THE GREAT, THE MOTHER OF HARLOTS, AND ABOMINATIONS OF THE EARTH."[3]

The ancient city of Babylon will never rise again, therefore Mystery Babylon must mean something else.

I am predicting here that a great World Church is rising now, and will link together with the spirit of Lucifer.

At the World Council of Churches gatherings we have the nuclei for this system. Some people involved do not see the repercussions of their actions and obviously have not read the prophets.

| LIST A | LIST B | LIST C |
|---|---|---|
| Anglicans | Roman Catholics | Occultists of |
| Presbyterians | Sikhs | all brands; |
| Methodists | Moslems | including |
| Associated Churches of Christ | Hindus | New Age |
| Congregationalists | Buddhists | Movement |

This great World Council is all embracing and is not averse even to Anton La Vey's church in California, The First Church of Satan.

All this is a beautiful description of Mystery Babylon on the rise again — religious — yes, and binding also.

Now the sad part is, that they will not last very long.

**STATEMENT**

The World Church will assist World Government to come to power, then World Government and their leader will destroy the World Church and make way for the final world religion which is — LUCIFER WORSHIP — there's that eye again.

**LIST OF CHARACTERS AGAIN EXPLAINED**

| | |
|---|---|
| 10 Horns | — E.E.C. leading on to World Government — 10 regions of the Club of Rome. |
| Beast | — The World Government leader named Antichrist. |
| Whore (Prostitute) | — Opposite of Bride — One World Church. |
| 7 Mountains | — Capital of the World Church — Rome. |

Now read, "And the ten horns which thou sawest upon the beast, these shall hate the whore, and shall make her desolate, and naked, and shall eat her flesh and burn her with fire."[4]

Very descriptive you will agree. Lucifer helps them rise, then uses them as a stepping stone to bring himself to power.

You see, this World Council of Churches group even now, are traitors to the cause of Christ.

(a) They do not preach the gospel of salvation through Christ alone.

(b) They do not believe the Bible 'is' the Word of God. They believe it 'contains' the Word of God. Find it if you can, is the game they play. Its title is "demythologizing in terms of existential encounter" (which means twisting it to make us say something different).

(c) They are bedmates with the communists. N.B. Every accredited clergyman in Russia is a member of the K.G.B.

(d) They are racial stirrers, looking for minority groups like the Aboriginals of Australia to use as pawns.

Dr McIntyre, 75, President of the Council of Christian Churches, in a newspaper article, said that "the W.C.C. uses racism as a cover to get money into the hands of guerillas. They originated out of Moscow, and have spent at least $10 million helping guerilla groups in Africa.

They have succeeded in helping the communists to take over Angola and Rhodesia.

The Aboriginals' biggest problem was the World Council of Churches attempt to 'agitate them' " he said.

"The World Council of Churches stands for:
(i) Deception
(ii) Disruption
(iii) Destruction

It is a spectacle to see them pounce on the Aboriginals." End quote.

(e) They are blasphemous in their statements about God and His Son our Lord Jesus Christ.

WCC's HYMN FROM HELL

"New Hymns for a New Day" by the Youth Departments of the WCC and the World Council of Christian Education:

1. It was on a Friday morning, that they took me from my cell,
And I saw they had a carpenter to crucify as well,
You can blame it on to Pilate, you can blame it on the Jews
You can blame it on the devil but it's God that I accuse.

Refrain
It's God they ought to crucify, instead of you and me
I said to the carpenter a-hanging on the tree.

2. You can blame it on to Adam, you can blame it on to Eve,
You can blame it on the apple, but that I can't believe,

It was God that made the devil and the woman and the man,
And there wouldn't be an apple, if it wasn't in the plan.

3. Now Barabbas was a killer and they let Barabbas go,
But you are being crucified for nothing here below,
But God is up in Heaven and He doesn't do a thing
With a million angels watching, and they never move a wing.

4. To hell with Jehovah to the carpenter I said,
I wish that a carpenter had made the world instead,
Goodbye and good luck to you, our way will soon divide,
Remember in heaven, the man you hung beside.

**ROMAN CATHOLICS**

Where do they fit in to all this? It is important to know as, obviously, the World Church will be based in Rome.

I have read much about 'differences' over the years, but we have many Roman Catholic friends. What is said here therefore will be 'facts' alone.

Many Protestant Pentecostals or charismatic folk continually ask me, "How can a Roman Catholic be born again and receive the baptism in the Holy Spirit, and still remain in this church system?"

That is a fair question and here is my answer:

(a) The Catholic charismatic movement is the thin end of the wedge that has enabled Catholics to have some fellowship with born again, Bible believing Christians. Therefore, it is the mercy of God that there is such a movement.

(b) The genuine Christian love for Christ and other believers shown by some of these dear folk has to be seen to be believed.

(c) Their lack of knowledge of the Bible comes from centuries of their ancestors having no Bibles at all. — These folk are delighted, excited and infectious in their enthusiasm for they are discovering this 'treasure hidden in the field' or the pearl of great price (i.e. salvation through Christ, and the baptism in the Holy Spirit).

(d) Moving into these two experiences makes them long and hunger after more of God. Many are not taught

about the true nature of their Roman Catholic doctrines and put up with the Sunday liturgy, all the while looking forward to their week night charismatic fellowship meetings where 'real things' take place.

As a younger man, I had far less wisdom and grace than I have today.

**RULE**

Remember that every church on earth has faults and errors, but, in the words of Dale Carnegie, "He who wishes to collect honey should not kick over the beehive."

(e) The basic problem, when dealing with religion, or Protestantism and Roman Catholicism in this case is to distinguish their

**Authority** — or Foundation for faith.

Fact No. 1: The Word of God is the one and only authority.

Remember — "The Word that I have spoken, the same shall judge him in the last day." [5]

Fact No. 2: Tradition cancels out the Word of God.

Jesus speaking, "Thus have ye made the commandment of God of NONE EFFECT by your tradition."[6]

Again — "But IN VAIN, they do worship me, teaching for doctrines, the commandments of men."[7] (Emphasis added.)

Long and hard, I prayed for a gentle spirit, that I may help and not hinder a seeking soul.

**MY PRAYER —** "Lord, please show me one doctrine only that is powerful enough to illustrate this point. This doctrine, must apply to both Protestant and Roman Catholic alike to avoid a wrong spirit.

I've found it!

**THE MASS** — This is taught by the High Anglicans (Protestants) and also by the Roman Catholics. Therefore, let none of us be offended, just thoughtful.

I remember lecturing in a large public hall in a certain town. Not knowing who was present, I launched into my message and apparently inadvertently made mention of the Mass as being blasphemous.

I said, "When Jesus partook of the emblems of bread and wine at the last supper, what is the true story?"

This is most important, as you will now see.

Let us read what Jesus said: "And He took bread, and gave thanks and break it, and gave unto them saying, this is my body which is given for you. This do in REMEMBRANCE of me." Likewise, also the cup after supper saying, This cup is the new testament in my blood which is shed for you."[8] (Emphasis added for clarity)

In the light of what we are now about to read, we are forced to the belief that this

(a) Communion Feast or Holy Eucharist in the Mass is In remembrance only — not a literal transformation of the bread and the wine.
because

| | |
|---|---|
| Here is Jesus | Here is a loaf of bread which is also Him. (His flesh.) |
| Here is Jesus, with blood in Him. | Here is His blood. |

**PROBLEM**

You now have two lots of Jesus' flesh.
You now have two lots of Jesus' blood, at the time of his speaking.
Would the true Jesus please stand up. Answer this. Don't dismiss it.

Now — going on. When Jesus spoke in the imperative, He was obviously using examples only:
e.g.
I am the door — not a piece of wood.
I am the way — not a road men walk on.
I am the light of the world — not a 200 watt bulb.
Therefore, this feast must be IN REMEMBRANCE only.

## A SHOCK FOR ROMAN CATHOLIC AND PROTESTANT ALIKE

Did you know that those who teach the transforming of the wine and bread into literal blood and flesh of Christ also teach

Ready now . . .

That Jesus is literally taken off His throne in heaven 200,000 times daily in all the Masses that are said around the world, to be personally present and involved at them all.

Herein lies the blasphemy.

When I made this statement, there was a great buzz of excitement, and after the meeting, a semi-circle of people called for me to come over and explain further.

**EXPLANATION GIVEN**

The mass and the ceremony of the Holy Eucharist is the SAME SACRIFICE as that which took place on Mount Calvary, many years ago.

You say, "I've never heard this before." — don't be surprised, neither have millions of others either.

"PROOF, PROOF," I hear you cry.

From "This is the Catholic Church" published by the Catholic Information Service, Knights of Columbus, Imprimatur Most Reverend John F. Whealon, Archbishop of Hartford . . . "Sacrifice is the very essence of religion. And it is only through sacrifice that union with the creator can be perfectly acquired. It was through sacrifice that Christ himself was able to achieve this for man. It is only through the PERPETUATION of that sacrifice that this union may be maintained." (Emphasis added.)

"What makes the Mass the most exalted of all sacrifices is the nature of the victim, Christ himself. For the Mass is the CONTINUATION of CHRIST'S SACRIFICE which he offered through his life and death. Jesus then is the priest, the offerer of the sacrifice. But Christ was not only the priest of this sacrifice (of the Cross), He was also the victim, the very object of this sacrifice. THE MASS IS THUS THE SAME AS THE SACRIFICE OF THE CROSS. No matter how many times it is offered, nor in how many places at one time, it is the same sacrifice of Christ. CHRIST IS FOREVER OFFERING HIMSELF IN THE MASS." End quote. (Emphasis added.)

Thank you Rev. Whealon.

How do we know that this man is correctly interpreting true Catholic Doctrine?

Quickly, over to the Council of Trent.

Passed in Session XXII. CAP. II

No. 4, "If any one shall say that a BLASPHEMY is ascribed to the most Holy sacrifice of Christ performed on the cross BY THE SACRIFICE OF THE MASS — let him be accursed."

Well, that is what I am saying.

The curse I return to the sender, unopened.

As the interest grew, this little group in the public hall grew also.

I took out my Bible and turned to the Book of Hebrews, inviting my listeners to do the same.

**EXPLANATION**

In the Old Testament, the High Priest continually offered sacrifices to temporarily cover sin until CHRIST should appear.

"Please take out your pens," I said "and underline the

following words in your Bibles. Remember, with this information, you are preparing yourself to interview your church leaders to find out whether I am telling the truth or not. Do it as a group. This will give you confidence — don't be afraid. Read Hebrews Chapter 9 verse 25.
V.26 underline 'ONCE'
V.28 underline 'ONCE OFFERED'
Read Hebrews Chapter 10 verse 11.
V.12 underline 'ONE SACRIFICE' for sins, 'FOREVER', 'SAT DOWN'.
V.14 underline 'ONE OFFERING he hath PERFECTED FOREVER.'

"No wonder Jesus said on the cross, IT IS FINISHED John 19:30."

There was a murmur of consternation at this point as I said, "There is only one more warning I bring you, and it is this. Do not RECRUCIFY Jesus please. It is your soul that I value."

Read Hebrews Chapter 6, verse 6.

"If they shall fall away, to renew them again unto repentance, seeing they CRUCIFY TO THEMSELVES THE SON OF GOD AFRESH, and put Him to an OPEN SHAME."[9] (Emphasis added.)

This now makes it clear why these churches have the sign of the crucifix prominently displayed. Christ is still suffering on the cross.

I'm so excited to tell you, Christ is OFF THE CROSS now. He has died. It's all over.

Each time you now attend the Mass and the Holy Eucharist, you are guilty of BLASPHEMY.

The Second Vatican Council 1963-65 says, Quote — "At the Last Supper . . . our Saviour instituted the Eucharist sacrifice of His body and blood. He did this in order to PERPETUATE THE SACRIFICE OF THE CROSS. . . ." end quote. P. 154 The Documents of Vatican II Walter M. Abbott S.J.

These dear folk sent a spokesperson around the next morning for a final interview. "If you are right, then we are wrong."

"No," I said, "Let's put it this way. If the Bible is the Word of God, let's do it His way."

These people later visited their priest, which I invite each doubtful reader to do and ask for clarification.

This man got angry and accused me of being Antichrist. This, however, did not satisfy these thinking godly people.

They said, "If that is your only explanation by way of defence, we are leaving your church."

"Is this what I must do?" I hear you ask.

Let the Word of God answer.

"Come out of her my people that ye be not partakers of her sins, and that ye receive not of her plagues."[10]

At this stage, some will criticise me. "Why don't you go and expose — expose — expose?"

My name is not God. He is quite able to lead a sincere seeker into the ways of truth through the constant reading of His Word.

"And you shall know the TRUTH, and the truth shall make you free."

When I was a younger man, I was less wise and during my preaching, I let fire with all barrels.

One day, I learnt an all-powerful lesson from God's Word. Here is a warning to over-zealous correctors of doctrine.

"The servants said unto Him, wilt thou that we go and gather them (tares) up.

"But he said nay, lest while ye gather up the tares, ye root up also the wheat with them."[11] (Word added for meaning.)

One night, whilst watching a T.V. programme with my family entitled, 'Dr Finlay's Case Book", one line spoken by old Doctor Cameron, hit me square in the heart . . . "Young Dr Finlay, remember the human spirit is very tender. When you walk on it, wear carpet slippers."

Sequel: The group I mentioned before are now rejoicing in this beautiful salvation, bought once and for all through the precious blood of Christ. They have joined up with a Bible believing church and are growing strongly in the Lord and His Word.

Are priests and nuns leaving too?

Yes, in Australia, between 1962 and 1982, over 400 Diocesan and religious priests left the ministry. The number of departing brothers and nuns is much larger.

In the last 20 years half a million lay Catholics have withdrawn from weekly attendance of Mass.

In a newspaper article before me, the writer points out that, "The more academically pretentious members have managed to filter a good deal of Marxism into Catholicism via sociology and liberation theology."

Prayer: "May all those who have come out, find something good, Bible-based and Spirit led-to go in to."

God never calls us out of something into nothing.

Here is a letter from a dear Christian sister that illustrates the difficulties yet the great blessings. This letter was written to a T.V. preacher in December 1983.

Dear Brother

I am a former Catholic nun. There is so much truth in what you say, but do you have any idea of the agony your Catholic friends and mine have to undergo when they have been taught that to leave their church means certain condemnation to hell? On the part of most priests and nuns, it also means the loss of all visible means of support, since there are no retirement benefits, health insurance, unemployment benefits, or social security for priests or nuns.

In my case when I knew I could no longer stay in the Catholic church, my reward for 22 years of service was $82.50 in cash and the clothes on my back. My family, except for one sister, acted as if I didn't exist. Without her, I would have starved. All of my work experience was tied to the Catholic church and at 40 years of age I started over at $1.65 per hour, working 12 hours a day and living on frozen chicken pies which cost 24 cents at that time. In spite of all this and so much more I have never for one moment regretted that decision. God has seen fit to call me to spiritual paths that would have been impossible for any believing Catholic to foresee.

I have a heavy burden for those that still remain within the Catholic church. Your exposition of biblical truth versus Catholic teaching is excellent and penetrating, but it still does not go far enough. You cannot describe or address the issue of the spiritual, psychological and emotional impact of discovering that the truths you have clung to in total security for a lifetime might not be so.

You speak accurately and correctly of the difference between "petros" and "petras". I can still feel the chills which ran down my spine the first time I heard this explanation. I remember my frantic search through the Scriptures and then checking the Catholic doctrine. But everything I found told me that Christ is the only Rock and that everything else is just pebbles. It was my first glimpse of light, but like coming into a bright sunshine out of the dark, it was so painful. I could not go back, but feared to surge on. If Peter was not the rock, then all my beliefs based on Catholic authority and tradition were built on sand. And so I found it to be. But it has taken 20 years of pain and joy to be able to write this letter.

Please consider this: if you encourage priests and nuns to leave their way of life, could you also reach out with the spiritual, emotional, psychological, and financial help they will need to start over? They need people in the born-again Christian community to welcome them and help them find a new Christian family.

I want you to be aware that the position of a defective Catholic is one with serious implications for every area of life. Can you establish a "help hotline" or an outreach programme or a rehabilitation centre for former priests and nuns? This type of support is essential for many if they are to survive intact. You must know that you have started down a path from which you cannot retreat. You must research, write, and reach out to the Catholic. God will be with you, because they need your help so desperately.

California

I have deliberately kept off too much doctrine (teaching) that the reader may give full attention to this one main point.

Later, this could lead on to the examination of a host of non-scriptural teachings which are taught in direct contrast to the Word of God, by both Protestants and Catholics alike.

i.e. The infallibility of the Pope — his own people argue with his decisions these days and start breakaway groups. Now in 1984, we learn that one was murdered by his own people, i.e. Pope John Paul 1st. See p.70 in my book 'Warning' printed in 1980.
Tradition v the Bible
Mary the Queen of Heaven — taken from paganism.
Mary not a virgin at time of her death. Jesus had brothers.
Priests — Bible teaches priesthood of all believers in Christ.
Nuns — not mentioned in Bible.
Baptism of babies (christening) — $1,000 cash reward for one direct Bible verse.
The Confessional — not in the Bible — comes from Babylon sungod worship.
Non-marriage of priests — doctrine of devils.
Religious robes — concept borrowed from Roman judiciary years ago.
Statues – forbidden by God. Ex. 20:2.
Candles – borrowed from heathen worship.
Prayers for the dead – no scriptural basis.
Purgatory — no such place.
Limbo — nothing there.
Blasphemous titles for Papacy.
Cloistered Nuns — what happens to them behind those walls.
The wafer — disc shaped like the sun. Egyptian sun god worship.

The Monstrance (sunburst design for holding wafer) from Osiris worship in Egypt.
The adoration of saints — not scriptural.
Confirmation — not in the Word of God.
Plenary Indulgence (time cancelled in Purgatory) — nonsense.
Penance — not in the Bible.
Merit system — dreamed up by dreamers.
Venial and mortal sin — who made this distinction up? Certainly not God.
The Saints — all believers in Christ are saints.
Miraculous medals, scapulars — no, it's not on.
Rosary beads — please, please — enough.
Monasteries with self inflicted bodily chastisement and being trodden on by other monks — what for?
In the Sydney Morning Herald 27th August 1982 we read: "OPUS DEI — THE 'INNER CHURCH' REBOUNDS. OD, as it is widely known within the church is an order for lay people which is tightly controlled by priests. . . . It has the enthusiastic support of Pope John Paul II. Numeraries are expected not only to take three monastic vows of poverty, chastity and obedience. . . . This includes one session of self-flagellation a week with a variation with the cat o' nine tails and the wearing for two hours a day of the cilis, a metal chain with links turned inward held in place by a thong. This is worn around the upper thigh so that it and the injuries it causes are not seen. The minimum recruiting age is 14½. The founder, Monsignor Escriva, said he received all this by direct inspiration from God in a vision." End quote. — What kind of a God is this? Satan yes, but certainly not the Father of Jesus Christ.

All this is doomed to failure. The priest or the layman takes his sinful nature with him into the cell — he needs "Jesus" poor man.

No wonder the Word of God says, "COME OUT OF HER MY PEOPLE."[12]

Some years ago I was holding meetings in a certain town together with many folk from different churches. A Catholic priest was also present, which pleased me greatly as I wished him to refute any errors in my message. If anything, at least I endeavour to be honest.

During the course of my message this man sat just in front of my wife and family. He complained about many of the statements and included swear words in his vocabulary which shocked others in the audience.

After the meeting, he came to see me to have a discussion. "Why do you speak like this?" he asked.

By way of an answer I turned to the first book of Timothy, Chapter 2 and verse 5. Herewith is a record of this discussion.

Self: "Do you believe in one God?"

Priest: "Yes, I do."

Self: "Do you believe that men are less than God?"

Priest: "Yes, certainly."

Self: "Right, now let us read the verse in question —

"For there is One God, and
One Mediator between
God and men,
The man Christ Jesus."[13]

"Now, because we both speak English, would you please explain to me, as a spokesman for your church, where your Pope fits in with the ONE MEDIATOR — CHRIST JESUS. One is one, you will agree. Please explain."

Priest: "To be perfectly honest, I have never considered the verse before. I will need to return home and examine it."

Gasp from assembled listeners.

When a Pope is crowned in Rome, so says the Encyclopaedia, these words are spoken over him.

"Receive the triple tiara and know that thou are:

(a) The Father of Kings and Princes.
(b) The Pastor of the Universe and the
(c) Vicar on earth of our Lord Jesus Christ." — End quote.

These names are all blasphemous, as no man should dare to claim such things. No wonder Pope Paul VI, when upon his deathbed, and it was recorded in the newspaper, screamed his way into eternity. David Yallop's book shows how involved he had become with

(a) Mafia.
(b) Vatican Bank.
(c) Freemasons in P2 Lodge.

He covered up a giantic conspiracy, poor man, and without Jesus' salvation how else could he be expected to leave this life.

Now, some will remember that in Greek, Hebrew and Latin, a system of numerics is built into their alphabets.

Let us look at the third blasphemous name, along with its numerics.

Here are the Latin words for statement "C".

| | | |
|---|---|---|
| V — 5 | F — no value | D — 500 |
| I — 1 | I — 1 | E — no value |
| C — 100 | L — 50 | I — 1 |
| A — no value | I — 1 | —— |
| R — no value | I — 1 | 501 |
| I — 1 | —— | |
| U — 5 | 53 | |
| S — no value | | |
| —— | | |
| 112 | | |

Add them together 112
53
501
——
666 connected to a name of blasphemy —
"One who stands in the place of the Son of God."

"Lies," I cry.

"ONE MEDIATOR" — remember.

I feel that all this information is sufficient to any person who is prepared to think.

My soul is okay. It's yours I worry about. This particular chapter was written in Launceston, Tasmania.

Last evening, coming in from the meeting, we turned on the T.V. to catch the late news and instead, to our great delight, picked up a documentary filmed in Ireland.

It presented testimony after testimony of Irish men who, under the deceptive banner of freedom, both fought against each other.

These men, to the obvious surprise of the reporter each claimed that they had been "BORN AGAIN". They were no longer Catholic or Protestant, just BORN AGAIN CHRISTIANS.

The scene, taken in their large church, showed them hands raised, tears running down their cheeks, singing to the one who gave them a

(a) Completed
(b) Final
(c) Life-changing
(d) Satisfying
(e) Non-Religious
(f) Enduring and Eternal Salvation.

Their preacher was full of the Holy Spirit's power. He preached from the

(a) Final Authority
(b) The only Book of God to men.

(c) Fully inspired of God.
(d) The Bible.

It was great. God is doing a new thing today. Calling people out of dead religion into a satisfying lifestyle through Jesus.

I picked up a young hitch-hiker one day, and by way of opening the conversation, I told him what I did. I said, "Are you a Christian. Do you attend a church?"

Here was his answer (not mine):

"I was raised in the . . . church. I no longer believe a word they say because the whole thing was so false. I only attend three or four times a year now because I am interested in drama. I ENJOY THE THEATRICALS."

In his book, "The Bible, The Supernatural and The Jew', McCandlish Philips, a Jewish man, uses the following illustration:

"A man goes into a restaurant and orders a meal including 'Special Carrots'. Upon eating some of these carrots he calls the waiter over: 'These carrots taste odd', he says.

'Oh yes Sir,' replies the waiter. 'That is because these are not real — they are our substitute carrots made from sawdust. Although they taste unusual, you must confess, they look like the real thing.'

"Upon hearing this, the man lays down his knife and fork, gets up and leaves, never again to return. He goes to a restaurant where they sold REAL FOOD.

It is strange that people will go, week by week, year by year to the same church, or synagogue where there is little or no reality. They miss the reality of Christ's presence in the Spirit — a word of prophecy — tongues — interpretations — miracles, but most of all the pure Word of God being preached."

**KEY STATEMENT**

In no other field, but in the field of religion would people tolerate such nonsense.

**WHY DO THEY CONTINUE ON LIKE THIS?**

(a) Familiarity with their surroundings — fear of change.
(b) Family pressure.
(c) My ancestors went here also. If your ancestors all took poison, would you?
(d) Fear from years of false teaching — damned if you leave, etc.
(e) Social status — it is respectable to go here.
(f) A habit — I feel better once I've been.

**FINALLY**

An explanation of salvation by Celso Muniz, former Professor and Principal of a major Roman Catholic Seminary.

"When I realised the total depravity of my sinful human nature, I felt like a shipwrecked man who sees the glittering shore at a distance. If only he can reach that shore he will be safe. The shore does not seem very far away, but that is only because things tend to look nearer when viewed across water. The man begins to swim, and at first does quite well, but as he reaches nearer to the shore he suddenly feels a current which sweeps him back out to sea.

He struggles all over again, for he must get through the currents and the breakers or he will die. He tries again and again but he cannot make it, and at last the inescapable conclusion presses into him — the law of nature will not permit him to reach his goal.

Desperate and broken he can only wait for the end. This is the experience of the man who discovers the inadequacy of his own human power to please or find God, and who realises that he can never save himself from the day of judgement.

On the eternal shore dwells a Holy God, and that Holy God maintains His holiness by His commandments. These are like the great waves and currents around the eternal coast, and man will never pass them by his own efforts because he is far too weak and sinful by nature."

To extend the picture, imagine that suddenly a helicopter is seen taking off from the shore. Will the pilot see the drowning man?

It approaches the place where the lonely man is battling hopelessly against the waves, and a rope is let down right over his head. If the drowning man will only grasp the rope then the helicopter can lift him out of the water and carry him over the waves and the boiling surf to safety.

Here is a perfect picture of what Jesus Christ has done. He was seated in the land of eternity at the right hand of the Father. Then He came to this world from the Father's side in order to save us. He entered into the boiling surf of God's wrath when He suffered the punishment of sin upon the Cross at Calvary.

And since that time He reaches down a hand to save 'shipwrecked' sinners. Countless times He has seen the sinner wrestling with the waves of God's law — and He has reached out with the hand of salvation. Every lost person who has completely trusted Him and believed His Word has been pulled out of the sea of condemnation and into a new life.

Returning to the illustration of the drowning man, supposing he had ignored the rope and tried his utmost to continue to reach the shore in his own strength? Obviously, he would have drowned.

Or, supposing he had only half trusted his rescuers. What if he had reached out to grasp the rope with one hand, and yet continued to swim with the other. He would have failed in both measures, and drowned.

We can never find salvation while part of us trusts in what Christ has done to take away the punishment of sin, and another part of us still trusts in sacraments, indulgences, and our own attempted good works. Real salvation comes only when we fully trust Christ.

What are you going to do?

One further note. From the Marlborough Express 12th December 1984: "Pope John Paul II in a 138 page document today attacked the idea that Roman Catholics can obtain forgiveness directly from God without going through the church." . . . End quote. How dare this man condemn millions with his lies.

**RECAP**

The Lord promises that all must be revealed. It is indeed. e.g. Freemasonry revealed in depth — Book: The Brotherhood by Stephen Knight; False Religion revealed in depth — Book: In God's Name by David Yallop; World Government — Book: Cosmic Conspiracy by Stan Deyo, Book: None Dare Call It Conspiracy by Gary Allen, Book: Mystery 666 by Don Stanton, Books: Warning and Second Warning by Barry Smith.

## CHAPTER TEN

# GO TO HELL

In the early 1960's, I was living in an old two-storied house in Apia, Western Samoa. This place was situated on the waterfront, just across the bridge from the town's most famous hotel, Aggie Grey's. Along with two other single men from New Zealand, we lived a life of comparative luxury, housegirls doing all the housework, cooking etc., leaving us free to really enjoy life.

One of my companions was into palmistry and every visitor who set foot on the property immediately had his palm read. As a committed Christian, I would not allow my palm to be read.

In contrast to this, I ran weekly Bible study groups, interspersed with bright singing, testimonies, etc., and would gather well over 100 young people to those meetings.

George, the palm reader, who incidentally also worked for the same firm as I did, Burns Philp (South Seas) Co. Ltd., complained about our meetings, explaining that it was stirring up the spirits in the house.

This, I had no trouble believing, as darkness never goes with light, but not only that, this particular house was haunted, some said, by the spirit of an old man who had died there some years before. Stories of creepy events abounded at that time and, although I was a born again Christian, I was not familiar with the power of God, revealed to Christians through an experience known as the Baptism in the Holy Spirit.

Examples of these stories were —

(a) A previous Australian-born occupant, along with his friends, would, on occasions, be very upset to observe a girl walking up the stairs, her head in her hand, combing her beautiful long hair with the other hand.

(b) Strange tapping sounds in the downstairs bathroom area where the old man was found hanging by the neck, many years before. George and I tried to trace these knockings by standing one on each side of the unlined walls but failed every time.

(c) People would rush in off the street and disturb our evening meal, from time to time, telling us that our kitchen was on fire but upon examination from within the house this would be found to be false.

(d) A previous occupant, also a personal friend who lived with George in the house before I arrived, told of sitting on the couch one night with his girlfriend. All the lights were off when suddenly the big refrigerator door in the kitchen was heard to slam shut.

They both leapt to their feet, peered through the gloom into the kitchen area, and to their mutual horror saw a cigarette end, glowing at about the height of an average man's body, but there was no one behind it. "I'm going home," she cried, "And I'm coming with you," retorted my friend.

(e) At nights, when both the other two were out, I occasionally heard the kitchen cupboard doors opening and closing, yet I was supposed to be the only person in the house.

On one such night I was in bed, when I heard footsteps come up the stairs, walk along the corridor and stop right outside my room, separated from the passageway by a wire screen, which assisted in keeping the air circulating. The hair on the back of my neck stood up as I called out, "Is that you Ron?" (the other boarder at the time). No answer. The footsteps turned around, walked back along the passageway and down the stairs.

All this I share by way of a background to my main story.

A few months went by and one night after one of my Bible meetings had concluded, I packed my Morris Oxford stationwagon (maximum capacity one night equalled 19 people — remember the silly things you did in your youth) and delivered the young people to their various families.

Arriving home, well after midnight, I parked the car in the carport under the house and proceeded inside. As I approached the front door I heard violent smashing sounds coming from inside. Thinking some of my housemates were involved in some sort of drunken punch-up and not really wishing to be involved I made my way to my bedroom — thoroughly exhausted after a very demanding day.

The noise downstairs grew louder. I went to George's room, knocked on his door and he appeared in his pyjamas with a very sleepy look in his eyes. After some discussion, we both concluded that the other boarder in the house must have been somehow involved. To our amazement, we found him, dead drunk, stretched out on his bed, fully clothed, certainly in no state to be involved in any fight.

Returning to my room which looked out over the road I observed a torch light flashing and saw a nervous little group from another family who lived about 250 yards away, standing just under my window.

"Mr Parry," cried the father. (The Samoans regularly confuse P's for 'B's — hence my name — Mr Parry). "What's the noise in your house? We can't sleep."

It occurred to me for the first time that there were no humans involved in this affair. It was definitely spiritual. I called out the window, in a loud voice, "Satan, in the Name of the Lord Jesus Christ, whom I serve, I command you to stop your noise, and go to hell, where you belong."

"Pardon, Mr Parry?" queried the man with the torch "Not you," I replied, "I'm talking to someone else."

Immediately on that word of command, the noise stopped abruptly. Picking up George at his bedroom door, by now, both of us quite nervous, we crept down the stairs, feeling our way along by the light of a torch and finally stood at the door of the front room from whence the noise had been coming.

We pushed open the door with trembing hands, and at that moment a giant dog tore its way through the solid lattice work wall of our house, shot past the family outside and set off across the bridge with a piece of timber in its mouth. This dog had also attacked a 6" x 8" corner post, and our dining room floor was littered with timber next to this great hole in the wall.

In Samoa and other Pacific islands, it is common for evil spirits to go into dogs. The newspaper made a full investigation and reported the story the next day along with photos, which I still possess in my old photograph album.

Upon telling the story to a fellow New Zealander the next day, he remarked, "Well that accounts for the very strange noise we heard passing our house after midnight last night. It went 'Whoo-oo-oo-oo' down the road and we all jumped out of bed thinking it was a tidal wave approaching."

This was my second main experience with this type of thing; the first taking place in Nelson, New Zealand, some years before when my bed, with me in it, was levitated off the floor by some strange power, whilst we were on a Gospel outreach with a group called 'Open Air Campaigners'. The name of the Lord Jesus Christ brought both the bed and me down with a crash. This wakened the others in the team and we held a powerful prayer meeting at that stage.

"For we wrestle not against flesh and blood, but against principalities and powers. . . ."[1]

This devil dog story, which I record in full herewith was written up in both English and Samoan languages in the local newspaper, and was a talking point for weeks amongst the locals who were not too surprised.

"DOG EATS HOLE IN WALL"

Translated from the Samoan Bulletin, 3rd February 1961:

FOUR LEGGED DEVIL — It was about midnight, Monday 30th January 1961, Mr Barry Smith could not sleep because of something akin to the noise of battle in the back room. A torch was shone on the wall which revealed a large hole in the wall of the room. A couple rushed out just in time to see a large black dog with a piece of wood from the wall in its mouth. B. Smith and others living in the house really believe it was an evil spirit because dogs do not eat wood.

Many nights, there were noises in the house. People who lived nearby gathered on that particular night to investigate the strange demonic noises coming from the house. (This house is situated opposite the Vaisigano Bridge, and Mr Brown, ex Manager of Burns Philp used to live in it.)" — End quote.— That house again —

To those who find it difficult to believe in spirits, etc., I say, "You should travel with us for a month. Our family regularly sees people set free from evil spirits in the Name of the Lord Jesus Christ."

It always angers me to hear of films like "The Exorcist" and the "Amityville Horror" where the so-called man of God loses, in both cases.

I say, send in a true servant of the Lord who knows his authority, and is familiar with the four weapons, and he will win 100% every time.

These weapons are:

(1) The Name of the Lord Jesus Christ
(2) The Blood of the Lord Jesus Christ
(3) The anointed praise of God's people
(4) The Word of the Living God

Even a born again believer has no guarantee of victory, when using faulty equipment.

In the book of Deuteronomy, God forbade his people to indulge in certain occult practices as he said,

"For all that do these things are an abomination unto the Lord."[2]

I herewith present that list along with other things which are weaker than, and therefore subject to, the name of the Lord Jesus Christ who said, ". . . All power is given unto me. . . ."[3]

If you, the reader is involved in any of these activities, it is important to RENOUNCE them with your lips, and claim cleansing from these evil things, in the precious name of the Lord Jesus Christ.

Remember, your soul is too important to play around with these occult practices.

**LIST OF ACTIVITIES TO BE RENOUNCED**

**1.** Believing accounts of after death experiences as recorded in Readers Digest and other magazines or publications. These teach — in a very subtle form that Christian and non believers in Christ all have a beautiful experience at death. This is simply not so.

At the point where the human spirit is about to leave the body, that individual knows where he or she is going.

In the year 1978 we were in the Cook Islands and one day a friend of mine, Evangelist Jack Lloyd, and myself, visited the Premier of those Islands, Sir Albert Henry, in his office.

Not long before this meeting, Sir Albert had taken a sudden heart attack whilst visiting Rotorua, New Zealand. I record herewith a record of our conversation:

Self: "Albert, I hear you nearly died whilst you were in Rotorua. What were your thoughts at that time?"

Albert: "I looked out the window at the gardens, and thought back to this my island, that I possibly would never see again. However, I didn't die and here I am."

Self: "Had your heart stopped at that time, where would you have gone?"

Albert: "To HAWAIIKI (the legendary abode of the spirits, in Polynesian culture.)

The Cook Islands people had no T.V. in those days and the radio was, and still is I believe, their main source of news gathering. These radios are normally turned up very loudly so that even a traveller, walking through a village, does not need a radio of his own as he can pick up a full programme listening to all the others. Most people including Sir Albert and his family listened in.

The next night, speaking over Cook Islands radio to over 7,800 square miles of territory, I said, "Yesterday I met a man who told me that when he dies he is going to a place called Hawaiiki. I wish to state here, that when a person dies, they go to one of two places. Both of these start with the letter "H" but neither of them is Hawaiiki."

Therefore, don't listen to anybody else — only the true source of authority — The Word of God.

Other books by so-called experts are strangely lacking from

my bookshelves, e.g. "How to Play Football" by One Who Has Never Played; "The Pill's Grim Progress" by the Pope, or "Love your Neighbour" by Idi Amin.

**2. OCCULT IN EVERY FORM NEEDS TO BE RENOUNCED**

This includes astrology.

(a) No witch can work without it.

(b) Nostrodamus was into it. Born France 1503 — an occultist.

(c) It is forbidden by God.

"There shall not be found among you *an observer of times* . . ."[4]

Any astrological gear should be destroyed immediately, if possible by fire. This includes:

(a) Books or magazines

(b) Occult signs on clothing

(c) Occult signs on jewellery

(d) Birth signs, etc. Signs of the zodiac.

(e) Be careful of health trips. Vegetarianism can become a religious, demonic trip. God has not made a mistake in giving us teeth to eat meat, and teeth to eat vegetables. We are carnivorous and herbivorous.

"In the latter times, some shall depart from the faith giving heed to seducing spirits and doctrines of devils."[5]

(a) Forbidding to marry (some churches are into this — it's demonic).

(b) Commanding to abstain from meats (foods) which God hath created to be received with thanksgiving of them which believe and know the truth. . . ." (word in bracket added for meaning)[6]

Conversation with vegetarian:

Self: "Why don't you eat meat?"

Vege: "Because you have to kill an animal to do so."

Self: "What do you eat?"

Vege: "Lettuce, etc."

Self: "Who gave you permission to kill that lettuce?"

**3. WITCHCRAFT**

Modern day witches say that there are two types:

(a) White — cast good spells (Wicca)

(b) Black — cast evil spells

(c) Actually, both are the same — satanic.

(d) Key witchcraft words — "natural force"

(e) Most clever witchcraft film — "Star Wars"

(f) Key phrase "The force be with you".

NO!

(g) The fallacy in witchcraft is that it is natural force that gives the power.

The manufacturer's handbook tells us very clearly that none of us is master of our own fate.

"To whom ye yield yourselves servants to obey, his servants ye are, whom ye obey, whether of

(a) Sin unto death or

(b) of obedience unto righteousness."[7]

During the course of our travels, we have seen many witches set free in the Name of Jesus and it matters not how highly ranked they think they are, their power is completely useless when confronted with the Lord Jesus Christ.

Any witch reading this had best recognise God's hatred for this ancient occult practice, by reading the following.

"Thou shalt not suffer a witch to live."[8]

Some dear folk are right into the study of genealogies but I have discovered that the homes of much witchcraft today are the Gaelic speaking countries, i.e. Scotland, Ireland and Wales, along with Stonehenge in England.

My advice therefore must be, because you cannot possibly know what your ancestors were into, forget them, and when you receive Jesus as your Saviour and Lord, START A NEW GENERATION.

"If any man be in Christ, he is a new creature. . . ."[9]

Witchcraft shows itself in the following ways:

(a) Domination

(b) Manipulation

(c) Jealousy

(d) Rebellion

(e) Stubbornness

(f) Cool behaviour is a byproduct of witchcraft, or rebellion.

Look at many of the young people's faces and see it written there.

"For rebellion is as the sin of witchcraft, and stubbornness is as iniquity and idolatry." [10]

Here is a challenge to all Christian young people. DON'T BE COOL — BE NATURAL.

"Rejoice with those that do rejoice, and weep with them that weep."[11]

We saw a queen witch of 20 years experience, set free one night, in the name of the Lord.

Rushing at me, fingers raking the air, eyes changing colour, challenges coming out of her mouth,

Evil spirit: "You'll never get rid of me, you mole. I'm not just any old witch, I'm a queen witch."

Self: "Don't you call me a mole. I've got news for you and it's all bad. You're coming out in Jesus' name."

Evil Spirit: "No I'm not. Others have tried and failed."

Self: "This is it. In the Name of the Lord Jesus Christ, set her free and come out now."

Result: Crash to the floor. Evil spirit of the queen witch leaves. Today, a fine Christian rejoining in her salvation.

Jesus said, "In my name, they shall cast out devils."[12]

**4. TEA CUP AND PALM READING** (remember my mate George).

**5. DIVINATION**

This includes colour therapy, water divining (water witching), swinging a button on a thread over pregnant lady to determine the sex of the unborn child.

"There shall not be found among you any one that . . . useth divination."[13]

**6. CONTACT WITH SPIRIT MEDIUMS**

In this way, through the natural grief involved in losing a loved one, some try to bring back the spirit of their dead loved one. Instead, the medium brings up a familiar spirit and puts the person in direct contact with a demon from hell. It speaks just like the deceased, knows the secrets of his life because it is familiar with his whole life, having followed him about secretly for years.

"Regard not them that have familiar spirits, neither seek after wizards to be defiled by them, I am the Lord your God."[14]

**7. ALL SPIRITUALIST CHURCHES ARE DEMONIC**

Even the so-called christian spiritualists. If you check their hymn-books, there will be absolutely no mention of the precious blood of our Lord Jesus Christ. A mention of this would cause many of them to manifest an evil spirit, or to vomit.

". . . The blood of Jesus Christ His Son cleanses from all sin."[15]

**8. FORTUNE TELLERS**

Fortune tellers at fairs, socials or any other place can bring you into bondage with fear.

Looking into a crystal ball, he or she reels off much good

news. Cunningly inserted in the midst of all this is bad news which brings fear.

The evil spirit then rides in on the fear and brings it to pass. That is why the text book says,

"For God hath not given to us the spirit of fear, but of power and of love and of a sound mind."[16]

The enemy loves fear. Some of you readers have fear of certain places, rooms, graveyards, death, going to the bathroom at night. This fear needs to go in Jesus name.

A warning from a man called Job.

"For the thing which I greatly feared is come upon me, and that which I was afraid of is come unto me."[17]

**9. HUMANISM**

Beware of intellectual trips in the fields of philosophy, psychology, psychiatry, sociology, etc.

Much of this knowledge contradicts God's plain Word, and is man's vain attempt, without God, to explain the meaning and the mysteries of life, and how to solve its problems leaving God, the originator of all life, out of the picture.

This desperate human intellectual struggle results in bankrupt nothingness.

I well remember, years ago, a Chinese speaker called Leland Wang came to New Zealand and gave a number of talks.

Herewith is his definition of a philosopher.

"A philosopher is one who studies more and more about less and less until he knows everything there is to know about nothing."

Once we receive the Lord into our lives, we no longer need to philosophise about the meaning of life. We receive the answer to that age old question in a moment of time.

Why are we here?

"Christ in you, the hope of glory"[18] again "And for thy pleasure, they are created." [19]

No wonder this clear warning is given to us, as many involved in solving problems of individuals lives, because they do not have the protection of the blood of Jesus Christ, finish up as bad as, or worse than the person they are counselling, and a man with a white coat leads them away, kicking and struggling.

"Beware lest any man spoil you through philosophy and vain deceit after the tradition of men, after the rudiments of the world, and not after Christ."[20]

**10. SEANCES AND OUIJA BOARDS**

Seances and ouija boards might look like a lot of fun kids (and oldies). They may sell under the heading of games, but oh, what a deadly game, that ends with you burning in the fire with no friends around to encourage or help.

Leave these strictly alone. One game, or contact is enough to bind you up.

A boy in Henderson, Auckland, told us the following story. He said, "I am not a Christian, but one night we were playing with a glass on a board, asking it questions. I asked it about the blood of Jesus Christ and the glass shattered into a thousand pieces. We were all terrified and I will never try that again."

## 11. ANCESTRAL SPIRITS

There is no doubt that our everyday lifestyles are affected by the actions of and the genetic makeup of our ancestors.

It is well written,

". . . visiting the iniquity of the fathers upon the children unto the third and fourth generation of them that hate me."[21]

All is not doom and gloom however, as we also pick up the good qualities along with the bad.

Do you fear certain things or places, e.g. going into a certain room or house, meeting certain people, or a certain uneasiness with authority figures?

Remember that many of our ancestors were into the occult and that even those of European stock aren't exempt.

During my public lectures, I recommend that when one becomes a born again Christian, it is important to forget the past and start a new series of generations based on the Lord. (I have mentioned this twice in this chapter for emphasis.)

Therefore, if any man be in Christ, he is a new creature; old things are passed away, behold all things become new.

(a) **Maori Illustration**

Some years ago, along with a group of Christians, I travelled to Paihia, in New Zealand's Bay of Islands to assist in the lifting of a Maori tribal curse from a small tree in the area. This curse had wrought much havoc to those who tampered with the tree. We marched around it, singing songs of praise to the Lord.

Our leader, evangelist Muri Thompson, then spoke to the evil spirit behind the curse in the name of the Lord Jesus. Immediately, on this calm day, a violent wind sprang up, battering us to such a degree that we needed to hold on to each other to stay upright.

Muri spoke words of authority over these spirits a second time, in the name of the Lord Jesus, and again this wind hit us, and battered us. Then again, the third time, and the wind thrashed around us again. Muri said, "In the name of the Lord

Jesus Christ whom we serve, I lift this curse, and set this area free." As we still clung onto one another to stay upright, the wind ceased. The oppression lifted, Muri tore off a branch, flung it against the tree, then stripped off some leaves and handed them around to those of us present. Some obviously felt a little nervous, yet Muri said, "There you are, you are all alive and well, aren't you?" We all had to agree and so I placed the leaf in my Bible where it stayed for some years alongside these words, ". . . upon this rock I will build my church, and the gates of hell shall not prevail against it."[22]

(b) **Cook Island illustration**

The year was 1978, we were on the island of Rarotonga, the capital of the Cook Islands. It was our second trip to that island that year, both trips within the period of three months. Our friend and minister Jack Lloyd was with us on both occasions and the Lord's power was shown mightly through his ministry. Such a lot had happened during our first visit, with many many people committing themselves to the Lord Jesus Christ. Satan was hopping mad and he didn't want us back on that island.

**Incident No. 1:**

Flying over from New Zealand we were nearing the airport when, suddenly, on a clear calm night, the DC8 aircraft was caught in an updraught, then it dropped, hundreds and hundreds of feet, the fuselage twisting from end to end. Beer glasses hit the ceiling, people screamed, and the hostesses fell heavily into the aisle, one girl hurting herself quite badly. I personally felt, 'This is it — it's all over.' One of our daughters was so upset by the experience that she spent the next two weeks in bed. Later, the pilot was reported as saying that there was no warning, or apparent reason for our experience. However, without trying to be dramatic, we, in our Christian team knew better.

"We wrestle not against flesh and blood, but against principalities, against powers. . . ."[23]

**Incident No. 2:**

Arriving at the airport, we were met by local officials, amongst them, the Immigration officer. "Mr Smith, you again," he muttered. "You are not preaching here any more."

"Yes I am," I replied. There was some debate over the non-stamping of my passport, but then with dire warnings of consequences, should I preach, or convene meetings, he stamped it, but grudgingly.

**Incident No. 3:**

We commenced meetings that very night in a large corrugated iron hall at Black Rock, around the coast from the main town.

I preached my first message and at the conclusion, as is my custom, gave the listeners an invitation to come forward and commit their lives to the Lord. At that stage, a sound of torrential rain came on the roof. People ran out to close their car windows, and came back in with amazed expressions on their faces. The noise was so loud, I turned the amplifier up as loud as it would go.

"Don't be distracted. Give yourself to the Lord Jesus," I repeated. Immediately down came another apparent cloud burst of rain on the roof, causing me to stop speaking. People went out and came in again as before, surprise written all over their faces.

"This is just the devil. He's angry," I said, as people began to move out to let Christ into their lives. There it came again, like rain mingled with hail (which simply doesn't happen in that part of the world). I stopped speaking and waited for it to pass, thinking all the time of a soaking wet seat in our borrowed truck.

After the meeting, we rushed out to inspect the damage, but to our surprise, there was no sign of any rain. The sand was dry, no water ran in the gutters. Our truck windows were left open, yet the seats were dry.

A senior sergeant of police who was himself a new convert to Christ, went to work the next day, where he held the following discussion with a fellow senior sergeant who had been on duty that day outside the hall as we held our meetings.

Christian Policeman: "How did you enjoy the meeting yesterday:"

Duty Policeman: "Really good. I stayed there right throughout the meeting. Only two things mystified me. Why did Barry stop speaking three times near the end of his message and why did people run out and then inside again?"

Christian Policeman: "Because of the rain storm of course. You couldn't hear yourself inside, and folk ran out to close their car windows."

Duty Policeman: "Oh no, there was no rain at all. I can't understand this."

Only those who are prepared to recognise the existence of a spiritual enemy will understand this particular chapter.

For those readers who doubt, do not be dismayed. I have no doubt that few would wish to call me a liar directly.

These stories are all explainable only in terms of the supernatural. Don't say, "I don't believe." Rather say, "I don't understand".

**(c) Samoan Illustration**

Anybody familiar with the islands of Western Samoa will also be familiar with the names of the national spirits who, from time to time, take on the forms of beautiful girls who go out in the night and trap unwary young men into a relationship of some kind or another.

The unsuspecting young man is picked up the next morning, his body twisted into grotesque positions, and a witch-doctor is normally called in to set the victim free.

The two spirit girls are named Sama'iafi and Telesā respectively. The witch-doctor rubs the victim with leaves, traps the spirit in one part of the body and reasons with it. The spirit then sets the terms, e.g. cut off the girl's hair if the victim is a girl, or take her or him to a certain place at a certain time and the evil spirit promises to come out. In other words, the evil spirit likes to set the terms.

The year was 1979. We were back on the island holding meetings. The night in question, I was preaching from the back of a truck to a crowd of about 1,000 people gathered on the reclaimed area on the Apia waterfront. I felt prompted to mention these two spirit girls.

"Many folk on this island are terrified of Sama'iafi and Telesā. If you call in the witch-doctor, the evil spirits will argue, come out on their terms and then return with seven others worse than themselves. If you do the job the Bible way, in the name of the Lord Jesus, the evil spirits will go, never again to return."

"And these signs shall follow them that believe, in my name shall they cast out devils." (said Jesus.)[24]

A policeman standing in the crowd asked a friend of ours, "How come this man can speak like this without getting a stone thrown at him?" Our friend answered, "No-one will hit that man with a stone until his time is ready."

The next night, a telephone call disturbed our meal, "Can you come quickly please," pleaded a girl's voice. "My brother has a nightly appointment at the graveyard with the spirits you spoke about last night. He covers himself with perfume, goes to meet them, after which they try to destroy him by drowning him in the river, from whence, he normally requires rescuing."

"Get the boys in the family to hold him until we arrive," I said. We set off and soon met at the house together with a dear friend, Max Rasmussen.

We found the boy sitting on the couch looking furtively at the clock.

Addressing the spirit in the Samoan language, I asked,

"Agaga leaga, o ai lou igoa i le suafa o Iesu?" (Evil spirit. What is your name, in the Name of Jesus?)

A girl's voice answered out of this boy's mouth. "Sama'iafi" — I answered, "You lying devil. In the Name of the Lord Jesus Christ, come out of him and set him free."

Immediately the boy jumped as the evil spirit left him and when he came down, he was a new man.

"I'm free," he breathed. "That's right," I answered and if you wish to stay that way you will need to be born again into the Lord's family. Are you agreeable? — He was and so we led him in the sinner's prayer.

His mother then burst into tears claiming to be the most wicked woman in the village. "I need the Lord," she sobbed, and so my wife May sat down and led her to Christ. Another sister said to me, "Barry, I received Christ recently at a Youth for Christ meeting. Will you please pray for me to receive the baptism in the Holy Spirit. I did and we left the house with the joy of the Lord — one delivered, two saved, one baptised in the Holy Spirit.

We then went home with happy hearts and finished the meal.

Lesson learnt so far: All evil spirits are subject to the name of the Lord Jesus Christ.

No matter how strong the curse, or the power of any witch-doctor, family sickness passed on down the generations, Jesus is the answer. Anybody involved in Aboriginal work in Australia needs to know that featherfoot curses are also weaker than the Lord's Name.

## 12. EASTERN RELIGION

Eastern religion does not provide a way of salvation.

Some years ago, I took Andrew, my son, and another young man, Derek Jones, to a rock festival cum eastern religious convention, entitled Nambassa. In the midst of all this was a large marquee being a witnessing point for the 350 Christians who were there. All around the grounds were hundreds of tents with larger ones being used by the eastern religious groups.

Half-way through the festival the rain came down and flooded the river on the property, washing away the bridges. Thousands of folk were stuck on our side of the river and, in their efforts to escape the rain, rushed into the Christian marquee. We had haybales for seats which most enjoyed sitting on, with the exception of the many nudists who were also present. Gurus, and priests and adherents from the many groups were also there.

I was handed the microphone and asked to speak. My

opening remark captured the attention of everybody present.

"All eastern religion is demonic."

There was a deathly silence as the statement went forth. Suddenly, in a burst of anger, the many gurus present surged forward in an attempt to refute my remarks. Andrew said later, "Gee Dad, I really thought you had overdone it at that point. Derek and I were getting ready to come and give you a hand." The gurus marched up in their long flowing robes, their faces contorted with rage behind their straggly long hair and bedraggled beards. I was so confident, I just continued on with my message. The gurus marched all around me, their hands reaching out fruitlessly for the microphone. I never moved it, as no-one could lay a hand on it. After their efforts failed they all turned around, faces registering frustration now, rather than anger, and returned to the back of the tent.

By these statements, we make it quite clear that Christ Jesus not only is Lord, but is the only way to God.

Every man in his own way is looking for God, but God has ordained that there is only one way that man will get to know him, i.e. through the Lord Jesus Christ, who said,

"I am the way, the truth and the life, no man cometh unto the Father but by me."[25]

| Possibilities | (Please tick appropriate square): YES | NO |
|---|---|---|
| (a) Jesus was a liar — was he? | ☐ | ☐ |
| (b) Jesus was a good man but deceived — was he? | ☐ | ☐ |
| (c) Jesus was mad — was he? | ☐ | ☐ |
| (d) Jesus was who He said He was. Was he? | ☐ | ☐ |

I once met a man who said words to this effect: "I believe in God. It's just the Jesus part I can't stand." I have bad news for any who believe this way.

Listen, ". . . All men should honour the Son, even as they honour the Father. He that honoureth not the Son, honoureth not the Father which hath sent him."[26]

It has been estimated that there are about 2,000 practising gurus posing as Christs, at present, and in America, one person in nine has been sucked into following these frauds. Dr Billy Graham said that there are about 400 of these people in Los

Angeles who have announced their divinity and managed to scrape up a following.

All these need to be renounced: Bahai, Hari Krishna, Divine Light, all Gurus (including Rajneesh Bagwan and Saibaba), Moslem, Hindu, Sikh, I Ching, Yoga, Burning of Incense, Haribol, Acupuncture (Yin and Yang concept — two needles). Also T.M. (correct name = Hinduism.)

Note also no eastern religion has a living leader and none offers forgiveness. Only the living Lord Jesus Christ forgives sin.

In 1978, on the island of Rarotonga, I was introduced to two fellow New Zealanders, whom I knew were T.M. teachers, recently expelled from Western Samoa, who were travelling the Pacific spreading their pernicious doctrines.

"Are you the Mr Smith that writes against us in the papers?" asked the younger man. "Yes, that's the one," I replied. When asked why this was, I explained that T.M. is Hinduism in disguise.

I went on,

1. "Isn't it true, when a candidate comes in to join up, he has placed in front of him or her a picture of a gentleman called Guru Dev, the Maharashi Yogi's teacher?" — He agreed.
2. "You then have the candidate offer up three to five pieces of fruit before that picture. This means that the candidate offers up the senses to the evil spirit behind that picture.
3. "The teacher then offers up a white linen handkerchief before the picture, which means the human spirit now surrenders to the demonic spirit behind the picture.
4. "A bunch of flowers is offered up by the teacher on behalf of the candidate. This is offered up to Guru Dev on the altar. All candidates must go through this to make it work.
5. "The candidate is then given a 'mantra' or secret word that he or she will use during periods of meditation. This mantra is given according to age and personality. Called Buja this word is the beginning of the name of a Hindu god. Later on under advanced technique the candidate says in Sanskrit the words 'Come in' at the beginning of the mantra. The aim is to attain God consciousness. A Hindu demon comes in to deceive the candidate.

   This mantra is the name of Hindu god and is the candidate's own personal devil — isn't that nice.
6. "Now the candidate repeats some words in the Sanskrit language which is understood only by those who teach.

   Meaning — 'Before you, oh spirit, I bow down — I bow down — I bow down.'

My word, the devil loves that, and thus the candidate stumbles on like an ox to the slaughter. It is not a religion, he is constantly reassured. 'No indeed', chuckles Maharashi Yogi — 'It is demonism in disguise'.

Having heard all this, the young teachers turned a green colour and said, 'We must be going.' "

Standing next to me all this time was a friend named Bobby. "Follow me," I said. "We will go around to these people's house and continue on with the conversation that they are apparently so keen to terminate." Arriving at the house, we found the younger men explaining what this dreadful man had said to them. Bobby and I knocked and walked straight in.

"Hello," I said. "We are the ones who have been talking to your friends. I haven't quite finished yet, so we came around here to explain something else. The next stage in this Hindu system is for you to become vegetarians."

There was a very real anger building up in the leaders by now, and so, having delivered the message, we left, satisfied that it was a job well done.

It will no doubt be of interest to the reader, that T.M. takes you on, stage after stage until you are ready for flying school (levitation). There is one of these places in New Zealand and others in various parts of the world, where the following takes place:

(a) The candidate goes up in stages, and when certain proficiency has been attained, he or she is ready to levitate. There are 20 different techniques and one is levitation. Yoga is compulsory.

(b) The candidate in every case undergoes a Dr Jekyll and Mr Hyde transformation. The features contort, and take on a completely diabolical look. The candidate at this stage, is becoming possessed of an evil spirit, who will give him or her flying ability.

(c) Suddenly a transformation takes place. The evil expression disappears and the candidate now takes on a beautiful expression, it has been described, "just like an angel".

"And no marvel, for Satan himself is transformed into an angel of light."

(d) The candidate may then take off from the polystyrene floor and fly.

Therefore, if you wish to be involved with evil spirits from hell, stick with the Transcendental Meditation way.

Remember, T.M. definitely works, but it is the way of death

according to God's true way of salvation, as revealed in His Book.

## 13. MARTIAL ARTS

Continuing on with my talk at the Nambassa Festival, I said, "All martial arts are demonic."

After a moment of shocked silence, there was a tremendous uproar. The top degree black belts were present of course, as they were there in a teaching capacity. Their language was disgusting, as they shouted back at me. I challenged them in the name of the Lord, "Don't you swear at me like that. Come up here and I'll prove to you that what I'm saying is true." They started marching down the aisle towards me. My son, Andy, said afterwards, "Hey Dad, you did it again. Derek and I were getting ready to give you a hand once more." Actually, I didn't need a hand, the Lord was there and his promise sustained me.

"Behold, I give you power . . . over all the power of the enemy, and nothing shall by any means hurt you."[27]

These top degree martial arts experts came very close, yet I felt no fear or apprehension. "Come on," I said, beckoning with my finger, but they didn't (or couldn't). Looking them squarely in the eyes, I knew that it was the Holy Spirit that stopped them. A look of fear came over their faces. as they turned around and made their way to the back of the tent. The Christians rose as one man and praised and glorified God.

A sceptic at this point may arise and say, "Oh yes, you were lucky that time. You wouldn't come off so well if you tried that again."

Well, it did happen again.

The year was 1981. We were on the island of Penang near the Thailand border, but still in Malaysia however. Visiting a Christian school, we learnt that some teachers were teaching karate as an exercise. The students, who in the main were children of missionaries, were the most rebellious looking bunch we had ever seen. These missionaries, many of them from the U.S.A., went out preaching to others and left their own children smouldering with bitterness and resentment, in the meantime.

These folk challenged me when I said,

(a) Martial arts are demonic.

(b) As you bow to the picture of the master, you bow to a spirit of violence, who is in that man.

(c) As you do your deep breathing exercises, you breathe in an eastern spirit of violence. Your breath is actually reserved for the Spirit of God.

(d) The continual longing for someone to attack you, comes from this proud spirit of violence that inhabits you, upon your clear invitation.

At this point, many disagreed with what I had said, and became very vocal.

I replied, "There is only one way to settle this argument. A direct confrontation. Do you have a top degree black belt master who instructs you? Secondly, does he break concrete blocks with his hands?"

They replied in the affirmative to both these questions.

I then commissioned an older boy to make his way to the Chinese master's home with the following challenge:

"Barry Smith from New Zealand is inviting you down to the school at any time of your choosing. A concrete block will be provided for you to chop, and just as you are about to do this, Barry Smith will bind up the violent devil in you in the name of the Lord Jesus Christ, and you will smash your hand on the block."

A tense group waited until the messenger returned, with the following message — "He won't come."

I remarked to the then startled congregation, "Of course he won't because the spirit in him knows that what I am saying is true."

Every time a blow is struck, the sound from the lips is the expression of the violent spirit within.

Get out of

(a) Kung Fu
(b) Karate
(c) Tae Kwon Do, etc.

Learn to use the name of the Lord as your protection.

"The name of the Lord is a strong tower; the righteous runneth into it and is safe."[28]

**14. FIRE WALKING**

"There shall not be found among you any one that maketh his son or his daughter to pass through the fire."[29]

It is strange, but many evangelical, apparently born again Christians who do not believe in the power of God through the baptism in the Holy Spirit will go to such countries as Fiji and will bring home coloured slides of the famous fire-walkers of Beqa Island — Now this is pure demonism. Therefore, these dear people believe in the power of satan but not in the power of God. It's really amazing.

These firewalkers came from Fiji to New Zealand some years ago to put on a performance at Lower Hutt. They dug a pit, heated the stones, went through their purification ceremonies, and then, in front of a live audience stepped on the stones.

Unfortunately for them, a friend of mine, born again and filled with the Holy Spirit of God, bound up the demons in them, and the firewalkers burnt their feet.

The newspaper recorded the next day, "Firewalking fails in New Zealand".

## 15. FALSE CULTS

How do we identify one of these?

It is very simple — they all have three things in common.

(a) They will always have a prophet or a leader who dominates their thinking, thus tampering with their free will.

(b) They will have a system of do's and don'ts which add to God's gift of salvation through Christ alone.

(c) They will all claim to be the one true way to God.

Who was it again who said, "I am the way, the truth and the life, no man cometh unto the Father, but by me."[30]

List of false cults to renounce and leave immediately.

(a) **Mormons**

(i) False prophet Joseph Smith, who with his brother Hiram climbed high and rapidly in the degrees of Freemasonry. He was expelled from the Masons for stealing their secrets and incorporating them in his new religion. Mormons are taught Jesus and Lucifer are brothers. Notice another Freemason angle here.

(ii) He also had a visitation from a demonic angel named Moroni, one of the one-third cast out of heaven with Lucifer.

(iii) He wrote his own holy book from the manuscripts of one Solomon Spaulding, a deposed minister. The name of the original publication was "Manuscript Found". It was a pseudo-christian publication, with the words — "and it came to pass" — liberally inserted throughout. The locals in Spaulding's town chuckled as he appeared in public and said, "There goes old — 'and it came to pass' Spaulding." Imagine how much louder the laughter became when they read Smith's new book which he claimed he got from Moroni's revelation on some golden plates, read with magic specs. — It was Spaulding's book refurbished all over again.

The origins of the book of Mormon then are,

(i) A demon angel called Moroni.

(ii) A well known stranger to the truth and one who had a very slender grasp on reality, one Joseph Smith (a documented fact).

(iii) Passages from Shakespeare's writings.

(iv) The story line from Manuscript Found ("and it came to pass") claims it came from reformed Egyptian which included little sail boats upside down and numbers 1-9 on their sides. Egyptologists said it meant absolutely nothing.

(v) Passages taken at random from the KING JAMES VERSION of the Bible (translated by scholars between 1604-1611, in the Old King James English) yet it supposedly came from ancient reformed Egyptian, thousands of years old.

Funny thing, wouldn't you agree. Imagine the slaves building the pyramids, speaking Egyptian with King James English accents — e.g. "Verily I say unto thee, I wot not that thou wouldest help me to build this structure in the wilderness."

Next, to any who are considering going through the Mormon secret temple ceremonies.

1. Your clothes will be removed.
2. A robe put on.
3. You will be washed, under your robe.
4. You will be anointed with oil under your robe.
5. You will be asked if you would like to leave at this point. Most will say, "No", because curiosity leads them on.
6. You will then move into the witchcraft realm with the Masonic symbolic
   (i) Slitting of the throat
   (ii) Tearing open of the chest
   (iii) Ripping open of the stomach
7. A new name is given. Yours will be the same as many others on that day, e.g. Joseph or Rebecca.

I would rather wait and get mine in heaven.

"To him that overcometh, will I . . . give him a white stone, and in the stone a new name written, which no man knoweth saving he that receiveth it."[31]

So then, to recap, we now see that Mormonism has a false prophet, witchcraft, Freemasonry, a false holy book, claims to be the one true church, denies that salvation is the gift of God through Jesus Christ our Lord, and it puts curses on people's lives.

A woman in New Zealand called Freda Stirling held a public

meeting in Hamilton some years ago. In this meeting, she pointed to the leader of the Mormon College at Tuhikaramea, who was also present at the meeting and said, "When I resigned from the church, that man over there said these words, 'May your body be found with its throat cut from ear to ear.' " You see — the old Freemason's curse again.

Leave it, and disassociate yourself from it.

(b) **Jehovah's Witnesses**

False prophet's name, Charles Taze Russell, and also another called Judge Rutherford (sometimes translated Judge nother fraud).

These people damn themselves and all those who follow their lies, using a clever twisting of the Scriptures. In their New World translation of the Scriptures, the word "a" is inserted in the gospel of John Ch. 1. v. 1.

"In the beginning was the Word, and the Word was with God, and the Word was a God." (wrong — wrong — wrong)

This is an attempt to take away from Jesus being God. My comment on this is as follows: If Jesus is not God, then there is unfortunately no salvation for any of us.

| | True | False |
|---|---|---|
| No man can save another man | ☐ | ☐ |

(Please tick appropriate square)

**Medical Facts**

When a baby is in the womb, the mother's blood does not touch the baby. Mary's blood, being normal human blood, was tainted with sin. Even she knew this when she confessed that the one within her womb would one day save her from sin.

She said, "My spirit hath rejoiced in God my Saviour."[32]

Only a sinner needs a saviour, right? — Right.

The blood that flowed in Jesus' veins was a special blood, containing the R.H. factors of God.

That's why Jesus could say, "He that hath seen me, hath seen the Father."[33]

Jesus was therefore equal with the Father. Each time He used the words I AM, He claimed this. Anything else would be blasphemy.

I AM the way

I AM the truth

I AM the door

I AM the life

On the night He was betrayed, the soldiers came looking for Jesus of Nazareth.

He called out, "I AM He"[34] (this latter word is in italics, not in the original) and the power of the Name of the Lord, spoken by Him who is God, knocked them all over backwards to the ground.

It is interesting to note that when I, or you, or anybody else calls out I AM, very few people fall to the ground.

Why? "Because Jesus Christ is Lord."

Because all the Jehovah's Witnesses doctrine is based on a false foundation, there is no forgiveness from sin.

They are taught, as do all the other cults, that theirs is the one true church. Salvation comes about through witnessing about Jehovah. This is sad, because Jesus said, "You shall be witnesses unto me."[35]

In Acts 4:10 and 12 we read, ". . . by the name of Jesus Christ of Nazareth, . . . neither is there salvation in any other, for there is NONE OTHER NAME under Heaven given among men, whereby we must be saved." (emphasis added)

These dear people are sucked in through clever talk. Continue on witnessing, witnessing, witnessing, every knock-back they are taught is a blessing or another star in their crown.

Their minds are filled with doom. Their opening phrase, "What do you think of the state of the world?" leads on to talk of Armageddon. Their witnessing is done parrot fashion. Any who want to talk to these folk about the Lord Jesus and His salvation must get them off the track. They report back regularly on all witnessing done, and results achieved.

All books they endeavour to sell they have first had to buy.

According to their doctrine, there is no definite salvation in this life. We must wait for death to find out whether we have it or not — how sad.

It is written, "He that hath the Son hath life, and he that hath not the Son of God, hath not life."[36]

These people need prayer and love. They are deceived and eternally lost.

If you belong to it, get out.

(c) **Armstrongism (The Worldwide Church of God)**

Herbert Armstrong, whose programme appears on T.V. in many countries, is a sad little old man. Often called Mr Confusion, he has ideas that he is God's gift to the world. Written up many times as the final end time voice, in his magazines he claims to have the divine revelation that he and his church alone are right, and that all others are wrong.

It's strange, I know, but I seem to have heard all this before.

Points to ponder.

Many years ago, he came in contact with a sabbath keeping neighbour who showed him some Judaistic teachings which he clung to.

(i) Sabbath keeping
(ii) Observance of certain health laws
(iii) Regular tithing to his work, etc.

Being one of the world's most clever advertisers, he built up his church by advertising through his glossy magazines and sales pitch.

In each message, he advertises these publications using such clever wording as

(i) No cost whatsoever, to you personally
(ii) We don't want your MONEY
(iii) The COST has been taken care of, etc. All this is called reverse advertising.

So clever is he at his skills, that he is literally rolling in wealth, as the human subconscious does the rest. People do not, generally speaking, like anything for nothing. Pride forces them to send much money to this man and his organisation.

Herbert has worries however.

(i) All is not well between him and his son, Garner Ted
(ii) There have been financial and leadership problems with various staff members
(iii) He is an old man, getting ready to die, yet he himself is not saved.

Listen to Jesus,

"Woe unto you lawyers, for ye have taken away the key of knowledge, ye entered not in yourselves, and THEM THAT WERE ENTERING IN, YE HINDERED."[37] (Emphasis added for meaning.)

Armstrong says that it is heresy to say that you can know that you are saved now. You must wait for death, to find out.

This means that the angel brought a false name for God's Son, when he called him

— JESUS = SAVIOUR

I tell you, here plainly and clearly, that our God has provided

(i) Salvation from sin
(ii) Assurance of salvation now; not later
(iii) A living vital communion with Himself through Jesus.

Please read this.

"These things have I written to you that believe on the name of the Son of God that ye may KNOW, that ye HAVE everlasting life. . . ."[38] (Emphasis added.)

I've got it now. How about you?

Therefore Herbert Armstrong is wrong, and God was right all the time.

Amongst his publications, Herbert has produced
"The Wonderful World of Tomorrow" and
"The Plain Truth"

Both publications mingle truth and error.

There is a book out entitled, "The Plain Truth about the Plain Truth". Upon reading this book, you will find that the: plain truth about the Plain Truth is that it is not the plain truth.

My advice is, burn them, cancel your subscription and return to good Christian reading exalting Jesus, and to His Word, the Bible.

(d) **Hare Krishna**

Barely requires any notes. Shaven heads, painted faces, shapeless robes and the ringing of bells accompanied by a strange little jig is hardly the type of thing that appeals to a normal person.

(e) **Moonies**

A group who has as their false prophet, the Rev. Sun Moon at present in prison on tax evasion charges. What a naughty false messiah! By now, the reader will realise that in order to keep the cult ball rolling, this group must also claim to be the only correct one. Mr F. M. Moon (F.M. = False Messiah) gets and holds his converts using the following methods.

Offers of friendship to lonely people.
A communal spirit of apparent love and caring.
This leads into domination (witchcraft) of lives.
Brainwashing techniques are then employed,
i.e. lack of sleep — late nights, very early mornings, lack of protein in the diet
Indoctrination in the beliefs of the group.

Using these three methods, folk who wish to leave need to be deprogrammed.

Salvation through Christ alone is missed out.

(f) **Rosacrucianism**

Is pure occult. Mind power is simply the work of psychic demons — terrible confusion is the result and when one tries to come to Christ Jesus as Lord and

Saviour, it is very difficult indeed. Deliverance is needed here.

(g) **Scientology**

Another weird person, Mr Hubbard, who is at present hiding from the authorities, has conned a large group of seeking people. In this system, you self-evaluate using a tick off list. — Result: despair, anguish, confusion, and no salvation. The use of an "E Meter' keeps people temporarily amused — come out please.

"There is a way which seemeth right unto a man, but the end thereof are the ways of death."[39]

(h) **Tongues for Salvation**

These groups are spreading all over the world. The people are taught that speaking in tongues is essential for salvation.

"Not true," I cry. Masses of people are turning themselves inside out to speak in tongues, in order that they might be saved.

I speak in tongues, but I was saved before I ever did. Speaking in tongues is a great gift from God, but it is not salvation.

"For by GRACE are ye SAVED, through FAITH and not of yourselves. It is the GIFT of God." (emphasis added.)[40]

(i) **Seventh Day Adventism**

I almost hesitate to include this group as God is doing a work amongst them today and clearing up their woolly thinking regarding salvation.

Their prophetess was Ellen G. White. She was the follower of a godly Baptist man who interpreted Dan. 8:14 to mean that Christ would return between 21st March 1843 and 21st March 1844. It never happened of course, so a new date was set — 22nd October 1844. This also turned out to be a fizzer and so William Miller confessed he was wrong.

On p.412 "History of the Advent Message", we read: "We expected the personal coming of Christ at the time and now to contend that we were not mistaken is dishonest. We should never be ashamed frankly to confess our errors. I have no confidence in any of the theories that grew out of the movement." (Miller)

The bad apple in the box apparently was Ellen G. White, as many S.D.A. folk are at present finding out, to their horror I might add. It has been discovered that she did not write her book, "The Great Controversy" under the inspiration of the Spirit of God, but plagiarised it from other books. In spite of this, many still believe that she was the "Lesser Light" linked to Jesus, the "Greater Light".

This means that her integrity and honour is in question. Therefore, the argument is, that her vision where she claims that God showed her Miller's figures, were as the Lord wanted them, and that His hand was over and hid a mistake in some of the figures, is also suspect.

A Mr Edson then took up the deception, built up on a mistake, covered by the hand of God ("Sick blasphemy", I cry) by explaining that actually Christ moved into the second apartment in the heavenly tabernacle to perform further work, prior to His second coming.

I am sad to relate that this makes Christ's sacrifice a perpetual, on-going one, similar to that which the Roman Catholics teach.

Some years ago, whilst we were living in Western Samoa, the following incident occurred during the time of revival; or the outpouring of God's Holy Spirit.

A Seventh Day Adventist man saw a girl lying on her back on the concrete with about 60-70 others, with her arms raised towards heaven. This continued on for about eight hours, from midnight until 8 a.m. the next morning. He came up to the girl saying, "This is not God. This is the devil," trying at the same time to bend one of her arms. He couldn't do so however, and at that very moment, a large dog jumped out of the bushes, sinking its four fangs into his arm. He yelled out, "Help, get me a doctor" but we called the pastor who prayed healing over him and salvation, in the Name of the Lord.

One night, as I was preaching soon after that, he came to me at the conclusion of the service and said that I didn't mention keeping the law.

I asked him the following question, as the congregation gathered around to watch and listen.

"Po ua lava le toto o Iesu e fa'amagalo ai agasala uma lava?" ("Is the blood of Jesus enough to forgive all sin?")

He answered, "Yes, but you must also keep the law."

I asked the question three times, and his answer was the same each time.

I then wrote the question, on a large sheet of white paper, using a red marker pen — I then handed him the pen and the crowd strained forward waiting for him to write his answer. He wrote only two words, and I stopped him.

"That's enough," I said.

He had written, "YES, BUT . . ."

I then pointed out that anybody with a knowledge of the English language would know immediately that,

"YES" is cancelled out by "BUT".

"What you really meant was 'No' I observed. Going on, I invited him to follow me in a prayer in the presence of the then crowded building.

Self: "Lord Jesus, I thank you for your precious blood which you shed on Calvary for me."

S.D.A. man: "Lord Jesus, I thank you for your precious blood, which you shed on Calvary for me."

Self: "But it is not enough to cleanse away all my sin."

S.D.A. man: "But it is . . ." gasp, gasp. "I can't say that to God."

Self: "Why not. You said it to us."

S.D.A. man: "I know, but it is different saying it to God."

I couldn't agree more. I really love the S.D.A. folk, but every time I read this verse, I tremble for them.

"Christ is become of no effect unto you, whosoever of you are justified by the law YE ARE FALLEN FROM GRACE."[41] (emphasis added).

God's law is one law. S.D.A's, without permission divide it up into Moral and Ceremonial in order to make their doctrines palatable. This endangers a clear and precise understanding of God's way of salvation through Christ alone.

I'll tell you what. It's all over. It's all done. "It is finished[42]," said Jesus — not "half finished".

Remember Matthew, Mark, Luke and John are all old testament books until the crucifixion of Christ. It is at that point, the new testament starts. Dwell on these old testament concepts and you are still under law — full of legalism.

A man bought his wife a beautiful mahogany table. He was horrified to walk in the gate one day and hear the sound of a wood plane being used. He rushed in.

Man: "What are you doing?"

Wife: "I thought I saw a small bump in the surface. I took your plane from the shed and I'm smoothing it off."

Man (tearing his hair): "Oh no, that table was finished. Anything you do wrecks it."

That's right. This applies to our salvation too.

"This man, after he had offered one sacrifice for sins forever, sat down at the right hand of God."[43]

Stop planing please.

Just one more point. What about the Sabbaths? They were only for Israel, not the Gentile nations.

"Speak thou unto the children of Israel saying, verily my sabbaths ye shall keep, *for it is a sign between me and you* throughout your generations."[44]

"Wherefore, the children of Israel shall keep the sabbath, to observe the sabbath throughout their generations for a perpetual covenant."[45]

"It is a sign between me and the children of Israel forever."[46]

When God speaks once, He says what He means, and means what He says.

When He speaks twice, it is emphasised. Three times, however, makes it irrefutable.

To keep the sabbath day therefore means that your mother must be a Jewess. If she is not, or if you have not been adopted into the Jewish faith by deed-poll, you have no right to get involved in the Sabbath issue.

Will you please stop butting in on other people's covenants.

Once we receive the Lord Jesus Christ as Saviour, days are no longer applicable to either Jew or Gentile.

"One man esteemeth one day above another, another esteemeth every day alike. Let every man be fully persuaded in his own mind. He that regardeth the day, regardeth it unto the Lord, and he that regardeth not the day, to the Lord he doth not regard it."[47]

If this is the truth, which it is, Tuesday could be quite suitable for believers in certain situations.

I meet many of these dear people, continually endeavouring to live up to this binding system. I'll be quite frank here. If it was at all scriptural, I would do it myself: but please read this.

"Let no man therefore judge you in meat, or in drink, or in respect of an holy day, or of the new moon, OR OF THE SABBATH DAYS which are a SHADOW of things to come but the BODY is of CHRIST." (Emphasis added.)[48]

Stick to your sabbath keeping and you are involved with the shadow.

Turn wholly to Jesus and get involved with the reality.

By the way, if it is true, and they teach that Jesus and the archangel Michael are the same person, why was it that at the burial of Moses, Michael (who is supposed to be Jesus) couldn't defeat the devil as he did at the temptations, using the Word of God.

Come on now. You are too intelligent to believe all this. Forget Mrs White.

I call on the leaders of this movement to re-clarify the main issues on salvation by faith in Christ alone, etc., and get involved with the millions of us who are born again, and love the Lord Jesus Christ.

Sunday worship is not the mark of the beast at all. It is now clear that the mark is an extension of the credit card (E.F.T. system) involving a laser mark on the hand or head, the future system to be used in buying and selling.

## 16. TAROT CARDS, E.S.P., NUMEROLOGY, PSYCHIC HEALING

It's all occult with some witchcraft.

## 17. HALLOWEEN, DRUIDS

Halloween, Druids, is out for the believer in Christ.

## 18. HYPNOTISM

Hypnotism is yielding up your will to a demonic occult source. Opening yourself up like this is very bad. In one meeting, in a certain town, two hypnotherapists who, incidently were doing very well in business, committed their lives to Christ and the next day cancelled all their clients and found new employment.

The Lord's promise applies here.

"Those who honour me, I will honour."[49]

## 19. HOMOSEXUALITY

Homosexuality is the only sin in the Bible that causes God to give people up.

Although the term "gay" is used, very few of these folk are gay. They are actually very sad, prisoners.

Christ alone can set them free to be the beautiful people they really want to be.

"Wherefore God also gave them up into vile affections for even their women did change the natural use into that which is against nature."[50]

Here is a picture of the lesbian spirit.

"And likewise the men, leaving the natural use of the woman, burned in their lust, one toward another, men with men, working that which is unseemly. . . ."[51]

Here is a picture of the male homosexual Spirit.

Is AIDS mentioned in the Bible?

". . . and receiving in themselves, that recompense of their error which was meet."[52]

I can't help thanking God for His textbook, the Bible.

Shouldn't we all be grateful for the Manufacturer's Handbook.

Never can we forget the night, years ago, when one of these unfortunate men stumbled into the lounge dripping wet. He was so disgusted and upset with his behaviour that he tried to commit suicide, by drowning in the sea. A group of Christian boys rescued him and brought him ashore.

To those with any feeling left, Christ is your escape route.

"If the Son therefore shall make you free, ye shall be free indeed."[53]

**20. ABORTION**

Abortion is not on. Psalm 139:13-16 points out that records are kept in heaven of the formation of a baby, and all its members.

Wicked men, cut them up, or inject a burning agent which causes the baby to writhe in agony in its death throes. They are then sucked out with a vacuum cleaner-like machine, deposited in the waste bin, sometimes still alive and crying, to be burnt in the hospital furnace.

"Murder," you cry — yes. A doctor who had performed many abortions recently told how he televised the procedure. A camera was inserted in the womb and as the knife began its dreadful work, the baby struggled to get away. Horrified, he refused to do another abortion. Can God forgive? Yes. "His mercy endureth forever."[54] Praise God.

**21. COMPULSIVE GAMBLING**

Some cannot keep away from the T.A.B. and other gambling joints. Jesus can help you — cry out to Him.

**22. DRUG TAKING**

Drug taking is sending thousands to hell. Do you realise that when God populates his eternal city, the New Jerusalem, there are certain folk who are not allowed in.

"For without are dogs<br>
sorcerers<br>
whoremongers

idolaters
and whosoever loveth and maketh a lie."[55]

This word, sorcerers, is the Greek word pharmecia which applies to drugs. Thus the person on a drug trip is on a witchcraft trip. In a book entitled "Death of a Guru", we read that the author discovered this fact and turned to Jesus, wholly disgusted with his old life.

Grass, smack, needles, junk — forget it — your soul is too precious. Remember, eternity lasts forever.

What is NOW, compared with the eternal THEN.

## 23. TOBACCO

One of the most powerful drugs is nicotine. One of the first ways we show our rebellious spirits as young people, is to smoke.

Some start with tree bark and brown paper, graduate to a gum nut and straw and then get into the real thing.

When we were kids, at least we tried to hide it. Not so the youth of today.

A person can be set free from every other evil thing, yet the cigarette is the last one to go, in many cases, and is the gateway for evil spirits to return again.

"What, know ye not that your body is the temple of the Holy Ghost which is in you, which ye have of God, and ye are not your own . . ."[56]

Message from the Lord: If you want to light a fire, do it in your own house and not in mine.

## 24. ALCOHOL

Some years ago in an open air meeting, a preacher stood outside a pub and preached to those assembled there. — "Booze is your worst enemy".

Drunk interjector — "Excuse me, doesn't the Bible say, love your enemies?"

Preacher — "Yes, it does say love them, but it doesn't say swallow them."

. . . "Drunkenness . . . they which do such things, shall not inherit the Kingdom of God."[57]

In most countries of the world there is a law which says a certain percentage of alcohol in the blood makes you a drunken driver. As we do not know what God's percentage is, better leave it alone.

If it doesn't hurt you, make sure it doesn't stumble somebody else.

"It is good, neither to eat flesh, nor to drink wine, nor

anything whereby thy brother stumbleth, or is offended, or is made weak."[58]

## 25. UFOLOGY

That is, God was an astronaut, Jesus came in a flying saucer. Von Daniken certainly made a lot of money out of the notion, yet it is clearly fiction.

God is so big — "Behold the heaven of heavens cannot contain thee. . . ."[59]

I therefore personally think that God would experience some difficulty in fitting into a space programme.

By the way, we know

(i) Flying saucers do exist — I've seen them.

(ii) Certain power groups are manufacturing them (see "Cosmic Conspiracy" by Stan Deyo.)

(iii) Some of these are demonic manifestations. We have a personal friend who was buzzed by one whilst driving in his car one evening near to our previous residence in northern New Zealand. So traumatic was this event that he sought salvation and peace through our Lord Jesus, and is now a bright Christian.

Christians should avoid reading psychic books (Edgar Cayce, etc.), science fiction and occult journals. The weird figures portrayed here are introductions to demonic spirits. Carvers, ancient and modern viewed these actual occult figures whilst they carved and that is why heathen gods of worship are repulsive to normal people (i.e. those who have not been perverted from wholesome Biblical standards for Christian living).

Astral travel is an occult practice, and as such is not acceptable to the believer in Christ. It is true that people appear to travel, having been inspired by books written by Lobsang Rampa and others. Your natural body is linked to some spiritual body, these folk are taught. Just learn to change bodies and it's "Hi Ho Silver — away". I hereby recommend the reading of Ecclesiastes 12:6 —

"or ever the silver cord be loosed . . ."[60] This provides a clue. It would be dreadful to go out, and not be able to return again.

## 26. SENSITIVITY TRAINING

— Touch for healing. Passing of hands over subject — this is all a mis-use of the scripture.

These signs shall follow:

". . . them that believe in my Name they shall lay hands ON the sick and they shall recover". (Emphasis added)[61]

## 27. WRONG READING AND VIEWING

Wrong reading and viewing can act as a catalyst to bring about altered behavioural patterns, e.g. arguing, fighting, despair. Care should be taken about T.V. viewing. Many are very vocal in pointing out that T.V. viewing does not alter behaviour, yet it can become as addictive as a drug.

Television producers will deny that their programmes have influence over the viewer's minds, yet charge business people thousands of dollars to present an advertisement in prime viewing time, promising that people will be influenced to buy their product.

## 28. ARTEFACTS

Some very well-meaning people will travel overseas and bring back objects of heathen worship in the form of carvings, statues or objects of death — e.g. statues — masks — prayer wheels — spears and arrows — witchcraft jewellery, etc. These same people wonder why they have continual problems in their homes and families.

Whilst on a speaking tour of Singapore, a Chinese Christian businessman asked me, "Do you have eastern religion in your country?"

I answered, "Yes we do."

"Do you know why?" he enquired and when I indicated that I didn't know why, he said, "It comes in with the statues that your tourists bring back from the east."

You see, an evil spirit is a personality without a body. If possible, it will inhabit one of these three, in the following order

(i) Humans
(ii) Animals and birds
(iii) An inanimate object

"Nonsense", cries the sceptic, to which I reply, "You stick to your area of knowledge, and I'll stick to mine."

A report in a well-known magazine told the story of a millionaire in the U.S.A. who lived in a mansion with a fence all the way around his property studded with gems, and heathen statues and artifacts wrought in silver and gold.

He became a born-again Christian and promptly called in a bulldozer to destroy his wall. Friends berated him saying, "Don't be a fool, save the gold and silver, have it melted down and sell it."

This man was no ignoramus. He had read a clear command in the Manufacturer's Handbook, and he stuck by it.

"The graven images of their gods shall ye burn with fire. Thou shalt not desire the silver or the gold that is on them, nor take it unto thee, lest thou be snared therein, for it is an abomination to the Lord thy God."[62]

Some folks give these statues an honoured place in their homes, or give talks on them to children's groups; in spite of the fact, the Book goes on to say,

"Neither shalt thou bring an abomination into thine house, lest thou be a cursed thing like it, but thou shalt utterly detest it, and thou shalt utterly abhor it, for it is a cursed thing."[63]

Hey! It looks as though God can't stand these statues. This by the way includes statues of Jesus, Joseph, Mary and all the saints.

"Thou shalt not make unto thee any graven image . . . Thou shalt not bow down thyself to them, or serve them for I the Lord thy God am a jealous God."[64]

Things to destroy — symbols or statues of . . . snakes — dragons — witches — ankh (a cross with a circle on top) — unicorns horn — pentagram (five pointed star, symbol of Satan) — hexagram (two triangles together — eastern concept of good and evil merging and mingling — sometimes called the Israeli "Star of David". One of the most powerful witchcraft symbols around. This was brought in amongst God's original people by Solomon who had about 1,000 women at his disposal.)

King Solomon had a thousand wives
and that's the reason why,
he often missed his business train
through kissing them all goodbye.

Once the Jewish nation accepts the Lord Jesus Christ as their Messiah, they will need to change their flag also.

To those who are still not convinced, try to discover where a witch's hex comes from. I remember a young man walking into one of our meetings, with a hexagram hanging around his neck. A number of interesting things happened in the meeting that night, and afterwards, he informed us that as I spoke on these subjects the hexagram symbol swung on its cord six times around his neck. Another girl was almost strangled by a cord holding a Maori tiki around her neck, the very same evening.

I often thank the Lord for a very wise earthly father who once said,

"Son, don't make sins out of things which are not sins. The devil has given us enough to contend with already."

This list is not complete. I might add, "And such like."[65]

A final word to the biggest fools of all —

## 29. SATANISTS

(a) Your boss will finish in the lake of fire and so will you.

(b) Your boss is defeated. A lion with no teeth. All that is left is a roar. Young, fit, virile lions don't roar. They act quickly. The old ones cover up for their lack of real power by making a noise.

"Your adversary the devil as a roaring lion walketh about seeking whom he may devour."[66]

(c) The Lord Jesus Christ beat him at the cross of Calvary,

"And having spoiled principalities and powers, He made a shew of them openly triumphing over them in it."[67]

That's Jesus you know.

Ex satanists tell us that they were taught that Jesus Christ was in fact just an ordinary man who could perform a few magic tricks and hypnotise people, yet if a satanist accepted Jesus Christ into their lives they were committing the ultimate sin.

The satanist Bible tells you how to destroy Christians. They are the people that satanists know have power enough to harm their existence.

Every person initiated into a Satanist coven was expected to publicly deny Jesus Christ, and publicly call him a deceiver.

There is also a "Communion Service" in an initiation process, and just as we Christians use bread and wine, a satanist uses a human foetus and human blood for communion.

In certain parts of Australia, it has been revealed that satanist girls are giving birth to illegitimate babies specifically to be used in human sacrifice to satan.

Much of this book has been written in the Australian states during a 1984 tour. Whilst writing this particular chapter in Northern Queensland, some of these strange people have been leaving notes written in blood on the doorstep of a local church. Then, they dropped a dead bandicoot there early last Sunday morning with letters written in blood on its side.

How stupid — fancy following a loser like satan.

His end is already decreed.

"And the devil that deceived them, was cast into the lake of fire and brimstone, where the beast and the false prophet are, and shall be tormented day and night forever and ever."[68]

Jesus however is very different — listen,

"And He had on His vesture, and on His thigh a name written KING OF KINGS and LORD OF LORDS."[69]

Choose carefully please.

## 30. ANTHROPOSOPHY

Rudolph Steiner was a master occultist. His schools and academies teach

> education, health, art, music, organic farming, philosophy, dance forms, etc., but it is very dangerous as the whole thing is riddled with the occult.

These folk have schools in Germany and other parts of the world including my little country, New Zealand. In Northern Queensland during the month of August 1984 I went to visit a man who was wasting away physically for no apparent reason. Doctors could find nothing wrong with him.

I walked into his bedroom and tried to talk to him about Jesus and the Bible. Here he was, emaciated to the point of looking repulsive, but instead of listening, began to tell me of his philosophies.

I broke in saying, "You've been into the occult, haven't you?"

He tried to deny it, but very soon he revealed that his father was a student of Rudolph Steiner. Poor man. On his way to the lake of fire. A special visit from a Christian man who could have helped him — still talking his philosophical nonsense.

Bio Dynamics is creeping into the farming scene. A cow's horn (symbol of power and strength) is filled with dung, etc., buried in the ground to break down into compost. First of all, however, witchcraft is involved.

(a) Incantations
(b) Astrology
(c) Cycles of moon observed.

Compost then is dug up, watered down and sprayed on property. Men involved in first stages get very sick and weak as this is occultish practice. Evil spirits come with the spray on your farm. REJECT IT.

## 31. SOAP OPERAS

A psychiatrist in Cairns said to a lady recently, "I cannot help you provided you continue to watch these programmes," i.e. Dynasty, Dallas, Sons and Daughters, etc., for you take on the problems in the programmes.

A man watched a programme called General Hospital where someone contracted a disease of the Lymph Glands and within three days he had the same symptoms.

Remember the first rule in computers — GARBAGE IN = GARBAGE OUT.

## OCCULT GLOSSARY

This is a useful list, sent to me by a friend.

ASTROLOGY — The belief that man's destiny is controlled by his horoscope.

AUTOMATIC WRITING — The gift of writing while under the spirit power of another. (The writing instrument moves of its own accord.)

BIOFEEDBACK — Use of electronic machines to train a student how to use his mind to control his physical and emotional outputs: is said to deepen one's self awareness and cosmic consciousness.

BIORHYTHM — The belief that one can chart his physical, emotional and intellectual cycle — kits and calculators allow one to 'compute' compatibility between self and others, to warn of good and critical days, and to assist one in planning his best possible schedule of activities.

CLAIRVOYANCE — The ability to perceive things that are not in sight.

LEVITATION — The ability through mind power to lift an object into the air.

MEDIUM — A person who goes into a trance and lets himself be possessed by another spirit. Supposedly the spirit of a deceased person with whom another wishes to communicate. Usually takes place when a group of people meet together for a seance.

MIND CONTROL — Ability to use the energies of the mind to control self and others.

MYSTICAL MEDITATION — A method whereby one alters his conscious state to reach cosmic consciousness. The vehicles of meditation is usually a secret word *(mantra)* which has been planted in the mind. The word is silently repeated over and over again and is believed.

OUIJA BOARD — A game used to give players 'guidance' they need for the direction of their lives. The board spells out words in answer to questions people ask.

PSYCHOMETRY — Art of tracing a client's past, present, future, by feeling 'vibrations' in a personal item.

REINCARNATION — Belief that a person has existed in a prior lifetime or lifetimes and that understanding one's previous life helps one understand fears about present life.

SELF HYPNOSIS — A self/induced state of suggestibility in which the conscious mind is partially or wholly inoperative. Suggestions put in the mind change one's way of behaviour, thoughts, etc.

SPIRITISM — Those involved seek to communicate with the dead for advice, information, etc. (Impersonating spirit, familiar with deceased persons life.)

TELEPATHY (ESP) — The ability to communicate or perceive through mind power.

TERAPHIM — Household gods, idols, images, etc.

YOGA — (literally 'YOKIN' union) aims to unite one with the divine through concentration and meditation aided by specific body postures, called by dedicated practitioners "the art of living". Physical yoga (hatha) is intimately related to, and part of, the other spiritual forms of yoga.

IRIS DIAGNOSIS — The eye is divided into 12 zones, corresponding to the astrological signs of the zodiac.

Some will take notice of the warnings in this chapter. Some won't. Here is an illustration — if there is a terrible traffic accident and you turn up at the scene of carnage, go to the people who are lying around and lift up their eyelids. If they are dead, no pulse, no life, leave them alone.

Go and help those who are only injured and request help.

In Jesus' words "Let the dead bury their dead."[70]

## CHAPTER ELEVEN

# CAN'T STOP THE MUSIC

Many people wonder whether the stories of my experiences over the years are true. I assure you — they are.

Some years ago, I remember setting a young man free from a number of evil spirits. As he lay writhing on the floor, the demon's voice revealed its identity.

"Drums", it screamed. I never knew there was such a thing, up until this point. On command, in the Name of Jesus, this spirit left. There was still one binding spirit there I knew and so I asked the Lord for its name, which was given to me immediately. This gift is called the discernment of spirits and is more than useful when releasing people from spiritual problems.

As soon as I named it, "Apollyon — come out in Jesus' Name," this thing wrenched his body around, almost strangled him to death and then left with a wild cry. A small group of us in the room heard this most amazing sound. It left the young man's lips, went across the room, through the wall and it continued on away down the road. "No-o-o-o-o-o-o"

He was free in Jesus' Name. I have had this same spirit leave another young man also upon another occasion.

The word 'Apollyon', I could have never guessed, so I looked it up in the Book of Revelation, chapter 9 and verse 11. This is what I discovered.

(a) Apollyon is a kingly angel in charge of the bottomless pit.
(b) His name in Hebrew is Abaddon.
(c) His initial name means Destroyer.

This devil is the king of a mass of devils who have the hair of women and the faces of men. It is no accident then that the rock groups of today look like this. The youth of today are being destroyed by this invasion from the pit.

It is difficult to go anywhere today without hearing the raucous Boom — Boom — Boom — Boom

Records and tape bars
Shops selling jeans and youth ware
Department stores
Parties at night
Portable transistor tape decks
Walkman portables and earphones invade the consciousness of the user, blocking out all natural sounds.

I read recently that some folk have now invented an underwater walkman.

Satan is roaring with laughter.

Remember music's intended order.

(a) Melody; (b) Harmony; (c) Beat.

Now the enemy has changed and perverted it, until the beat comes first.

One film which really encouraged this excessive beat was entitled, "Saturday Night Fever". Recently in Perth, a number of visiting American ships came into the port of Fremantle. We observed many of the sailors with portable stereo tape decks, turned up full blast, dancing in the malls and streets completely taken over, and oblivious to all else.

Anyone who has studied African music or drumming arts will know that the drums are used to call up the spirits.

In describing Lucifer, God said,

"They have filled the midst of thee with violence."[1]

Our young people are being led on, step after step into violence and destruction.

**STAGES OF MUSICAL DISINTEGRATION**

Rock and Roll — Elvis — Beatles — Acid Rock — Disco — Punk — New Wave — Head Bangers.

Such is the power of music I've given this subject a chapter all on its own.

Points to ponder:

(a) Whenever the children of Israel marched, the musicians always went in front.

(b) Lucifer was involved in the music of heaven. He therefore knows its power. Tabrets and pipes were prepared in him in the day that he was created. He was a type of musical instrument. See Ezek. 28:13.

(c) Once he fell through wisdom and beauty, his music began to stink. Worms spread under him and worms covered him. See Isaiah 14:11

(d) His music became noise and bred violence. See Ezek. 28:16.

(e) His music destroys people. See Revelation 9:7-11.

(f) In the secular music scene today, the bands or individuals who hope to make it to the top, sell their souls to satan.

(g) Inspiration for words and music then comes from one of three sources.

(1) Drugs

(2) T.M.
(3) Automatic writing

(h) The group cuts their master tape, then place it inside a hexagram and dedicate it to satan.

Any person then buying a copy of that tape or record receives a bonus. Just think of it. Their own personal demon spirit.

That is why the majority of groups today specialise in
(i) Smoke
(ii) Fire
(iii) An obsession with death
(iv) Weird makeup
(v) Occult symbols
(vi) Bible verses
(vii) Lack of real joy

By the way, over 80% of rock music is in a minor key (depressive).

Music is made up of these three elements.

1. Melody — with no harmony — minor key = dead depression
2. Harmony — with melody distorted, rhythm varied = rebellion
3. Beat — melody and harmony not considered = sensuality

Leading on from this thought we see record covers with terrible perversions printed on them.

Certain persons and groups make no effort to hide their occult links, and some of the records when played backwards have satanic messages built in.

e.g. Stairway to Heaven — Led Zeppelin
Electric Light Orchestra
Stray Cats
Queen

Others are just blatantly evil in the Christian's view.

e.g. AC/DC
Alice Cooper (sold himself to the devil)
Rolling Stones
Meatloaf
Kiss
Black Sabbath
Iron Maiden
The Dead Kennedys

Unfortunately, many of these artists are hell bound and are influencing others in the same direction.

Christians who listen to music like this would be well advised to destroy records and tapes forthwith.

"The thief cometh not, but for to steal, and to kill and to

destroy, but I am come that they might have life, and that they might have it more abundantly."[2]

As was mentioned before, over 80% of today's "so-called" music is in a minor key.

(a) In the dark ages, the Gregorian chants were in minor keys. Also Jewish music is in minor (sad) keys as they await the return of their Messiah.

(b) When the reformation came, with Martin Luther, the music changed also. Great hymns of faith were composed in major keys, e.g. "A Mighty Fortress is our God."

(c) The church continued on with great music over the years, with men like Sankey, singing at the great D.L. Moody crusades. Evangelical revivals were accompanied by great singing (happy music) in major keys.

This made the devil angry so he aimed to infiltrate the music of the churches, through the congregation.

SATAN'S MASTER STROKE

(d) He has succeeded in some Christian groups. They are back to minor key (sad) hymns again. The rock beat is in through excessive bass and drums and satan is rubbing his hands. When confronted with this truth, the Christian musos say, "Oh, but the words are beautiful", to which I reply, "The devils don't listen to the words, it is the beat that calls them up".

Herman Riffel tells of visiting an American missionary in the Zaire. "How's your work going brother?" he asked.

The Baptist missionary replied, "Terrible. Most of the people have left the church. When I asked a leading elder why this was, he replied, "Pastor, as long as your son calls up spirits in his bedroom, we will not return to church."

Actually this pastor's son had just been home to the U.S.A. where he had purchased some so-called Christian rock tapes. The African elder continued, "We don't understand the words, but we would recognise that beat anywhere."

Major keys — happy, bright, victorious.

God the Father = 1st note
God the Son = 3rd note
God the Holy Spirit = 5th note
Played together = Harmony
It is easy to go off into praise
and worship — singing in the spirit.

Minor keys — sad, wistful, sometimes depressing.

God the Father = 1st note

God the Son (Jesus) = 3rd note lowered half a tone
God the Holy Spirit = 5th note

Notice that in the minor key, Jesus is displaced from His position. It is now difficult and almost impossible to lead a group of Christians off into praise and worship and singing in the Spirit, from a minor key.

Eastern Music — Take Jesus out altogether and all that is left is the first and the fifth played in conjunction. Hark to the eastern sound.

To all Christians, I bring this word.

When you are born again into God's family, it is a happy experience. Minors should be used very sparingly. Pacific Island people are very joyous folk. Their traditional music does not have any minor chords at all.

Go through your records and tapes.

Destroy any that

(a) Have a depressing effect.
(b) Have a loud pounding beat.
(c) Have a sound of wailing guitars (i.e. a corruption of the eastern sitar).

A Christian man, Dr Eby told recently of being carried to heaven in the spirit. He listened to the music of heaven which was so beautiful, he felt bound to enquire as to the source of its beauty.

The Lord Jesus told him to listen again, and find out for himself.

"It's got no beat," exclaimed the man, excitedly.

"That is correct", replied Jesus. "How can it have. The music of heaven is the music of the Spirit. It is timeless, as heaven is not connected with time, but eternity, that is why it cannot have, nor does it require any beat."

Whilst we live on this earth, the Lord recognises our need for time. He allows "beat" but it must always take third place, subservient always to melody and harmony.

This in turn, very gently prepares us for eternity.

"And the angel which I saw . . . sware . . . that there should be time no longer."[3]

Did you know that you are

(a) Spirit — God conscious — the telephone link to God's spirit.
(b) Soul — Self conscious — mind, will and emotions.
(c) Body — world conscious.

The spirit in you gives you the ability to worship God. This is the essential difference between you and an animal. It is very rarely, you will agree, that you ever catch a dog saying his prayers.

Did you know that when you claim to be born again, only your spirit is born again.

The soul and body require constant attending to and working on to make them fit in with the now new aims of your spirit.

"And His Spirit bears witness with our spirit, that we are the children of God."[4]

Did you know that your music in the soul realm can bless, or wreck your spiritual growth.

Did you know that you as a muso can be so wilful that you can deny all this, assault me verbally and by mail, but the still small voice within you reminds you saying, "You don't like it, but he's correct you know. Your spirituality is all on the surface. There is no depth."

My brother and my sister, do yourself a favour,

WATCH YOUR MUSIC

To those of you with bedroom walls covered with posters of —

> Greasy, demonic, evil, disgusting, ludicrous, dirty pop stars, or even of those who look sauve, cool, slick, clean and appealing, my advice would be,
>
> "If they do not bring honour and praise to our Lord Jesus Christ, rip them down, and light a big fire."

Finally, brethren whatsoever things are

True<br>
Honest<br>
Just<br>
Pure<br>
Lovely<br>
Good report<br>
Virtuous<br>
Praiseworthy<br>
Think on these things.[5] (Abbreviated)

## CHAPTER TWELVE

# WHAT ABOUT THE RUSSIANS?

As a boy, I can remember wending my weary way up a narrow track on my way home at the end of each school day. This path led me past the backyard of the Russian Embassy. The whole area was surrounded by a high wrought iron fence, but what really interested me was the back lawn. Rising up all over it were ventilators coming from underground and tall radio aerials. A buzzing sound from beneath this lawn told me that I was listening to either the buzz of conversation at a worms convention, or sounds from an underground radio room. Quite an unusual place for it to be situated you will agree.

My curiosity aroused, I made further investigations and found the following.

(a) Russia is a vast country, with many different language groups.

(b) The Russians are, in most cases, normal, loving, happy, family orientated people.

(c) In 1917, their royal family was brutally put to death and the reign of the Czars came to an end.

(d) Two political characters, Lenin and Trotsky, financed from the U.S.A. by a group called the Illuminati, proceeded into Russia and brought about the Revolution. This was to be a test case, to prove Adam Weishaupts theory that the masses could be controlled by a small "Eye in a Triangle Group", originally called by the Illuminati's founder, the Insinuating Brethren, but later on, the K.G.B.

This K.G.B. group are simply a group of mindless thugs who, along with a highly sophisticated surveillance system makes everyone's lives miserable, using violence, spying and lies. Claiming to be atheistic, satan uses these people to prepare the world for his takeover bid.

Communism is not then as many people suppose, an effort to improve conditions for the underprivileged, but a spiritual force out to confuse people, and finally to take them to the grave, and finally the lake of fire, without hope and without God.

Secondly, it is not a classless society. All that is a myth, and the commos well know it. Only the leaders get the caviar, the world trips, the parties, etc., while the masses live on in their dull, drab, meaningless, godless existence. It is little wonder alcohol is such a problem to them. In a state which allows no other political parties, no elections, and no light at the end of the tunnel, getting oneself "boozed to the eyeballs" is a popular pastime.

While teaching school one day a boy asked me, "Which is better, Mr Smith — Capitalism or Communism?"

"Oh that's easy," I replied. "Have you heard of the Berlin Wall, son?" When he replied that he had, I continued on, "Which way do the people jump?"

Most will agree that very few people get shot jumping into a communist state. Most are jumping out. It was for this reason alone that the U.S.S.R. boycotted the Olympic Games held in L.A. in 1984. This would have proved another embarrassment when crowds of their athletes would have defected. After all, who wants to experience freedom and return to a "Paradise" surrounded by secret police, spies (even within the family group), midnight raids, governmental lies, food queues, a disastrous agricultural policy. Who would have ever believed that these words would come true.

"And the brother shall deliver up the brother to death, and the father the child, and the children shall rise up against their parents and cause them to be put to death."[1]

As we have already learnt, satan was cast out of heaven with one third of the angels, and has now placed a demonic angel over each country.

The name of this chief prince over Russia is revealed to us in the Word of God as 'Gog'.

Now, the Russian communists are generally very unpopular in the world today, for a number of reasons.

(a) There are no human rights.

(b) They have interfered in and invaded such countries as Czechoslovakia, Poland and Afghanistan.

(c) They shot down the Korean jet liner with no word of apology, just words like, "Never mind, you'll forget it shortly." None of the world's governments did a thing about it. Why? you ask. Because the nations are fearful of Russia and their armed might.

God is not impressed, however, and has decreed their judgement.

"Vengeance belongeth unto me, I will recompense, saith the Lord."[2]

In their stupidity and ignorance, these poor people teach the little children in their schools against the concept of God. This is a terrible mistake as God promises.

"But whoso shall offend one of these little ones which believe in Me, it were better for him that a millstone were hanged about his neck and that he were drowned in the depth of the sea."[3]

A little Christian girl, living in a Communist state refused to obey her teacher's command to repeat the words, along with her classmates, "There is no God". She was threatened, then sent home to write out 1,000 times, "There is no God." The teacher read the lines, "There is a God", written out 1,000 times and was very angry.

Seizing a stick, he said to the little girl, "If you truly believe in your God, you had better pray to him now."

"Help me Jesus," cried the little girl. A knock was heard, and a child answered the door to find no-one there. The teacher threatened, "Someone is playing the fool here," and prepared to thrash the little girl. Another knock came on the door, and a child answered it to find no-one there.

Furious by now the teacher dragged the little girl across a desk, and raised the stick, only to be stopped by a third knock on the classroom door. The teacher himself flung open the door, a look of terror came over his face and before the eyes of his startled students, he dropped dead in the doorway.

Result: The whole area heard about it, and crowds and crowds turned to the Lord. To those readers trying to suppress a knowing laugh, remember,

"Be not deceived, God is not mocked, for whatsoever a man soweth that shall he also reap."[4]

When the Russians announced their Olympic boycott, a man from Hungary wrote to the newspaper saying in effect that the Olympics were "well rid of the Russians. He said that the powerful alliance of exiled East European people, most of them U.S. citizens, have raised their voice to deny the Soviet propagandists a forum at the L.A. games (the voice of the free people in the communist dictionary is terrorism; if it is Soviet-inspired or organised, it is a peace movement). — Has the free world really lost anything by their absence," he asked.

Well, I agree, however, a matter of concern is as follows.

Three countries at present are playing right into communist hands, i.e. New Zealand, Australia, Great Britain.

The communist parties some time ago in these three countries agreed that they could do a better job by infiltrating the Labour Governments. Clever eh?

Now, in Australia, the commos in the left wing call each other comrade this, and comrade that. The word "struggle" is part of their jargon also. Mr Hayden, jealous because he was pipped at the post for the Prime Minister's job, by Mr Bob Hawke, has now publicly made the statement the U.S. bases may have to be removed from Australia.

**ANZUS**

This word means Australia, New Zealand, United States Defence Agreement. Co-operation in time of war.

Now the ANZUS treaty is collapsing, because the communists boast that they will one day take over the world without a shot being fired.

On to New Zealand. The new Labour government led by Prime Minister Lange, who was reared in a beautiful Christian home, knew the dangers of this policy and was not personally against the idea of US nuclear powered ships coming into New Zealand ports, but is committed to his communist influenced left faction policies. What a dreadful position for the poor man to be in. Please pray for him, that the few sensible ones in the new Labour party will be able to soon deal a death blow to the Judas's trying to wreck our country.

Even Mr Bob Hawke is smart enough to smell the danger and tried to change Mr Lange's mind during discussions held at Port Moresby, Papua New Guinea, in 1984, but Mr Lange was trapped by his own party's communistic policies, and remained firm.

1. Let's face it. ANZUS is over. If New Zealand does not co-operate, why should the U.S.A.
2. New Zealand is in the process of losing a powerful ally and laying herself open to Russian designs and objectives in the South Pacific. We are glad that Fiji has seen the light and welcomed the American nuclear ships.
3. If New Zealand fell, Australia is only a hop, skip and jump away — watch out Aussie.
4. The British Labour Party has promised that if elected to power they will tell the United States to remove all nuclear weapons from the country (Australian 8.8.84).

   Then in the Australian 14.8.84 we read, "Politicians are supposed to learn lessons from mistakes . . . honesty, or perhaps lunacy repeating itself perhaps. . . . Apart from being an exercise in dreaming, it now plans to lay before the British public, an election platform in which it would pledge, in effect, to leave the only nuclear weapons in Europe in the hands of the Soviet Union and its Warsaw Pact allies.

   It shows a trust in the Kremlin which is not shared by many outside the Left wing of the British Labour leadership." — end quote.

Otago Daily Times 27th November 1984 entitled "CND Ducks Move Against Soviets," we read, "Britain's Campaign for Nuclear Disarmament has refused to commit itself against Soviet nuclear weapons. . . .

The motion said that it was absolutely vital to apply our arguments consistently and publicly to all nuclear weapon states. . . .

The conference then voted on a show of hands to move on to the next item of business without taking a vote on the motion. . . .

Other delegates said they worried that the motion would be seen as a CONDEMNATION OF THE SOVIET PEOPLE AND SOVIET PEACE INITIATIVES." End quote. (Emphasis added.)

It is interesting to note that the majority of these groups aid the communist cause.

When a communist speaks of "Peace" he puts a peaceful bullet in a peaceful gun, and you die a peaceful death.

5. Even Israel's latest elections bring us a heading in the weekend Australian, July 28-29 1984 — "Israel's latest cloud is Moscow's silver lining." — The elections there were just confusion.

   Quote — "The elections provided Israel with another year of instability at this crucial time in modern history." — End quote. They of course, have elected a coalition government.
6. Russia is in financial trouble. From the Canberra Times, 19th May 1984 quote — "After an absence of fours years the Soviet Union has returned to the Western capital market, signing a $A222 million loan with a consortium of 31 non-American banks.'
7. From the Australian newspaper 9th August 1984: "The Russians did not go to the Los Angeles Olympics: They went to the Chicago Board of Trade instead. During the last month, the Soviet Union has bought more than 14 million tonnes of grain in America's biggest market place. That is even faster work than during the GREAT GRAIN ROBBERY of 1972-73, when the Russians took six months to buy up less than 20 million tonnes." End quote.

   In other words, the Russian agricultural policy is no good. On p.42 of my book "Warning" written in 1980, I referred to this, also on p. 85 I said,

   "Rule — if you really wish to destroy something — don't feed it."
8. Russian diplomats come in, do some spying, get caught, try to bluster their way out of it, get expelled, and then comes

the next spy, and round and round go the wheels again. It is called — Musical Spies.

Why does this happen, asks Mr AMITS (average man in the street)?

Trade is the one and only answer. We put up with these outrageous scoundrels within our fair shores just so that we can collect some of their roubles. What a terrible cost, don't you agree?

Australian, 15th May 1984. Quote — "Soviet Mutton Ban Triggers Crisis — The Soviet Union is by far New Zealand's biggest market for mutton . . .

The Soviet Embassy in New Zealand, soon to have an Ambassador, after the last one was expelled, appears to be denying there is a ban. . . ." end quote.

9. The one man the Soviets fear and hate is President Reagan. He knows their aims for world domination and says so.

   Motto — When dealing with the Soviets and their spirit leader Gog, fight fire with fire.

   The Lord help America once Reagan goes, particularly if a softy like Jimmy Carter was, comes to power. Mondale does not have any punch, not only that, he is a World Government man, as is George Bush, Reagan's running mate.

Friends, we all need the Lord now, as never before. Karl Marx said, years ago, "Politicians are errand boys." From a newspaper article, 29th September 1983 we read,

"The View from the U.S.S.R.

"When a former Hollywood actor was elected President of the United States, the Soviets were not necessarily surprised. In a sense, every western politician is viewed by them as an actor who is only playing a role on the basis of a script written by others. . . . The picture of the west which unfolds before Soviet eyes is not unlike a giant puppet show. What one observes is the marionettes who purport to move about freely or to be engaged in spontaneous discourse, but in actuality, the sounds emitted are not their own, and they are manipulated from above, by those pulling the strings." End quote.

I agree.

World Government figures manipulate Capitalism.

A demonic spirit manipulates the Communists.

Only the Christians are free. We are under God's government.

"If the Son therefore shall make you free, ye shall be free indeed."[5]

Henry Kissinger is reported as saying, "The communist and

the democratic worlds are condemned to co-existence."

This is not true.

Russian Communism can apparently never be defeated, even although the vast majority living under its intolerable regime hate it like poison.

However, Russian communism is doomed to defeat on the mountains of Israel. Points to ponder:

Quote — In the case of battle, none of the Russian's armed forces would fight with enthusiasm, but rather with gloom. They are under a compulsion of sorts. It is impossible to explain because they themselves can't. They don't like the Secret Police, but nonetheless accept it as inevitably Russian. . . . The generals are also gloomy because they know they can't use their nuclear devices because,

(i) There would be deadly retaliation. Nothing worthwhile would be left of Russia and Russians deeply love Russia.
(ii) It is not possible to use such devices against a conventional enemy, because thereafter their own forces could not advance.
(iii) Such devices cannot be used against America, because that would mean the starvation of Russia (grain) even without U.S. retaliation.
(iv) What would be the value to Russia of a nuclear devastated Europe, Middle East or Africa? None at all." end quote.

However, they have clearly spoken. They desire South Africa (minerals and strategic position) and Israel.

Why would Russia want the Middle East, and Israel in particular?

(a) An all-year-round warm water port.
(b) The minerals (potash, etc.) from the Dead Sea.
(c) Middle East oil.
(d) An inexplicable desire to take Jerusalem (Satanic.)

**A SHOCKING REPORT**

Readers will possibly remember the U.S. Forces joining the Israelies in Lebanon and the interesting thing is that they didn't leave for a very long time.

**REASON:**

These forces found great underground caverns tunnelled out under the village of SAIDA. There the largest SECRET MILITARY BASE in the world was tunnelled out. The tunnels were steel reinforced with miles and miles of other tunnels holding enough weapons to arm a half million to one million troops.

There were steel doors that could only be opened by emissions by radio waves from submarines.

Russian Invasion Date: 4th August 1982 — Documents by the score were seized, all written in the Russian language.

Yasser Arafat hung around right until the last minute, but the Soviets let him down, and went back on their word, until he was finally forced to leave.

The Israelis spent month after month trucking all this equipment back to Israel.

God spoke in 1982 — "Not yet Soviets. You'll come when I say. I'll put hooks in your jaws and bring you down to your destruction. There is a full record in the prophets Ezekiel and Daniel and herewith is that record. See chapters 38-39 of Ezekiel.

1. A peace treaty will be signed in the Middle East lasting for 7 years. This will cause the Israelies to lay aside their weaponry (apparently).
2. The following countries will be involved in the invasion of Israel.
   Russia (King of the North)
   Black African Communist Countries (King of the South)
   Iran
   North African Countries. N.B. In August 1984 Libya linked hands with Morocco.
   East Germany.
   Turkish Mountain people and many others including Cossacks.
3. The evil demonic prince called Gog leads these forces on to their destruction.
4. Initially troops will come up from Africa, join with the Arabs and attack Israel.
5. Next Russia, Iran, East Germany and Cossacks come through
   (a) Iran by land
   (b) A Mediterranean amphibious attack
   (c) By air, paratroops
6. Russia double crosses Egypt and invades it as well.
7. The only areas that escape this invasion are Edom, Moab and Ammon, down the Jordan valley. The ancient fortress, Petra is in this area, and many Jews will hide there at this time.
8. Whilst in Egypt, Russia hears bad news from home in the north about threats from China in the East. This unsettles the Russians and makes them feel insecure.
9. Russia and allies move back to Israel for their total destruction.

## DETAILED DESCRIPTION OF THE DESTRUCTION OF RUSSIAN COMMUNISM

1. Suddenly, a devastating earthquake hits the Middle East. It is so violent that the effects are felt world-wide. This is an introduction to an unbelieving world of the wrath of God unleashed. It has been well said,

   "There are no atheists in an earthquake."

   "The earth shall reel to and fro like a drunkard. . . ."[6]

2. Terrible confusion will then erupt amongst the communist troops. The problem is that there are so many language groups involved (even in Russia alone) that they will not comprehend any orders given. Communist will fight communist, and the Lord will see to it.

3. Next comes a terrible plague amongst the troops, which at a cursory glance looks suspiciously like a neutron bomb blast — yet we now believe it will be far worse than this as atomic warfare would make the land uninhabitable for years, also destroy the local populace. — No, a secret weapon will be used — more later!!

   "And this will be the plague wherewith the Lord will smite all the people that have fought against Jerusalem

   (i) Their flesh shall consume away while they stand upon their feet

   (ii) And their eyes shall consume away in their holes

   (iii) And their tongue shall consume away in their mouth."[7]

   As a result of this amazing blast, the results will be:

4. Floods, great hailstones (caused by ice being continually caught in updraughts and picking up more bulk before it finally falls to the earth), fire, sulphur and blood.

5. It should be noted here however that the new Israeli secret weapon will probably be used and herewith is a description of the results. The name of the weapon is —

### THE VELOCITY FACTOR

Readers will be interested to note that although Israel does not possess this weapon, it will be at their disposal at the appropriate time.

During our school days, many of us remember being taught that the speed of light was constant — i.e. 186,000 miles per second.

This has now been proven to be wrong.

Einstein's theory of relativity says that nothing can travel faster than the speed of light. It has now been found that the Quantum Theory is correct, but relativity is not, i.e. there is a tendency for two very distant sub-atomic particles to behave "harmoniously" as though each knew what the other was doing. Thus, if the behaviour of one such particle was altered, the other could be expected instantaneously to change in exactly the same way — with no apparent force or signal linking to them.

The result as predicted by Quantum Theory, demonstrated that whenever proton A was measured, proton B behaved as though it too had been disturbed. Therefore, it is clear that even two distant protons are linked by some sort of signal travelling faster than light.

David Bohm, Professor of Theoretical studies at London's Birkbeck College says, "Everything in the universe is in a kind of total rapport, so that whatever happens is related to everything else, or it may mean there is some kind of information that can travel faster than the speed of light, or it may mean that our concepts of "space" and "time" have to be modified in some way. . . ."

Mr Barry Setterfield in his manual "The Velocity of Light and the Age of the Universe", tells us that "from 1675-1960 there were 45 observations of the speed of light." He says,

". . . it is overwhelmingly likely that light was travelling much faster in the past, and that its speed has decreased rapidly at first, then gradually in a mathematically predictable way, until it reached a constant level in 1960 A.D."

By studying the curve he drew in relation to these 45 observations, Mr Setterfield shows in his book that by going back from 1960 the mathematical starting point turns out to be 4082 B.C. plus or minus 100 years.

"This date at which light appears to have begun to slow down matches very well with the Biblical date of creation, obtained by adding up the ages of father-son chronologies from Adam to Jesus Christ."

This new information cancels out much of the information we were taught at school.

I give this definition of a scientist to my family: "A scientist is a person who 'is discovering' some of the things which God has made."

This book mentioned above, will clearly show any honest truth seeker that light travelling at a constant speed from distant galaxies would take thousands of millions of years to reach us.

This is simply not so. The universe is only about 6,000 years old as shown us in the Word of God. The speed of light is not constant. Poor unbelievers. "Professing themselves to be wise, they became fools."[8]

Light initially travelled very much faster, and this allows for creation to fit into a 6,000 year pattern.

Just a little word of explanation on the Quantum Theory

"Light appears to be a steady stream, or a continuous flow of energy. Actually, light is not given off, or absorbed in one continuous process, but it is a series of many small actions, that may be compared to the filming of a motion picture, in which each movement is photographed in many small pictures. But, when shown on the screen, the motion picture appears as one continuous movement.

"Light, is therefore a series of tiny definite units called photons or quanta."

Now, back to the Velocity Factor.

If this factor of "7" system is used in the battle against the Russians which it will be, the velocity of light can be exceeded and therefore our conventional ideas of time will be completely destroyed.

For further inforfmation on this subject, please read on to the chapter entitled 'Bits & Pieces'.

**RESULTS**

1. Weapons of war can be stopped and destroyed at infinite speeds.
2. Transmitted events now travelling to infinity at the speed of light can be overtaken and played back. So we will eventually see the actual events of the past.
3. In the light of this information, it is now impossible to accept the conventional view of time.
4. The question may now be asked, when Israel receives access to this super weapon, will they use it against any aggressors, and quieten down the whole world scene.

   Answer — they won't until the communist invasion, for the following reasons: Once brought into use, this factor weapon will alter the whole earth's time cycle, by a factor of 7. The whole economy and lifestyle will therefore be changed right around the world.
5. Information to hand is that the Russians do not believe that there is such a weapon. It is this attitude that will bring about their complete destruction on Israeli territory. A force field around Israel will protect those within its boundaries but destroy all aggressors who will die violently.

   By the way, the authority who has this information tells us: "It is an established fact, impossible to question."

   I personally have had this vindicated through another source.

6. All the Communist forces will be destroyed. None will survive, who come against Israel.
7. The vultures will gorge themselves on the corpses lying around in the open. (N.B. Take no notice of the tract speaking of the multiplication of vulture's eggs — it is simply not so.)
8. Russian and African communism will be destroyed. These two continents will be ripe for the gospel.
9. The whole population of Israel will be seven months burying the dead as these decaying bodies will pose a major health hazard.
10. After seven months, the populace return to normal life, and special government employees, no doubt connected with the Israeli Health Department will supervise the final clean up. People travelling by bus or car through the area will assist in burying the rest of the bones and rotting corpses, yet those who are in a hurry will have permission to erect little signs alongside human remains, to enable the full-time workers to locate and bury them at a later date.

    No doubt, families and tour groups will pick up shovels and especially prepared signs before leaving town. Picture, if you will, this scene in an average family car.

    Child looking eagerly out window. "I spy with my little eye, something beginning with B."
11. The Israelis will not need to cut down wood out of their vast forests at all for a period of seven years.

    They will burn the weapons and stores belonging to their enemies. The Russians, by the way, in their efforts to avoid heat seeking missiles and those attracted by metal are using a Dutch invention "lignostone" in much of their weaponry. It is as hard as metal, yet it burns like coal.
12. From the prophecies, it is apparent that this Russian wipe-out is the prelude to the destruction of Chinese and Asian communism. About three and a half years later at the end of the period called Great Tribulation, the great dam built on the Euphrates river in Syria by the Russians will be closed off and these armies numbering 200,000,000 will cross over the dry river bed of this ancient natural barrier into Israel to fight against the Lord. This river is the North Eastern boundary of Israel's promised territory.

This is called —

13. The Battle of Armageddon

    The prophecies tell us that the Lord Jesus Christ himself, will fight the battle alone, accompanied up this valley 200 miles long from Haifa in the north down to Bozrah in Southern Jordan, by

(a) His Bride whom he has brought back from the marriage supper in Heaven
(b) The Jewish remnant who have been hiding in the caves of Petra
(c) The armies of Heaven on white horses.

14. Result — Defeat for Eastern Communism — Victory for Christ and His people. A river of blood, human and animal measuring up to a horse's bridle for 200 miles.

One third of this mighty army killed
i.e. 3 ) 200,000,000 = 66,666,666 killed.

## CHAPTER THIRTEEN

# WHAT ABOUT AMERICA?

Now for the other super power, the U.S.A.

At the time of writing, this nation is approaching their election in 1984.

Readers of my first book "Warning" may remember reading the following quote on p. 169.

Websters Dictionary has listed Ronald Reagan as the 40th President of the U.S.A. even before the elections were held.

Quote — "The presumption or genuine mistake by the Chicago publishers Consolidated Book Publishers has dumbfounded the American Consul-General in Auckland, Mr Peter Higgins. Unbelievable! was his first word.

Auckland representatives of the publishers were just as surprised and had no explanations." — End quote.

This now raises the question, "are American Presidents elected, or chosen?" The general populace can be easily manipulated through subliminal means, i.e. the secret message being incorporated in advertisements or programmes so that only the subconscious picks it up. The illustration is old yet true. Using subliminal means, "popcorn and coke" was advertised in a large picture theatre. At half time the audience arose and went to purchase "popcorn and coke". These subliminal tapes are now being promoted all over the U.S., Australia, New Zealand and other countries. (Date of writing — 17th August, 1984.)

Now, a number of interesting points arise. In all probability, the President of the U.S.A. will be

(a) Ronald Reagan, who claims to be a born again Christian is the one man who is smart enough to hold up the Russian plans for world domination. Meanwhile — the computers are working on his behalf to guarantee him the job. His speeches are arranged by the computers. Those States that want a "hawk" President get hawkish tough speeches. Those who want a dove President hear words like peace, love, dialogue, etc. The computer virtually guarantees his success. Its operator is the greatest.

May the Lord help America when Reagan goes and a softy comes into power.

Here is an outline of Russia's aims which Reagan clearly understands.

1. Freeze Europe into a terrified neutrality.

2. Occupy the United States in Central American problems.
3. Gain naval control of the ocean routes.
4. These are Russian devices used:
   (i) Marxism
   (ii) Pacifism
   (iii) Nuclear fears
   (iv) Terrorist activities
   (v) Industrial disruptions
   (vi) The skills of pro Russians
   (vii) Anti Zionism
   (viii) Islamic ambitions

(b) George Bush is another in the running for the presidential office. He is a World Government man.
   (i) Notice, he has been in three World Government groups.
   i.e. Council on Foreign Relations
   Trilateral Commission
   Ex-Director of the CIA — World Government police force
   (ii) He has power already to carry cypher cards which allow him to unleash America's nuclear forces if President Reagan were to die or became incapacitated and war broke out.
   (iii) He has been very strongly advised on various matters by a woman — some fear that this may cloud his judgement. (An important point in these days of militant feminism.)
   (iv) Up until 1984, he has remained fiercely loyal to Ronald Reagan, and makes a very good Vice President.

(c) Walter Mondale is next on the list.
A World Government man.
Notice he has been in at least three World Government groups.
i.e. Council of Foreign Relations
Trilateral Commission
Attended Bilderberger Meetings (Europe)

Soft, easy, kind to the Russians. Takes the position of a fly who wishes to enter into meaningful dialogue with the spider. A great danger to the freedom of America, yet a useful puppet in certain hands — could return to Nixon's and Carter's policy of Detente.

Remember p.95 of my book Warning, a quotation of

Brezhnev, taken from the Washington Post, 12th February 1977.

"Trust us Comrades, for by 1985, as a consequence of what we are now achieving with DETENTE (peaceful co-existence), we will have achieved most of our objectives in Western Europe. We will have consolidated our position. We will have improved our economy, and a decisive shift in the correlation of forces will be such, that come 1985 we will be able to exert our will wherever we need to.

We are achieving with Detente what our predecessors have been unable to do with the mailed fist. . . ." — End quote.

(d) Geraldine Ferraro — is a woman. This is no doubt of great rejoicing to the women's libbers.

Geraldine at the time of writing is experiencing some difficulty in explaining some irregularities in the field of finance.

I have in my possession a document dealing with the seven visions as seen by an outstanding man of God in the year 1933.

Five have come to pass, and it appears that No. 6 is now taking place symbolically through Women's Liberation.

Vision No. 1: The rise of Mussolini and his horrible end.
Vision No. 2: The rise of Hitler and his mysterious end.
Vision No. 3: Three great ISMS — Facism, Naziism, Communism the voice said "Watch Russia. Watch Russia."
Vision No. 4: Science advances — a plastic bubble-topped car invented.
Vision No. 5: The moral problem. Women get the vote. Cut hair. Wear men's clothes, then stripped off to a fig leaf apron. Terrible perversion resulted.
Vision No. 6: A woman rose up to run America. (In my opinion this has happened already in America as in many cases the husbands are controlled by the wives. — This is not God's plan for the Christian family.)
Vision No. 7: A terrible explosion. Debris, craters and smoke all over America.

Regarding this last vision. Other godly folk have seen this too, yet America will continue on. The U.S. flag arises through the confusion.

N.B. George Washington, Oral Roberts and Daisy Osborne have all seen similar visions.

Therefore, out of these four contenders, for the presidency, only two are World Government advocates, and Reagan who is a non World Government advocate has already been chosen, for a season.

The new monetary system needs to be in place first and then he can be replaced. (See further explanation in Bits & Pieces.)

The United States is the most difficult country in the world to subdue for World Government purposes. A trojan horse is needed to infiltrate from within.

Remember, when Poland was over-run by the commos, the first things that were confiscated were all communications sets, plus weapons and ammunition. In other words, so long as people are armed and can communicate with others, they are virtually impossible to subdue.

1. Whenever the Trojan Horse President is chosen by the one-worlders, you can be sure that one of the first bills to be pursued will be of strict gun laws and control.

2. The American people are, generally speaking, very patriotic and nationalistic. This spirit has to be undermined as is happening in other countries.

   Under World Government concepts, Independence must give way to Interdependence. — Thus the family and home must be attacked in a subtle way.

3. Miles must become kilometres.
   Gallons must become litres.
   Fahrenheit must change to celsius, otherwise people will not become confused, as they are in other countries around the world.

Now, please notice, that once the two superpowers are dealt with, either externally or internally, this will give the 10 countries of the E.E.C. a chance to rise, and together with their Antichrist leader, dominate all world trade through this new world monetary system.

Only born-again Christians will be in a place of safety at this time.

Remember, the prayer of salvation is in the last chapter of this book.

For more news on America, please turn to Chapter entitled "Bits and Pieces".

Never forget that in the measure America honours God, God will honour America.

The minority rabble are trying to destroy it, yet there is a strong sense of patriotism there that is seldom seen anywhere else in the world.

# CHAPTER FOURTEEN

# DYNAMITE AVAILABLE

I tied my outrigger canoe to the ring of steel on top of the marker buoy, and climbed up on to it. Another evening was ahead of me, seeking through prayer, the answer to tapping the power of God. The venue was the inner harbour close to the reef in Apia, Western Samoa.

Some months before this, my friend David Garratt and I had climbed the stairs to the office of a Pastor Trevor Chandler, a marine assessor and also a Baptist minister who told of being woken one night from a deep sleep and prompted to read this verse from the Word of God.

"It's not by might, nor by power, but by my Spirit saith the Lord of hosts."[1]

He had received a remarkable experience called the baptism in the Holy Spirit, and spoke in a new language which he had never learned. The power of God accompanied his messages from then on, and remarkable results became the norm in his meetings.

Trevor gave us a number of talks at a convention I attended and told us of the great Christian preachers like Moody, Whitfield and John Wesley all having had a touch from God, after they had become born again. This made me hungry for God as the world is a big place, and people desperately need Jesus and his salvation. As one had said, "One miracle is better than 1,000 words in gaining people's attention." — This pastor laid hands on both David and I and prophesied over each of us. The prophecy over me went like this:

"You shall seek for me and you shall find me, when you seek for me with all your heart. You shall find my joy and I will lead you into a fruitful field."

It was with a grateful heart to God that I watched my friend David and his dear wife Dale move into a God-given ministry entitled "Scripture in Song" and this has spread to many countries around the world.

I, in turn travelled to the Pacific Islands, and it was up there that the prophecy was fulfilled.

The trips to the steel buoy became regular. Night after night, rocking around out there, just God and me. I can still visualise the scene, with a warm tropical breeze stirring the lagoon waters, the lights along the waterfront from Aggie's Hotel to the town clock, reflecting in the dark waters by the sea-wall, and the occasional clank of the big chain, anchoring the buoy to the reef far below. — I knew the promise,

"Blessed are they which do hunger and thirst after righteousness for they shall be filled."[2]

On other nights of the week, I would pray with a very dear American friend from Sacramento, California, named Maurice Luce. This man became like a second father to me, and taught me about the Holy Spirit and His power for today. After about two years of good friendship, this brother in Christ and missionary from California, returned to the States and revival broke out.

**First Night**

We were having an Easter convention in a large thatched house, and kerosene lamps illuminated the meetings. At midnight, a boy ran outside and shouted, "I can see the cross of Christ in the sky". — The people rushed outside and before my startled eyes, I saw 60 people fall flat on their backs on the concrete. No-one was hurt, as it was the power of God that put them there. I had heard of this phenomena taking place under the preaching of the Wesleys, Whitfield and Finney and now I was seeing it with my own eyes. (By the way, it is happening frequently all around the world in the 1980's.)

Is it Scriptural? — YES!!

1. The priests ministering in Solomon's temple fell down under God's power.
2. Saul on the road to Damascus fell to the ground.
3. The soldiers searching for Jesus, in the garden, fell backwards to the ground when Jesus declared, "I AM he".

I walked amongst these people all through the night from midnight until 8 a.m. the next morning.

I was shocked as I heard them speaking in different languages, which they had never learnt. I knew this was spoken of in the Word of God, but at that time I didn't know much about it.

People sang in the heavenly choirs in different languages. The music was just fantastic. Others described scenes in heaven with the golden streets, the heavenly buildings, the Lamb on the throne, and the precious blood of Christ pulsing through his veins.

A little boy, aged about 12, stood to his feet, eyes closed, arms out-stretched like an Old Testament prophet, and spoke in his own language the following message from the Lord (possibly this needs to be heeded in other countries also).

"Samoa is a land of DEAD CHURCHES

with DEAD PASTORS
preaching DEAD SERMONS
over DEAD PULPITS
to DEAD PEOPLE

I have brought my servants from over the seas to restore the gospel of salvation to these islands. When this gospel has gone around these shores, I will return and judge the world with such destruction as has never been known since the days of Sodom and Gomorrah."

Another prophecy was given, in this camp in 1962.

"Many of you will not die, but you will see me coming in the clouds with great glory."

It's getting close now.

God has given mankind 6000 years to live on this earth. The number applying to man in Bible study is always No. 6. Man was created on the 6th day. The Antichrist world leader's number is 666, just short of 7 which is God's number of perfection.

Remember reading these words about how God views time.

". . . one day is with the Lord as a thousand years and a thousand years as one day."[3]

Now remembering what you have read about 6,000 years of creation being now proven (as the speed of light was originally much faster than it is today) I tell the following story.

During those years in the islands, I one day met an old pastor in a back village who said kindly,

"Simifi, alala mai i lalo." (Smith, sit down.)

This old man then passed on the following information.

From Adam — Abraham = 2,000 years
From Abraham — Christ = 2,000 years
From Christ — today = 1984 years (at time of writing)

therefore 5,984 years from Adam until today

Therefore we are almost at the end of the alotted period of 6,000 years.

Watch —

6,000
—5,984
= 16 years

In Matthew's gospel, chapter 24 we read about a dreadful period of earth's history called the Great Tribulation. This period lasts for 3½ years. It will be so bad that

"And except those days should be shortened there should no flesh be saved, but for the elect's sake, those days shall be shortened."

Less than 16 years then until the end of man's allotted time to choose God or satan. (Now this is approximate of course, depending on which calendar is used, i.e. Roman or Jewish. The Jews utilise a 360 day lunar year.)

There are a number of promises in the prophets which tell us that when we reach a period where God's enemy promotes occult practices everywhere, God will also move.

"When the enemy shall come in like a flood, the Spirit of the Lord shall raise up a standard against him."[4]

In other words, supernatural v supernatural.

Many of you readers have attended church services where you have been bored out of your brain and the only comfort you have is that it must end sometime.

It is likened to banging your head on a brick wall. It is beautiful when it stops.

No wonder it is difficult to encourage some folk out to a lively service where things really happen, because old memories die hard.

Thank God for His promise,

"And it shall come to pass afterward that I will pour out my Spirit upon all flesh. . . ."[5]

I'm excited to tell you that during these few remaining years, if you can receive it, the day of Pentecost will be repeated over and over on a much grander scale.

"Be glad then ye children of Zion, and rejoice in the Lord your God, for He hath given you THE FORMER RAIN — moderately (Day of Pentecost, 3,000 saved) and He will cause to come down for you the rain, the FORMER RAIN and the LATTER RAIN (Pentecost plus much more) in the first month." (Words in brackets and emphasis added to assist meaning.)[6]

**Second Night**

The next night in this island revival, at the close of the service, there was much weeping as people observed a heavenly figure dressed in white, move amongst the congregation, touching people gently on their heads. Each of those touched responded to the Lord and committed their lives to him and were born again that night.

**Third Night**

I was so keen this night to receive a touch from the Lord and

His power that I stood under a cocoa tree and prayed a miserable prayer.

"Lord, you've touched all the brown people. How about me? I can't help it if my skin is white." Just a few seconds went by and my name was called, so I ran across to where a group of Samoan men were praying. One of these reached forth his hand, touched me on the head and a word of prophecy came forth, through his lips from the Lord to me.

"My Son, do not say unto me because you have a white skin, I don't love you. You will receive my power soon," etc., etc., with more information (personal information for me alone). "You will receive my joy soon." — What a promise.

**Fourth Night**

The meetings were packed with people from then on. Hundreds and hundreds came in and listened to the powerful, annointed preaching of Samoan evangelist, "Makisua Fatialofa" and others of us whom God graciously used.

This night, it was my turn to preach. About three years had gone by since Trevor Chandler's prophecy.

I took my place at the pulpit. The thatched house at Lotopa was packed, and crowds stood or sat around outside in the warm tropical air. Suddenly, two people at the back of the building stood, spoke to one another in a strange language, laughed, nodded one to the other, stepped forward over the heads of those who were seated on mats on the floor, and stood directly in front of me, now preparing to preach.

"What's going on here?" I thought. "What are these two up to? I'm the preacher here." Speaking again in this new language, the two nodded once more, placed the tips of their fingers lightly on my forehead and I received the baptism in the Holy Spirit.

This power went through my being; twice. The Lord's voice spoke within my spirit. "This is my power you have longed for. Your left hand will remind you of the blood of the Lord Jesus Christ, whilst your right hand will remind you of the Name of the Lord Jesus Christ. With these two weapons, nothing will stand before you."

I laughed, cried, rejoiced and then thought, "Well, I'd better stop all this laughing and crying and get on with preaching the Word of God". I opened my Bible and started to say, "Let us turn to the Gospel of John." Out from my lips came another language I had never learnt. That night, try as I might, it was impossible for me to speak English or Samoan, only this new language given to me by the Lord. The congregation laughed and rejoiced with me as I sat down. The chairman stood to close the meeting, but also spoke in a language that he had never learned. He looked so frustrated as he also sat down.

Someone else closed the meeting.

Some time ago, I met a Christian lady, a Baptist pastor's wife, who told me of her vision. She had seen a mountain with a conical shaped peak, snow around the top and water streaming out from the volcano and washing rapidly down the sides.

A voice spoke, "Men have stopped my Spirit in the past, but they will never stop me now."

Are visions scriptural? Referring to these last days again, the prophet speaks. In the words of the prophet Joel, prophecy, dreams, and visions are promised for this period of history. His Spirit will be poured out on all flesh.

Another well-known Bible teacher from overseas came to New Zealand and told us of his vision. — A broad fast flowing stream, carrying all before it. A voice admonished, "Tell the people to get into the stream of my Spirit and stop splashing around in their little puddles on the side."

In the Middle East, it has been the custom to carry wine in animal skin bottles. Jesus referred to these when speaking of the new wine joy of the Holy Spirit.

"Neither do men put new wine into old bottles, else the bottles break, and the wine runneth out, and the bottles perish, but they put new wine into new bottles and both are preserved."[7]

It has been interesting to tour Australia in the 1980's and amongst many of the evangelical, Bible-based fundamentalist groups, hear these dear folk expressing exactly what their counterparts in New Zealand expressed during the 1970's. If it weren't so serious, it could be laughable. The old stiff, dried out, brittle wine-skins cry out, "Not for today. Not for today. The power has gone. Do all things decently and in order. Not for today."

Why is there such a proliferation of new Christian fellowships springing up all over the world today?

Many wish to expand spiritually, and allow the new wine to permeate their gatherings. There is no doubt about the tremendous joy that comes with this wine.

This is in no way a slight on those gracious people who belong to Christ's body who don't want it, or who do not have the capacity yet to receive it. God still blesses them in measure, and let us never forget that. — Grace is called for, as all this is a whole new realm to some Christians.

It has been well said that the evangelical believers, fundamental in doctrine and Bible belief, resemble a man with plenty of money in the bank, but who does not have the cheque book to draw it out.

Those who believe in the dynamic power of the Holy Spirit, unless they study the Word of God, are likened to a man with a cheque book, but with no money in the bank.

My word, satan is clever. Over the past decades he has prevented these two groups from mixing together, because he well knows that the man with money in the bank who also has a cheque book with which to draw it out, is a threat to his kingdom.

Evangelist Billy Graham says that God raised up the pentecostals to restore this power to the church. A satanist church member, recently converted, freely admits that the only people the satanists fear are those who acknowledge the power of God through the baptism in the Holy Spirit. These are the people that satanists know have the power to harm their existence.

Some say the power of God people become fanatical.

I well recall the words of a dear Christian man, Neville Winger, now passed on to be with the Lord.

"It is easier to cool down a fanatic, than to warm up a corpse."

Readers will recall that the early church had the power of God operating, regularly.

It has been predicted that Christ will not return from heaven until all this power has been restored.

"And He shall send Jesus Christ, which before was preached unto you whom the heaven must receive until the TIMES OF RESTITUTION of all things, which God hath spoken by the mouth of all his holy prophets since the world began." (Words in capitals for emphasis.)[8]

Years ago I asked my dad, a born-again Christian man about the Bible teaching called SPEAKING IN TONGUES. Like most others of his generation, he just laughed and said, "Well son, we don't talk about it very much, but anything that is good and provided it comes from God, go for it."

However, once it happened to me and I received this gift from God, I now understand what it is that out of the nine gifts of the Spirit, the only one that is continually hammered, bashed and pummelled by your average good evangelical is the gift of speaking in tongues.

**Reasons:**

1. Satan was cast out of heaven with his followers.
2. Satan is called "the god of this world."
3. His powerful followers are called "the princes of this world."

4. These princes have a ruler over each country of the world, e.g. Persia, Greece, Russia and all other countries.
5. They also have minor rulers over cities and towns.
6. God's throne is on the sides of the north. Above the north magnetic pole, there is a great space which astronomers have located. This space has no stars, but a luminous glow coming from around the outsides.

   "Beautiful for situation, the joy of the whole earth, is Mount Zion on the SIDES OF THE NORTH, the city of the great king." (Emphasis added for meaning.)[9]
7. Satan is also in charge of the atmosphere surrounding this earth. He is sometimes called the prince of the power of the air. Remember this next time you fly in a plane. Pray for protection.
8. Satan and his evil princes understand earthly languages and can interfere in people's plans.
9. When a Christian prays in his or her own language, the devils understand, make notes and act accordingly to frustrate those plans.

   For example, if I say to a friend, "I'm going to cast an evil spirit out of Bill this afternoon at 3.00 p.m. in the name of the Lord Jesus", the spirits will then warn Bill's evil spirit and he will take off in his car at 2.55 p.m. Experience has taught us that this is a fact.
10. Now, when a Christian prays in tongues, by the Spirit,
    (a) His understanding is not involved. It is his spirit praying.
    (b) No other person understands.
    (c) He speaks mystery words in a code known only to God.
    (d) The devil does not understand. Demons, satan and princes of this world do not have revelation knowledge.

"Proof, proof", I hear you cry.

"For he that speaketh in an unknown tongue speaketh not unto men, but unto God, for NO MAN understandeth him, howbeit in the spirit he speaketh MYSTERIES." (Emphasis added for meaning.)[10]

"Oh ho", I hear the sceptic cry. "No man understands but satan does."

Try this then.

"But we speak the wisdom of God in a MYSTERY, even the hidden wisdom which God ordained before the world unto our glory, which NONE OF THE PRINCES OF THIS WORLD KNEW, for had they known it, they would not have crucified the Lord of glory." (Emphasis added for meaning.)[11]

Get it? Satan and his co-workers do not have revelation knowledge.

When Jesus hung on the cross, these demonic forces no doubt laughed, thinking that they had defeated God's plans.

Actually it was the very opposite. The first prophecy in the scriptures was being fulfilled. Remember the Lord's talk with the snake in the garden of Eden.

"And I will put enmity between thee and the woman; and between thy seed and her seed. It shall bruise thy head, and thou shalt bruise his heel."[12]

True, true. When Jesus hung on the cross, satan was not smart enough. He did not have relevation knowledge and therefore lost the battle once and for all on that day.

Comparatively speaking, Jesus only bruised his heel whilst jumping on satan's head, which leads us on to the question.

Which is worse, to get your heel bruised, or to have your head jumped on?

(e) Now that we have found satan does not have knowledge of these mysteries that we speak in the spirit, he uses supposedly reliable men of the word to speak against and put people off this experience.

(f) We will now go a step further and say that every one of these persons who militantly fight and preach against this experience must of course have an evil spirit of deception working in their lives, no matter how godly they appear to be.

Rule — God does not fight God — correct?

The Word of God even tells us not to associate with these people, who

"Having a form of godliness but, denying the POWER thereof, FROM SUCH TURN AWAY". (Emphasis added for meaning)[13]

James tells us that the tongue is a small member, set on fire from hell. It is true we use it to bless God on Sundays, but curse others from Monday-Saturday.

"The tongue, can no man tame . . ."[14]

But praise be to God — he can and does.

Q. Do all who are baptised in the Holy Spirit have to speak with tongues?

A. All have the ability to do so. I would not be satisfied unless I did. This gift moves you into the realm of the Holy Spirit, with the gifts (See 1 Cor. 14.)

Some of these dear unbelieving believers even run around with tapes, endeavouring to frighten people with stories such as

"Here is a man speaking in tongues, but actually he is swearing in Chinese, etc." (depending on who is telling the story.) This, to my mind is very close to blasphemy against the Holy Spirit — be careful please.

As a result of this experience, life is far more exciting. Church becomes a place of life and spiritual excitement. The Lord's presence is revealed as He speaks through prophecy, tongues and interpretation.

One preacher I heard speaking on this subject said, "Criticism of the baptism in the Holy Ghost is like a man riding a bicycle criticising a jet plane."

Remember these words of John the Baptist,

". . . He that cometh after me is mightier than I, whose shoes I am not worthy to bear, He SHALL BAPTISE you with the HOLY GHOST and with fire." (Emphasis added for meaning)[15]

As one who was brought up anti (and I am not at all bitter — just sad about it) and as one who had to seek hard to find the true facts, to any doubters I say,

It is a matter of being prepared to allow the Lord to take control of you, your congregation, your services and not to fear that it will fly out of control. You can then move into the realm of the Holy Spirit.

"Oh dear," you cry, "What happens if I get a devil instead?"

Listen —

"If a son shall ask bread of any of you that is a father, will he give him a stone, or if he ask a fish will he for a fish give him a serpent?

Or if he shall ask an egg, will he offer him a scorpion, If ye then being evil know how to give good gifts unto your children, how much more than your heavenly father give the HOLY SPIRIT to them that ask Him."[16] (Emphasis added for meaning.)

1. This experience is as far removed from salvation as a saint is from a sinner.

   i.e. 1. = Life<br>
   2. = Power — Same Spirit, different operation.

   Illustrations.

**Saul/Paul**

(a) Life on the road to Damascus.
(b) Power in the house of Judas (Ananias lays on hands).

**The Lord Jesus Christ**

(a) Life in the womb of Mary. (Never needed a new birth — sinless.)
(b) Power in the river Jordan (start of public ministry.)

If it's good enough for Paul, it's good enough for me.
If it's good enough for the Lord Jesus, it should be good enough for us all.

2. It makes Christ a loving reality.
3. It moves the believer into a new realm.
4. Gives an awareness of spiritual forces.
5. Takes the drudgery out of Christianity.
6. Leaves the believer expectant for more blessing in the realm of revelation through the gifts of the Holy Spirit.
7. Gives tremendous joy and praising ability.
8. Gives confidence in spiritual crisis.
9. When a fellowship moves into this realm, strong discipline and Bible teaching is necessary to curb excess.
10. Your Christian love become demonstrative.

Simple early church truths are being restored.

A man of God travelling on a train was seated next to a monk. Herewith is a copy of their conversation.

Christian man: "Are you a follower of Jesus sir?"

Monk: "Yes I certainly am."

Christian man: "Are you following Jesus from the cradle to the river, or from the river to the cross?"

Monk (after some thought): "I hope I am following Jesus from the river to the cross."

Christian man: "Then you'll need the baptism of power that Jesus had in the river."

**Recap**

If you the reader object to this chapter, then it is probable that you will need help, in the form of prayer and deliverance in the name of the Lord Jesus Christ.

You have clearly received wrong teaching regarding the power of God. This is summed up in a book titled, "We've Been Robbed".

The true and living God never changes.

(a) Miraculous in the past.
(b) Miraculous in the present.
(c) Miraculous in the future.

# CHAPTER FIFTEEN

# BITS AND PIECES

(N.B. Information from many countries pours in continually. Much of it from people I have never met.)

When I wrote my last book, "Warning", I kept frustrating the typesetter by continually adding new information. I said then and I say again, "Prophecy turns into history even as I write."

**VERY IMPORTANT NEWS**
**PLASTIC CARDS**

AUSTRALIAN GUINEA PIGS. (April 1984 — First launching.)

The world's first national E.F.T. system is firmly established in the above country, with little New Zealand following along as No. 2 in the world on a national basis.

You will remember reading that the initiators were:

1. Westpac Banks
   Woolworths Supermarkets — One card — Credit and Debit Master Card
   Food Plus Stores
   British Petroleum Service Stations (BP)
   Now the others are getting in on the act.

2. National Australia Banks
   Ampol Total and Esso Oil Companies
   Safeway Supermarkets
   McEwans Hardware Stores — The biggest so far
   Myer Stores
   Target Discount Stores

3. Commonwealth Bank is linking with Mobil Oil.

There are arrangements being made to make all cards useable at any outlet.

EFT POS means — Electronic Funds Transfer at Point of Sale.

**GOODBYE CHEQUES**

This scheme is being extended to all states in a determined effort to make Australia cashless as soon as possible.

The N.Z. Post Office is closely involved in this new national system (EFT—POS). The Bank of N.Z. had the system operating in Wellington and Dunedin in October 1984, and hopes to have it operating in all branches by October 1985. They say it is a further step towards a "cashless society".

A Mr Tom Tennant of the B.N.Z. says "It was a step towards making banking hassle free, and towards putting a HUMAN FACE on banking." (Emphasis added.)

New Zealand readers please note that Woolworths had this system operating in Auckland and Wellington in 1984 and New Zealand has so many computer link-ups all ready to go, it is possible that this small country may even outstrip Australia and be the first National Cashless Society in the world.

**COMPUTERS**

Details on the expansion of these machines are taking up page after page of information in national newspapers. As we have already explained, these machines are being used in every realm.

Computer access code numbers are being assigned to every citizen. In Australia this has been done through a system called Medicare. This national health system has been proven to be a failure in Great Britain and other countries, yet has been installed right throughout this country. It has already caused massive problems between the doctors and the government of New South Wales, yet it was made clear that it cannot be scrapped.

Why?

Because Medicare has nothing to do with medicine. It is to do with collating information on each individual for the computer files. — This is not speculation. It is a verified fact.

New Zealanders — watch out — we're next.

To catch the young families, $10 extra per child was offered by the government in late 1984. All that was required was the filling in of a computer form — aha — clever eh? It's called "Family Care". Superannuitants now need to fill in a form to collect their super. These forms will continue to be foisted on an unsuspecting public. — These World Government people really CARE, don't they?

**Recap**

(a) A master card will be assigned first to the individual.
(b) This card has a link number which links to all other computer files.
(c) The average person cannot wipe his or her link number.
(d) The only ones who can wipe their link numbers are those involved in the setting up of the system. These

people no doubt have the ability to become non persons as far as the computer system is concerned.

These folk involved in servicing the machines must have service personnel codes for computer access. The computer crime of the future could well involve some of these people, or others who gain access to these codes. Even kids in the U.S.A. are into this area.

The mafia staff will be in on this, to be sure, plus crooked government officials and politicians to cover their payoffs. (No more brown paper parcels, containing banknotes eh boys?)

It is sad yet the Bible is correct.

"The heart is deceitful above all things and desperately wicked . . ."[1] Jesus is coming — you'd better believe it.

There is no real privacy in a computer. They are radiating devices, and if one could get alongside one with a tape-recorder this data could be copied on to a computer tape later on and replayed elsewhere.

Ultimately, access to each individual's file will be available to this world leader called Antichrist and he will be able to control individuals through a simple push of a button. — Nice isn't it?

**CREATION — BIG BANG THEORY**

In the light of Barry Setterfield's discoveries, we now see that the big bang theory never happened.

He says that this universe is not flying apart. On the contrary it is flying into a black hole. Actually we are on the dark side of the universe. This can be proven very easily. Absence of light on earth, when the sun goes down each night equals darkness.

Quote: "With the universe collapsing, and already a black hole as the above considerations suggest, its final fate is assured. The Scriptures give us the picture of the finale. 'The earth and the heavens fled away and there was no place found for them (i.e. they disappeared from sight)' Rev. 20:11. Exactly as would be the case for a collapsing black hole. Also, 'The heavens shall pass away with a great noise, and the elements shall melt with fervent heat and the heavens being on fire will be dissolved . . . nevertheless we look for a new heaven and a new earth wherein dwells righteousness . . .' (2 Peter 3:10-13). This scriptural picture is in total accord with the above model. Here is a warning and a challenge for us all. We will only partake in the new creation if we are right with the Creator Himself."

Now having learnt that Einstein was mistaken regarding the constancy of the speed of light, informed persons are now finding out that Darwin's works on the origins of the species should never have been taken seriously.

Here is a portion of an account of Charles Darwin's last days as recorded by Lady Hope of Northfield, England. In his hand he held an open Bible, which he was always studying.

"Hebrews," he said. "The Royal Book, I call it."

**EVOLUTION DOWN THE TUBES** — Remember Ch. 3 notes on Darwin

Lady Hope went on: "I made some allusion to the strong opinions expressed by many on the history of the creation, and then their earlier treatment of the earlier chapters of the book of Genesis.

"He seemed distressed, his fingers twitched nervously and a look of agony came over his face as he said,

'I WAS A YOUNG MAN WITH UNINFORMED IDEAS. I THREW OUT QUERIES, SUGGESTIONS, WONDERING ALL THE TIME ABOUT EVERYTHING. TO MY ASTONISHMENT, THE IDEAS TOOK ON LIKE WILDFIRE, PEOPLE MADE A RELIGION OF THEM.' " (Emphasis added.)

"He went on, 'I want you very much to speak here to the servants, some tenants and a few neighbours.' "

Lady Hope asked, "What shall I speak about?"

He answered in a clear emphatic tone. "JESUS CHRIST", adding in a lower tone, "AND HIS SALVATION". (Emphasis added.)

I have in front of me a large article from the Australian newspaper dated 22 August 1984 entitled, "Humans and apes just one big family". When will they ever learn?

I remember a man telling me the same thing years ago. I fixed him with a piercing gaze and replied, "I have heard the theory that we sprang from apes, but it is my opinion that some of us didn't spring far enough."

**COMPUTERS PROVE EVOLUTION TO BE NONSENSE or ANY SCHOOL CHILD CAN FIND OUT**

According to the Readers Digest Great World Atlas, man's evolutionary journey began 20 or 30 million years ago (making the Biblical account totally false.)

To show how silly all this is,

Ask the children to set up the school computers to tell you what the world population ought to be in 1984:

(a) If only 100 pairs existed 30,000 years ago, or

(b) If only 10 pairs existed 30,000 years ago.

— 30,000 is being very conservative when compared to 30,000,000 you will agree.

The calculations shown here allow for the decimation of population through war, famine, pestilence and disease.

Then ask your children's teachers to explain the figures. They won't like the request. Then ask your religious ministers who believe in evolution to explain, and if none can, ask the authorities to cease teaching contrary to the computer.

According to the Reader's Digest, in 1984 there was a world population of about four thousand million. It ought to be vast billions more. Science is supposed to be accurate and precise. It cannot urge the computer upon us, and rely upon it to take us to the moon and back, and then say the computer is not correct. It is their invention. At least one Middle East university is panic stricken by what the computer has said about the Darwinian hypothesis.

— Just ask the children, folks. Please turn to the postscript.

A certain Professor Sedgwick, a Cambridge geologist, upon reading Darwin's book, at once recognised Darwin's motive in writing it. This was whilst Darwin was still in his ungodly state. — "A dish of rank materialism cleverly cooked and served up merely to make us independent of a creator." — True enough you will agree.

He went on to say that if Darwin's teachings were accepted, humanity "would suffer a damage that might brutalise it, and sink the human race into a lower grade of degradation than any to which it has fallen since its written records tell us of its history."

1984 is proof of this prophecy being fulfilled. The computer will tell you the truth, sir or madam, if you are honest enough to apply the above test.

Charles Darwin will then from his vantage point in paradise, look down, metaphorically speaking, wipe the sweat from his brow and say a fervent, "Praise God another fool turned from the error of my ways."

**MONEY**

Cash is being manipulated. In Australia a $100 bill has just been introduced, and at the same time in New Zealand a $50 bill for the first time. This is causing problems with shopkeepers not prepared to give change when a small item is bought.

The U.S. economy is geared up for the use of these denominations, but our economy and thought patterns are not. Also in Australia, the $1 bill is gone, and in its place a small golden coin about the size of a 10 cent piece has appeared. — More confusion adding to the demise of cash, and the popularity of plastic cards.

There are many parts of the world now where cash is no longer acceptable when hiring cars, etc. Cards give instant information to the hirer should anything go wrong.

Stamp duty of bank cheques has also gone up — cunning isn't it?

**WOMEN'S LIB**

— or satan's fib to Adam's rib is gaining momentum in destroying lives.

Their aim, as explained before in this book, is not equality, but domination of men. An illustration of this may be gleaned from the Auckland Star, November 5 1984. Under the heading, "Women MPs will be boss in the House", we read, "Women will be in the majority in Parliament in about 40 years, Women's Affairs Minister, Mrs Hercus believes."

The two countries of Australia and New Zealand have been chosen as the GUINEA PIGS or first in the world on a National basis for the New Economic Order, or new World Monetary System.

Hand in hand along with all this, some horrific U.N. Bills are being forced upon the citizens of these two countries. One such is,

"The United Nations Convention on the Elimination of all Forms of Discrimination Against Women". Australia has passed this bill and at the time of writing New Zealand has ratified it. — The N.Z. Government made a pretense of listening to opinions but passed it regardless of that.

IT IS ALL PART OF THE PLAN.

Dr Martin Viney, a very clear thinking man, tells us why this bill is not necessary. Christchurch Press 5th December 1984 — Quote: "Matters concerning genuine discrimination — such as equality before the law — are adequately dealt with in these other covenants: strip away the repetition and what remains is pure feminist doctrine which has nothing to do with real discrimination. . . . Feminist rhetoric is that you must not discriminate against women. Discriminaton consists of denying women their rights. . . . Why should schools train children in feminists thinking . . . New Zealand is being affected by the policies of the convention even before ratification, disproving the claim that ratification is for the benefit of the oppressed women overseas." End quote.

Thank you, Dr Viney. I appreciate a person who can give a clear presentation of facts, without waffling around in obscure arguments.

The interesting thing is, that the longer women indulge in this

Wicca lifestyle in trying to move into masculine territory, scientists and others are alarmed to note that many of these women are experiencing

(a) Lowering of the voice
(b) Male gestures and habits
(c) The growing of added hair on the face and body.

This could be misconstrued as a deviation of "person-a-pause".

The Dominion newspaper, Wellington, on September 22nd, 1984 told how Erica Jong agrees with fellow feminist Germaine Greer that she and the rest of "liberated" womanhood have sold themselves short. "Women have been liberated to be externally exhausted, earning their own living and raising the children alone."

At 42, Erica is picking up the broken strands of her third divorce — end quote.

Never forget, radical feminism is satanic witchcraft which brings in a measure of temporary freedom, so-called, then comes the grief and the despair. Jesus waits gently to pick up the pieces. The Christchurch Press November 22nd 1984 reports that these women are trying to change school textbooks to make them non-sexist, e.g. Mum going to work, Dad wearing an apron. Yuk!!

Equality actually comes through Christ.

"We are heirs together of the grace of life."[2]

Some believe that any person using the initials Ms is immediately suspect, as we all know Mrs = married, and Miss = unmarried.

These two latter terms of address are adequate for the normal average person.

Is there a third group really? What are they trying to prove? Men normally appreciate feminine women. Very few men would wish to take on a wharfie as a life-long partner.

**STRANGE BILLS AND LAWS BEING PASSED**

The A.B.C. in Australia has now made it legal for travelling expenses to be paid to homosexual partners of its employees. This makes some of the other employees victims of cruel jokes, e.g. Do you work for the Gay B.C? — This is antidiscrimination in reverse.

It is like a national madness coming over the countries of New Zealand and Australia. No doubt, it all links with satan's world government plans and the new world monetary system in these countries.

Mr Neville Wran's Labour N.S.W. government passed a law

to make homosexual acts between consenting adult males legal. Now with the AIDS scare and even babies dying because of this disease, Mr Wran is now showing an interest in restricting the AIDS advance — this will strike the average person as being very queer.

**NINETEEN WORDS IN FEDERAL RESERVE CONSTITUTION**

In the first chapter of this book, I refer to this, and now, by way of proof, ex-Prime Minister Fraser of Australia confirms the truth of it for us.

From the 'Courier Mail' newspaper, Brisbane, July 14th, 1984:

Quote: "He (Mr Fraser) branded as a bad solution rumours of an overall buying out of problem loans by the U.S. Central Bank, The Federal Reserve Board.

"I hoped that story was false," Mr Fraser said, "It seems like an effort to bail out the banks rather than deal with the overall problem."

I humbly say, "Thank you Malcolm. Both you and I know it is not a rumour, don't we?" If it was, you would not have elaborated on it.

**RED HERRINGS**

In order to keep people's minds off what is really happening, i.e. the bringing in of world government, it is important to distract the populace with non-important issues.

(a) Nuclear and uranium issues. — We as Christians know, the world will not be destroyed for at least 1,007 years. Once nuclear weapons are used, that country where they are used becomes useless to all. — Marches, banners, confrontation = red herrings except of course for the U.S.A. and Russia. They will attack each other.

(b) Environmental issues (greenies). These folk, provided they are genuine, and are not just hiding a patch of marijuana in the bush have one main problem. Here it is.

"Who changed the truth of God into a lie, and worshipped and served the creature more than the Creator, who is blessed forever amen."[3]

These greenies love their trees, their animals, their soil, mountains, rivers and lakes, yet talk to them about JESUS, and they say — "No thanks".

That is really sad, because all the things they seek to save will perish, whilst Jesus and His salvation goes on forever.

I would rather fall at the feet of Jesus and worship him anytime than lie in front of a bulldozer.

## WORLD GOVERNMENT EXPANSION

Now in order for World Government to come in, at the right time, please remember the key words — "A GRADUAL TRANSFER OF POWER".

This power cannot be transferred if there are strong national leaders who will interfere.

Leaders who must go (Examples):

**Robert Muldoon — New Zealand** (gone)

**Crimes:** Too straight — too authoritarian — too clever. He intended to borrow until the inevitable crash came which he knew must come and thus keep his country afloat artificially. He would not submit to minority pressure groups and thus weaken the moral fibre of the country. From the Christchurch Press 7th December 1984, we see that the new Labour Government, not understanding the arts of borrowing, are making the mistake of trying to repay the loans. This is fatal at this stage in the history of N.Z.

Quote: ". . . New Zealand may be able to repay some Government debt next year for the first time in about 12 years, according to the Minister of Finance, Mr Douglas." End quote.

**Methods used against him:** A manipulative press and trojan horses within his own party who revealed themselves at the appropriate time.

**Result:** A weak, flabby Government now in power submitting to every immoral minority group, passing bills as quickly as possible, as if they know their time in power is limited. Resulting in — a pushover for world government. Some of this new Labour Government even belong to a power group calling themselves "Parliamentarians for World Order", e.g. Mr Richard Prebble.

**Malcolm Fraser — Australia** (gone)

**Crimes:** Too stable to be swayed by minority groups. Constantly on watch for weakening of moral fibre. His country experienced tremendous economic growth under his leadership. Australia was called — the lucky country.

Dignified, authoritarian, father figure, a curse to liberal destroyers.

**Methods used against him:** Media says, "Too old, out of touch with realities in a modern society." Media attack again. Whoever controls the media, sways the masses.

The alternative Mr Hawke was really boosted up by the media as a friend to all, including capitalist bosses and union workers.

Communists knowing that they could not win, threw in their lot with the left wing of the Labour Party (they even refer to each other as Comrade).

**Result:** A weak, flabby government led by Bob Hawke. He is a Rhodes Scholar who submits to world government plans and submits to international power groups as they use him like a puppet on a string, e.g. the closing down of the Franklin Dam in Tasmania – directed from overseas through Canberra to Tasmania, thus for the first time in history interfering with a state policy from overseas. Next to come in from overseas is a Federal Bill of Rights, giving power to Federal Government to cancel out state laws as they are passed. (Planned to be introduced in 1985.)

This bill will be passed and get rid of our next strong man — Joh Bjelke-Petersen. Articles in this bill will give more communist inspired rights to radicals (mostly whites and half castes) with regards to Aboriginal Land Rights.

"• Encourage homosexual marriages
- Legalise abortion
- Dismantle existing controls over pornography and street marches, and destroy state rights," Mr Petersen says.

Watch for it readers. There is a mad scramble in Australia to pass every disgusting bill as quickly as possible. The flood gates are open in both that country and New Zealand, e.g.

- Legalise homosexual acts between consenting males
- Homosexual marriages.
- U.N. Charter to eliminate all forms of discrimination against women — destroy male-female relationships and marriage.
- Destroy the stable home environment.
- Strange people allowed to teach sex to our young children.
- 50-50 job allocation, etc., etc.
- No mums or dads, just names will be used, summed up under the title, getting rid of stereotyped roles.

Kiwis note — The N.Z. Bill of Rights will be introduced in March 1985. The Government will pretend to listen to public opinion first and then pass it anyway. More subversive claptrap assisting with this "gradual transfer of power".

**Margaret Thatcher — Great Britain:**

**Crimes:** Says what she means and means what she says. Authoritarian and a leader of her nation towards good principles.

A threat to world government plans. Arthur Scargill is a communist who worked very hard with Russia, Libya and other rebels to try and destroy her through the miners strike.

**Aim:** To put in a Labour Government which will dismantle all nuclear bases in Britain and try to influence Europe to do the same; thus leaving all nuclear weapons in the hands of Russia and their allies.

The communists love this, as we found out when Mr Lange of the N.Z. Labour Government banned American ships into our ports.

In an article in the Christchurch Press 18.9.84 we read "Eastern Europe Applauds N.Z."

Dr Brash said, "New Zealand was not often mentioned in the news in Eastern Europe. But the delegation found New Zealand's stand on the nuclear issue was known everywhere."

This man led a 25 member delegation to the following countries, under the auspices of the N.C.C. (a liberal, pseudo-Christian group).

(a) Soviet Union — Communist.
(b) Bulgaria — Communist.
(c) Rumania — Communist.
(d) Hungary — Communist.
(e) East Germany — Communist.

To continue his quote: "People congratulated us on the government's strong stand," he said. "We got the impression it had made a significant mark for New Zealand on the world scene. Peace groups were active in most places." End quote.

Quite right Alan. It's made its mark all right — but not in the way you and your cobbers think.

When a communist speaks of "peace" he puts a peaceful bullet in a peaceful gun and you die a peaceful death.

Now — **Ronald Reagan — U.S.A:**

Chosen before the elections, a strong man with a strong authoritarian party behind him.

Others in the Presidential race — nice people but, pitiful, pliable and plausible.

**THE U.S. ELECTIONS**

In Chapter 12 I mentioned that the U.S.A. was a real thorn in the flesh for world government advocates. I am writing this section with today's Australian newspaper commenting on the Republican Convention at present being held in Dallas, Texas. (Shades of J.F.K. and L. H. Oswald.)

The very points I had written about earlier are all mentioned here.

Quote: "Republicans take a sharp right turn."

The Republican Party yesterday adopted its most right-wing policy platform in 130 years.

(a) Its call for a return to the gold standard . . . represents the adoption of a new political philosophy by the Republicans." End quote.

Now, those who follow the news may remember President Jimmy Carter's initial error which assisted in his removal from the White House. He tried to stop the plastic card and retain cash as a commodity. Reagan will not go yet, however. There are special plans for him.

(b) "Gun Control. — Republicans will continue to defend the constitution right to keep and bear arms."

Remember what we said in Chapter 12. For world government, the gun laws must come into force. That is exactly the opposite to this policy.

(c) "Education — The Republicans want to get back to basics and excellence."

This is exactly the opposite to world government plans. They want a bunch of illiterates brought up the modern way — all out of control.

(d) "Defence — we shall keep our peace by keeping our country stronger than any potential adversary. . . ."

This is no good to world government people. They want America brought to its knees. A weak, trembling, jelly-like structure.

(e) "Middle East — Israel must be helped to maintain a qualitative edge over its adversaries."

The world government people hate this. Israel is the key. Satan hates Jerusalem and the God of Israel. The prophets point out it will be continually attacked until Christ returns to rule.

By the way, if America does continue to assist Israel, it has God's continuous promises of blessings.

The world government manipulators put Reagan back into power in 1984 for one reason. To try to bring about the crash of the U.S. dollar during his term of office, and do him and his authoritarian party maximum damage. — We'll watch and see. God may have other plans.

Regarding Israel, God said,

"I will bless them that bless thee, and curse them that curse thee."[4]

**RUSSIA**

So devilish is this atheistic government filled with Darwin's now proven false theory of evolution, where men are no more than beasts, that it has now been reported in the Australian newspaper.

August 23rd, 1984: Quote "At least 30,000 people were killed in secret 'guinea pig' tests as the Soviet Union developed a huge arsenal of chemical and biological weapons. . . ."

How low can you get? Even animals don't behave like this.

The authors said the article was based on top-secret intelligence data.

Also, Cuban defectors had described Soviet chemical units and underground storage sites in Cuba. . . . end quote.

Now, these Russians have underground facilities in many parts of the world, e.g. Lebanon and Cuba and why is it, do you think, that Russian submarines are always snooping around the Scandinavian fjords?

### ABORIGINAL LAND RIGHTS

The evidence shows that much of this "movement" is being directed by communists and sympathisers in Australia. Aim: to divide Australia and bring in a black republic so that these people can bring the commos in.

Ayers Rock has already been given away.

A book called 'Red over 'Black' written by Geoff McDonald, an ex communist, makes all this clear.

### WHAT ABOUT NEW ZEALAND?

The uttermost part from Jerusalem.

From the Dominion newspaper, June 28th, 1984: "Cashless system makes N.Z. Debut."

"The Auckland Savings Bank yesterday launched the country's first 'cashless' purchase system at two Auckland petrol stations (EFT—POS)." End quote.

In the month of November, Woolworths in Auckland got in on the act. Shell Oil is moving in this direction also. It's all on folks.

### VIDEOS

Children in many countries are playing filthy video porn before their parents arrive home from work, and then acting out the scenes in the school playground the next day. Teachers are becoming alarmed.

### ART AND MUSIC

Many of us have noticed ugly art, shapeless figures, etc., and strange way-out music. I used to laugh and criticise, but no longer.

Pity, not laughter, is in order here. These dear people are

revealing through their repulsive art forms the dreadful turmoil going on inside.

So next time you see an ugly picture, a shapeless sculpture, or a horrible noise meant to be music, pray for and try to contact the author of it. This is an unconscious cry — HELP ME.

Jesus will fix them up.

We are living in strange days. Old foundations are crumbling, but there is one unchanging rock.

His name is JESUS

It is time now for a decision — a commitment, a born again experience.

**Recap**

It is impossible to keep up with events taking place in Australia and New Zealand.

1. Chosen as test cases for world government.
2. Have parliamentarians sneaking around in Parliament saying such things as "We must give up some of our national sovereignty. . . ."
3. Surreptitious laws coming in continually from U.N. sources. Any argument against these issues is cleverly squashed and made light of.
4. Woolworth's leads all in New Zealand with EFT. Banks and oil companies are joining in, on a trial basis they say.
5. "Ha ha", I say. Are we, the public, supposed to be ignorant or silly? You can't fool all the people all of the time.

PLEASE
TURN
THE
PAGE.

## CHAPTER SIXTEEN

# WHAT TO DO

It is one thing to hear all the bad news, but it is another thing to know what to do.

In the light of the coming monetary crash, this section is addressed mainly to "born again" believers in Christ.

To those readers who are not sure of their spiritual standing with the Lord, your only escape avenue is to humble yourself, turn to the last page NOW, become one of God's children through our Lord Jesus Christ, and then turn back to this chapter.

**RULES**

1. If you have been ripping off the tax department, stop, as the computer can now do quick checks of assets and related income. Please notice that the governments are bringing in asset tests regularly. In New Zealand, for example, even Family Care is revised with the filling in of a new form every 28 weeks.
2. Learn to live honestly, as God must now become your source. (In Australia and New Zealand at least, all information on bank interest goes straight to the Tax Department. Declare it.)
3. Do not hoard food, etc., or get in on the dehydrated food business. A brother in Christ from Texas once offered to make me a millionaire, selling "Doomsday Food" in Australia and New Zealand. — I listened to his offer, but obeyed the inner voice of God's Spirit.

   I replied, "Thank you for the offer dear brother, but I believe God has something else for us."

   Here is God's promise:

   "TAKE NO THOUGHT, saying what shall we eat (i.e. food, drink and clothing) or what shall we drink or wherewithal shall we be clothed (for after all these things do the Gentiles seek) for your heavenly father KNOWETH that ye have need of all these things, but seek ye FIRST the kingdom of God and His righteousness, and all these things shall be added unto you." (Emphasis added for clárity.)[1]

   "What things?" you ask — Food, drink and clothing.

   The same God that provided for the children of Israel during their 40 year sojourn in the desert is the same God that will supply for you and me.

4. Learn that of his 10 Yahweh titles in the Old Testament, one such is "JAHWEH JIREH" (Jehovah Jireh).

   "The Lord will provide."[2]

   Learn Philippians Chapter 4 verse 19 by heart.

   "But my God shall supply ALL your need according to His riches in glory by Christ Jesus. (Emphasis added for clarity.)

5. Don't run away and hide.

   God loves the people in town as much as he loves those who live in the country.

   Years ago, a group of "doomsday cultists" in Europe thought the end of the world was nigh. It was advertised in the paper, "End of the World at Midnight Tonight."

   The next morning it read, "End of the World Fails to Eventuate."

   These sad people had given away their houses and taken their furniture and belongings up Mont Blanc. When it all fell through, they trudged back to town and reclaimed their homes from the jeering crowds — what foolishness.

   Christians, keep on working. Work with more zeal than ever before. In the words of Jesus.

   "Occupy till I come."[3]

6. Don't invest as usual. Businesses will collapse shortly, as will banks, insurance companies, etc.

   Invest your money in the precious souls of men and women.

   "He that winneth souls is wise."[4]

   Don't leave your capital in the bank to await the inevitable crash. Use it wisely and well.

   If you can't go and preach — give, give and give again.

   Require that those you give to, return you information from time to time if possible, so that you may all rejoice together. Make the evangelist your partner.

   "So then, neither is he that planteth anything, neither he that watereth, but God that giveth the increase. Now he that planteth, and he that watereth are one, and every man shall receive his own reward, according to his own labour. For we are labourers together with God. . . ."[5]

   Imagine in the judgement as you are walking towards the judgement seat of Christ, hearing people lining the way saying, "Thank you brother, thank you sister, God bless you dear one." You ask an angel who is standing nearby, "Who are all these?"

   He answers, these are the souls who were saved through your money freely given to evangelism.

"And they that be wise, shall shine as the brightness of the firmament, and they that turn many to righteousness as the stars for ever and ever."[6]

7. What about insurance?

   I will not legislate here.

   To your own master you stand or fall. Some have a stronger measure of faith than others. Ask the Lord about your situation. The principle thing is wisdom.

8. If you do not have a home, in most cases, not all, it is wise to endeavour to purchase one. Although the world government people intend to take over all land and real estate, it is nice to have a home base. You will be allowed to live in your home, but you will not own it any longer.

   Don't worry. It is all very temporary.

   We have homes prepared for us in heaven, Jesus tells us.

   ". . . God is not ashamed to be called their God for He hath prepared for them a city."[7]

   "Is it far away?" you ask.

   No! Only a heart beat away.

9. Try to get a good car as it is becoming difficult to obtain car parts, and maintenance is expensive.

10. When all looks black, know that your God is the God of the supernatural.

Buy the life story of George Mueller from Bristol in your nearest Christian bookstore. Edited by A. Sims and printed by Moody Press Chicago, it tells of his collecting orphans from the streets of Bristol.

In answer to prayer for over 50 years, God met his every need. He fed 9,500 orphans and $7,500,000 came in, in answer to prayer.

God is not bound by our financial system. When Jesus wanted tax money it came out of the mouth of a fish. How did it get there? Very few fish go shopping, using their mouths as purses.

I had just finished reading this great book about Mueller some years ago whilst living in Western Samoa. One Sunday we asked our pastor and his wife around for dinner.

Unfortunately we discovered too late that there was no food. Pastor Makisua Fatialofa and his wife Mau duly arrived. I explained the situation and asked him to give thanks for the food.

He had just finished praying, when there came a loud knock on the door.

"There it is, just like the book," I exclaimed.

Racing to the door, I opened it, passed a large cardboard box of steaming hot food on the porch, ran out on the road, looked left, right, forwards, backwards and there was not a sign of a person anywhere. There was simply no time for anyone to get away.

Now there was only one way to look — UPWARDS.

I believe we had experienced a miraculous God-sent angel visitation.

There was never a meal like that one.

Remember . . . "God is no respecter of persons."[8]

He loves you as He loves me.

If one gets an icecream, we all get an icecream.

Praise His Name.

Our God is without partiality. God bless you.

**Recap**

At the time of revision, serious restrictions are coming into Australia and New Zealand. It is important to realise that the whole aim of this world government plan is to entrap one group in particular, i.e. THE CHRISTIANS.

We born again believers can be sure of one thing — that the numbers of government agencies will pool all information and find some crime with which to charge certain individuals. They will name the defendant and then order a crime to be tailored to him. — The Lord's promises of protection will stand us in good stead in those days.

Our faith needs to be firmly on our Lord Jesus Christ. Revival is just around the corner.

Christians prepare!

## CHAPTER SEVENTEEN

# THE KEY CHAPTER

Some years ago a Christian doctor, strolling across the moors in Britain, came across a patch of long grass and in the middle of this area sat a small boy with a cage full of skylarks.

Here is a record of their conversation.

Dr: "Hello my boy. What do you have there?"

Boy: "A cage full of skylarks I have caught sir."

Dr: "They don't look very happy. Look at them. Their feathers are ruffled and they are all unhappy, huddled in the corner of that cage. I'm sure God never made them to be like that — how much for the lot?"

Boy: "Two pounds sir, and I'll throw in the cage for free."

Giving the lad two crisp notes, the Christian doctor took the cage, opened the door, pointed the cage skywards and said these words,

Dr: "Little birds. God made you, not to live in a cage like this, but to fly high in the sky, happy, singing and joyful. I have bought you, at my own expense. You are now free."

He gave the cage a little shake and the first bird nervously crept to the door, as if he couldn't believe it. With a flutter of wings he was off and the other birds flew off in quick pursuit.

Within two or three minutes, the sky was filled with these birds, soaring and wheeling on the thermals, each of them singing their own happy song of freedom.

The doctor turned to the boy and explained.

Dr: This is a picture of people without God in a cage built by satan, desperately trying to enjoy themselves yet still trapped by their sin. Some commit suicide. Others just exist, on and on, while others again try to escape in pleasure and money trips. Still trapped, in their quieter moments they become honest, and ask, "Why are we here? What is it all about?"

Then, because they become genuine in their search they hear a voice quoting some very illuminating words.

"And for thy pleasure, they are and were created. . . ."[1]

Again, "If the Son therefore shall make you free ye shall be free indeed."[2]

The voice continues. "You were trapped in, and by your sin. — I bought you back at my own expense — with my own precious blood. I set you free, the moment you are willing to pray this prayer, and commit your life openly to me.

"By praying this prayer and publicly confessing to others that you are mine, I save you, on the spot."

Two organs must be used.

"If thou shalt confess with thy MOUTH Jesus as Lord, and shalt believe in thine HEART that God hath raised Him from the dead, thou shalt be SAVED." (Emphasis added for meaning.)[3]

Let the money crash come — world government — satanism — false religion — we Christians are going up to be with Jesus.

"For the Lord Himself shall descend from heaven with a shout, with the voice of the arch angel and with the trumpet of God, and the dead in Christ shall rise first, then we which are alive and remain shall be caught up together with them in the clouds to meet the Lord in the air, and so shall we ever be with the Lord.

"Wherefore comfort one another with these words."[4]

The price for your salvation has been paid.

Who is this wonderful Saviour? His name is the LORD JESUS CHRIST.

Your time of decision — please read on.

Remember, that the price of blood has already been offered and in the words of Scripture:

"For God so loved the world *(your name)..................................................... that He gave His only begotten Son (Jesus) that whosoever *(your name)............................................... believeth in Him (Jesus) should not perish (or go to hell) but have (not wait for, hope for, or think about) everlasting life." John 3:16 (Words in brackets added for meaning).

*Put your name here.

It is as clear as that.

The Bible teaches that there are three steps, plus one, to possess this life from God.

Find a quiet place;

Kneel down, or get into an attitude of prayer.

(Sit if necessary);

Start praying;

Here are the three steps —

1. Repent of your sin. Turn to Jesus.
2. Believe that He died for you.
3. Receive Him — Invite Him into your heart. Plus —
4. Tell someone what you have done.

If you find that you do not know how to pray, here is the prayer of Salvation:

## PRAYER OF SALVATION

**Part One**

(Say out loud;

"Lord Jesus Christ — I come to you now — because I am a sinner.

Today Lord Jesus — I repent of my sin — I turn away from my sin — and I turn to you."

**Part Two**

**"I believe, dear Lord — that you died for me** *.............................. I thank you Lord — because your blood covers all my sins. No one else can save me — only Jesus."

* (your name)

**Part Three**

"Right now — I open the door of my heart (put your hand to your chest and open outwards) — Come into my heart Lord Jesus — Wash me — Cleanse me — and make me your child — I receive you now by faith.

Help me to live for you every day until you come again.

I close the door (use our hand again, bring it back towards your chest) and Jesus is on the inside.

I thank you Lord Jesus, because today, by faith, I have received you — and you have received me.

(Pause.)

Amen".

HERE IS THE PROMISE —

"To as many (anybody) as **received** Him (Jesus), to them gave He power to become the Sons of God." John 1:12. (Emphasis added.)

Your choice this day gives you that power, and right, to call yourself a Son of God – Praise Him now in your own words.

In order that you may never forget this great day, I include here a copy of your New Birth Certificate:

## NEW BIRTH CERTIFICATE

At.............................on..........................................................................
(Time) (Date)

I.........................................................................................................................
(Name)

received the Lord Jesus Christ as my own Saviour.
I thank Him.

Signed: ..................................................

If you filled this Certificate in, please:

1. Copy it out again into the front page of your Bible;
2. Send another copy to me immediately, so that I can send you further assistance;
3. Go and tell someone what you have done.
   "That if thou shalt confess with thy MOUTH, the Lord Jesus, and shalt believe in thine HEART that God has raised Him from the dead, thou shalt be saved." Rom. 10:9 (Emphasis added)

That which is in your heart, must come out of your mouth. This is your starting point.

Now: Steps to help you continue on for Christ —

1. Pray daily.
2. Read your Bible daily. Start in John's Gospel, because it speaks about salvation and everlasting life.
3. Witness, or tell others about Christ.
4. Link up with a Bible-based Christian group or Church.
   (I may be able to help you here, as I have friends in many different groups and denominations.)

Welcome to the Family of God. I look forward to meeting you up there.

Your friend,

Barry Smith.

# CHAPTER NUMBERS

## Introduction

[1] Rev. 22:4

## Chapter 1:

[1] Rev. 13:16-18
[2] Prov. 22:7
[3] Jas 5:1-3

## Chapter 2:

[1] Jer. 17:9
[2] Rev. 16:2
[3] Joel 2:28-29
[4] Joel 2:23
[5] Lk 12:45-46
[6] Heb. 10:25
[7] 1 Thess. 4:16-17
[8] Dan. 12:11
[9] Rev. 22:4
[10] Rev. 14:9-11
[11] Math. 25:41
[12] Rom. 6:23

## Chapter 3:

[1] Ps. 14:1
[2] Rom. 1:20
[3] Gen. 1:11
[4] Gen. 1:29
[5] Gen. 8:22
[6] Hos. 8:7
[7] Jn. 8:36

## Chapter 4:

[1] Hos. 4:6
[2] Jas. 3:1
[3] Jn 5:22
[4] Jn 12:47-48
[5] Dan. 11:38a
[6] Dan. 11:37 Also check amplified version
[7] Job. 5:12-14
[8] Ps. 91:9-10
[9] Hab. 1:4

## Chapter 5:

[1] Is. 14:13
[2] Rev. 19:20
[3] Rev. 20:10
[4] Ps. 111:10a
[5] Prov. 14:12

## Chapter 6:

[1] Ps. 75:7
[2] Acts 4:10 & 12
[3] Jn. 5:22-23
[4] Rom. 6:23b

## Chapter 7:

[1] Matt. 12:37
[2] Ex. 20:5b
[3] Ex. 20:5
[4] Is. 48:11b
[5] 1 Jn. 1:5b
[6] Phil. 2:10-11
[7] Math. 4:4a
[8] Is. 14:12
[9] Rev. 22:16
[10] Rev. 20:10
[11] Phil 2:9-11
[12] Math. 10:26

## Chapter 8:

[1] John 8:12
[2] Acts 10:15b

## Chapter 9:

[1] Rev. 13:11
[2] Jn. 8:36
[3] Rev. 17:5
[4] Rev. 17:16
[5] Jn. 12:48b
[6] Math. 15:6b
[7] Math. 15:9
[8] Lk 22:19-20
[9] Heb. 6:6
[10] Rev. 18:4
[11] Math. 13:28-29
[12] Rev. 18:4
[13] 1 Tim. 2:5

## Chapter 10:

[1] Eph. 6:12a
[2] Deut. 18:12a
[3] Math. 28:18
[4] Deut. 18:10
[5] 1 Tim 4:1
[6] 1 Tim 4:3
[7] Rom. 6:16
[8] Ex. 22:18
[9] II Cor. 5:17a
[10] 1 Sam. 15:23a

[11] Rom. 12:15
[12] Mk. 16:17
[13] Deut. 18:10
[14] Lev. 19:31
[15] 1 Jn. 1:7b
[16] II Tim. 1:7
[17] Job 3:25
[18] Col 1.27b
[19] Rev. 4:11b
[20] Col. 2:8
[21] Ex. 20:5b
[22] Math. 16:18b
[23] Eph. 6:12a
[24] Mk. 16:17a
[25] Jn. 14:6
[26] Jn. 5:23
[27] Lk. 10:19
[28] Prov. 18:10
[29] Deut. 18:10a
[30] Jn. 14:6
[31] Rev. 2:17b
[32] Lk. 1:47
[33] Jn. 14:9b
[34] Jn. 18:5
[35] Acts 1:8
[36] 1 Jn 5:12
[37] Lk 11:52
[38] 1 Jn 5:13
[39] Prov. 14:12
[40] Eph. 2:8
[41] Gal. 5:4
[42] Jn. 19:30
[43] Heb. 10:12
[44] Ex. 31:13
[45] Ex. 31:16
[46] Ex. 31:17a
[47] Rom. 14:5-6a
[48] Col. 2:16-17
[49] 1 Sam. 2:30b
[50] Rom 1:26
[51] Rom. 1:27a
[52] Rom. 1:27b
[53] Jn. 8:36
[54] II Chron. 5:13
[55] Rev. 22:15
[56] 1 Cor. 6:19
[57] Gal. 5:21
[58] Rom. 14:21
[59] 1 Kgs. 8:27b
[60] Eccl. 12:6a
[61] Mk. 16:17-18
[62] Deut. 7:25
[63] Deut. 7:26
[64] Ex. 20:4-5
[65] Gal. 5:21
[66] 1 Pet. 5:8b
[67] Col. 2:15
[68] Rev. 20:10
[69] Rev. 19:16
[70] Math. 8:22

## Chapter 11:

[1] Ezek. 28:16
[2] Jn. 10:10
[3] Rev. 10:5-6
[4] Rom. 8:16
[5] Phil. 4:8

## Chapter 12:

[1] Math. 10:21
[2] Heb. 10:30
[3] Math. 18:6
[4] Gal. 6:7
[5] Jn. 8:36
[6] Isai. 24:20a
[7] Zech. 14:12
[8] Rom. 1:22

## Chapter 14:

[1] Zech. 4:6b
[2] Math. 5:6
[3] II Pet. 3:8b
[4] Isai. 59:19b
[5] Joel 2:28a
[6] Joel 2:23
[7] Math. 9:17
[8] Acts 3:20-21
[9] Ps. 48:2
[10] 1 Cor. 14:2
[11] 1 Cor. 2:7-8
[12] Gen. 3:15
[13] II Tim 3:5
[14] Jas. 3:8a
[15] Math. 3:11
[16] Lk 11:11-13

## Chapter 15

[1] Jer. 17:9a
[2] 1 Pet. 3:7b
[3] Rom 1:25
[4] Gen. 12:3a

## Chapter 16

[1] Math. 6:31-33
[2] Gen. 22:14
[3] Luke 19:13b
[4] Prov. 11:30b
[5] 1 Cor. 3:7-9a
[6] Dan. 12:3
[7] Heb. 11:16b
[8] Acts 10:34b

## Chapter 17

[1] Rev. 4:11b
[2] Jn 8:36
[3] Rom. 10:9
[4] 1 Thess 4:16-18

# POSTSCRIPT ON EVOLUTION

## CALCULATION COMMENCING WITH 100 PAIRS 30,000 YEARS AGO

100 couples producing 4 children each.
Reproduction at 20 year cycles. Death after 3rd generation (70 years).
Population after 30,000 years = ?
There are 1500 generations in 30,000 years.
To calculate population at any given generation:—
Add all generations minus all generations back except the latest 3 —
e.g. $2^1 + 2^2 + 2^3 + 2^4 + 2^5 + 2^6 — 2^1 + 2^2 + 2^3 = 11,200$
After 6 generations there are 11,200 people.
To calculate use chart below. Add two zeros at any time.

| | | | |
|---|---|---|---|
| $2^{1}$ | = 2 | $2^{28}$ | = 268,435,456 |
| $2^{2}$ | = 4 | $2^{29}$ | = 536,870,912 |
| $2^{3}$ | = 8 | $2^{30}$ | = 1,073,741,824 |
| $2^{4}$ | = 16 | $2^{31}$ | = 2,147,483,648 |
| $2^{5}$ | = 32 | $2^{32}$ | = 4,294,967,296 |
| $2^{6}$ | = 64 | $2^{33}$ | = 8,589,934,592 |
| $2^{7}$ | = 128 | $2^{34}$ | = 17,179,869,184 |
| $2^{8}$ | = 256 | $2^{35}$ | = 34,359,738,368 |
| $2^{9}$ | = 512 | $2^{36}$ | = 68,719,476,736 |
| $2^{10}$ | = 1,024 | $2^{37}$ | = 137,438,953,472 |
| $2^{11}$ | = 2,048 | $2^{38}$ | = 274,877,906,944 |
| $2^{12}$ | = 4,096 | $2^{39}$ | = 549,755,813,888 |
| $2^{13}$ | = 8,192 | $2^{40}$ | = 1,099,511,627,776 |
| $2^{14}$ | = 16,384 | $2^{41}$ | = 2,199,023,255,552 |
| $2^{15}$ | = 32,768 | $2^{42}$ | = 4,398,046,511,104 |
| $2^{16}$ | = 65,536 | $2^{43}$ | = 8,796,093,022,208 |
| $2^{17}$ | = 131,072 | $2^{44}$ | = 17,592,186,044,416 |
| $2^{18}$ | = 262,144 | $2^{45}$ | = 35,184,372,088,832 |
| $2^{19}$ | = 524,288 | $2^{46}$ | = 70,368,744,177,664 |
| $2^{20}$ | = 1,048,576 | $2^{47}$ | = 140,737,488,355,328 |
| $2^{21}$ | = 2,097,152 | $2^{48}$ | = 281,474,976,710,656 |
| $2^{22}$ | = 4,194,304 | $2^{49}$ | = 562,949,953,421,312 |
| $2^{23}$ | = 8,388,608 | $2^{50}$ | = 1,125,899,906,842,624 |
| $2^{24}$ | = 16,777,216 | $2^{51}$ | = 2,251,799,813,685,248 |
| $2^{25}$ | = 33,554,432 | $2^{52}$ | = 4,503,599,627,370,496 |
| $2^{26}$ | = 67,108,864 | $2^{53}$ | = 9,007,199,254,740,992 |
| $2^{27}$ | = 134,217,728 | $2^{54}$ | = 18,014,398,509,481,984 |

This, for example, is the 54th generation leaving us 1,446 generations to go.

At the 32nd generation we have the world population as it is in 1984. This leaves us 1,467 generations to go, making the result ridiculous, even allowing for wars, disease and decimation of population. Should the reader wish to calculate this problem using 10 pairs, simply move the decimal point back 2 places. Therefore any person who persists in arguing the case for evolution is a candidate waiting to be led away by a man with a white coat.

For a catalogue of other books and videos by Barry Smith, please write to:

International Support Ministries
Pelorus Bridge
Rai Valley 7156
NEW ZEALAND

Telephone: 64 (03) 571 6046
Facsimile: 64 (03) 571 6135